I0522272

Limitations of Liability/ Disclaimer of Warranty

Published by Diverse Dimensions, LLC

979-8-9862184-1-0 (Hardback)

979-8-9862184-2-7 (Paperback)

979-8-9862184-3-4 (eBook)

Visit us at: www.thediversedimensions.com

Write to us at: contact@thediversedimensions.com

THE BLACK MALE TRIUMPH STORY:

SUCCESSFULLY ACHIEVING GRADUATE DEGREES

Third Edition

DR. ALBERT C. FURLOW III
DOCTOR OF PHILOSOPHY

DEDICATION

I want to thank my parents: my mother, who always instilled in me the importance of believing in oneself, and my father, thank you for teaching me the importance of hard work. To my younger sister, Amelia, I want you to know that you can do anything you put your mind to, and it is an honor to be your big brother. To my older sister, Barbara, I thank you for being the go-getter that you are. You inspire me always. To my family and extended family: I appreciate your support and the love you all have shown me throughout this process. To my beloved wife, Lauren, I thank you for the abundance of love and graciousness you bring to our family. To my daughter Avianna, I want you to know that it takes endurance to succeed, as well as a strong faith in yourself and faith in the will of God. To the participants, I want to thank you all for your honesty and willingness to assist me with the bigger picture. Love is felt, and this is my reciprocity as we continue to sustain community love. Lastly, I would like to thank the University of the Incarnate Word and the professors who assisted me during this process.

ACKNOWLEDGEMENTS

I want to give many thanks and acknowledge Dr. Herbers, Dr. Labay Marquez, Dr. Norman St. Clair, Dr. Denise Staudt, Dr. Kevin Vichcales, Dr. Raul Zendejas, Dr. Danielle Alsandor, Dr. Hernandez, and Dr. Ortiz. You have all contributed to the implementation of this research. You all greatly enriched my book, and for that, I will always be humble and grateful.

PREFACE

The headlines of mainstream news media and even journal articles create a narrative of educated Black males as an "endangered species" and the education pipeline for Black males as "leaking rapidly." While the dire circumstances and dismal numbers of Black men in higher education are an unfortunate reality, this research study seeks to provide a counter-narrative to the plight of Black males in education, to inspire future students and educators to attain higher education degrees. The findings in this study provide a counterpoint to deficit-oriented research on Black males in graduate school. To better understand and identify the reasons why Black male graduate students persist through a post-baccalaureate program, it is necessary to learn the intricacies of their experiences which, among other things, necessitates a qualitative examination into the effects, if any, of participation and mentorship on Black male graduate students. As a theoretical guide, this study utilizes Alexander Astin's Student Involvement Theory and Gloria Ladson-Billing's and William Tate's Critical Race Theory in Education. It is vital to note that decades of research are decisive and uphold intellectual and collective alliances. Themes that emerged, such as why Black mentorship and representation matter, imposter syndrome, and the fact that employment viability trumps all, yielded the findings of these resilient leaders.

This study aimed to collect and make sense of the lived experiences of 16 Black males who have received a master's degree or higher in any academic discipline in the last 5 years. Participants in the study came from places like Ohio State, the University of Wisconsin— Madison, Texas A&M, the University of Texas, and the University of Iowa, some of the top universities in the country.

Participants also come from HBCUs with a national reputation, like Texas Southern University and North Carolina A&T State University (Thurgood Marshall Law). Moreover, others studied at Fordham University, Arizona State University, Trinity University, Cornell University, Kent State University, LSU (Louisiana State University), and UIW (Incarnate Word University). The Furlow Engagement and Endurance Theory (FEET) is the apex of this research and is the culmination of the findings that led to the development of the Successful Black Males Post-Baccalaureate Degree (SBMPD) Model. This theory was derived from a few theoretical frameworks, as well as my own lived experiences.

Table of Contents

Chapter 1

Introduction to the Black Male Story

A Pakistani teen named Malala Yousafzai was shot in the forehead by a Taliban terrorist as she was traveling with her friends to a school that her father had started. Malala was targeted because she wrote a blog that advocated for education in her country. After her recovery, the resilient Malala Yousafzai proclaimed,

One child, one teacher, one book, and one pen can change the world. Education is the only solution. Education first. We realized the importance of pens and books when we saw guns. The extremists are afraid of books and pens. (Scherer, 2013, p. 7)

The realization that education trumps fear is a realization that creates freedom. Malala went on:

They thought that the bullets would silence us, but they failed. Out of the silence came thousands of voices. The terrorists thought they would change my aims and stop my ambitions. But nothing changed in my life except this: Weakness, fear, and hopelessness died; strength, fervor, and courage were born. (Scherer, 2013, p. 7) They thought that the bullets would silence us, but they failed. Out of the silence came thousands of voices. The terrorists thought they would change my aims and stop my ambitions. But nothing changed in my life except this: Weakness, fear, and hopelessness died; strength, fervor, and courage were born. (Scherer, 2013, p. 7)

In her poetic words, Malala asserted the importance of education, especially in populations where it is taboo to seek it. Rather than aspire, women of her society and other populations are to be silenced by guns, gangs, drugs, and violence, as the idea of formal education became a threat to others who did not want her or others like her to be vocal about receiving education. Unfortunately, this is also true of populations in our current society in the United States of America, which is why all need to have the opportunity for education. In America, specific population sub-sets have faced limitations in accessing this opportunity. The Black male has more statistics that negatively portray them than that positively impact them regarding educational success. According to Bauknight (2020),

Researching the essential components of positive experiences and success in higher education for Black males was important because most existing research is negative and focuses on disparities that do not necessarily offer insight into achieving educational goals. (p. 6)

This study intended to show a positive perspective—a counter-story—of how other Black males have attained a post-baccalaureate degree. It is important to tell this story through research due to the multiple factors included. According to Druery and Brooms (2019),

In the last 25 years, Black male experiences in college have received significant attention in educational research (Cuyjet, 2006; Harper, 2012; Strayhorn, 2016). This research has revealed important factors that impact students' college success, such as access (Cuyjet, 2006), peer associations, and social support. (Harper, 2006; Strayhorn, 2008), Engagement on campus. (Brooms, 2016a; Harris & Harper, 2014, p. 1)

With additional research, the data can emphasize graduate school experiences as undergraduate school experiences. Rather than letting society, the world, the statisticians, and the cynics tell Black men what education would do for them, these men sought education, fought through hardships, and accomplished what they did not think was possible based on the number of predecessors before them.

Statement of the Problem

Remarkably, W.E.B. Du Bois (1898) had the discernment to visualize the effectiveness of higher education as a resource for the Black community to diminish the dreadful economic, political, and social conditions—referred to as the "Negro Problem" (p. 20)—that existed throughout his lifetime and is outlined in a collection of essays by prominent Black American writers that cover law, education, disenfranchisement, and Black Americans' place in American society. Du Bois states that it is no secret that "all candid people know there does not exist today in the center of Negro population a single first-class fully equipped institution devoted to the higher education of Negroes" (p. 22), highlighting the historical underrepresentation of Black males.

According to author Brown (2017), institutional racism begins in the educational pipeline, even today, with "African American students representing 16 percent of the public- school student population but making up 42 percent of those suspended more than once, and 34 percent of students expelled" (p. 3). News headlines often highlight the challenges Black males face in America from youth to adulthood, from school to the prison pipeline, from over-diagnosis and placement in special education to receiving more school office referrals, suspensions, and expulsions than any other group for lesser fractions and behavioral issues, profiling, and scores (Brown, 2017). According to Astin (1993), "quality of life tends to be highly correlated with one's educational attainment" (p. 4). Jackson & Moore (2006) specify that "for the last two decades, African American males' educational achievement has received serious research and attention as it relates to their experiences in education" (p. 202). The current body of knowledge is constrained because researchers fail to explore Black males throughout the educational pipeline properly. This emphasis on Black males' academic journeys assists in exploring how each stage of the educational pipeline influences other stages.

These pipeline experiences evolve into the fact that some school districts have a 50% or less graduation rate for boys of color, which then directly affects their quality of life, knowing that "a Black baby boy born 25 years ago has a 1 in 2 chance of being employed today" (Brown, 2017, p. 1). President Obama's administration established an initiative called My Brother's Keeper for this express purpose. My Brother's Keeper aimed to create jobs in the United States for Black males by enhancing their retention rates in higher education and employment (Brown, 2017). Education must be a priority, and through it, the former president's goal of increasing levels of education for Black males will lead to higher wages and, in turn, increase tax revenues for the government (Brown,2017). In addition, it will assist in furthering the professional goals of individuals through graduate programs that will make these goals possible. By increasing the likelihood of advanced job opportunities, we can minimize the gap and defeat the barriers hindering Black males' full potential. Institutions will gain partnerships and be able to incorporate specific skills and resources that will help prepare students for future employment when the presence of Black males in graduate schools all over the nation increases.

The success of these Black males will contribute to economic wealth, civic involvement, personal development, and increased health benefits (Ma et al., 2016). Blacks have faced prejudice, racism, discrimination, and even dehumanization. It is necessary to acknowledge such issues along with the breadth and depth of systemic and historic laws and practices controlling everything from where to live to the lack of fresh produce in areas where people of color live to public schools and educational access. This study contributes to the literature on Black males in higher education by looking at those who earned a graduate degree and examining how to increase the success rate of Black males in post-baccalaureate programs. By researching the successful characteristics of those individuals, themes emerged on which attributes commonly contribute to graduation in post-baccalaureate degrees. Researchers still need to explore the success of Black males who earn their post-baccalaureate degrees. Earning a doctorate allows Black men to join the academy. Gibbs and Griffin (2013) suggest that "faculty diversity has been shown to improve learning outcomes for all students, with a particularly positive influence on the retention and persistence of students from underrepresented backgrounds" (p. 712).

Additionally, joining the academy enables one to conduct research, train the next generation of scholars, impact policy, and have a voice where curriculum, policies, and procedures are discussed and implemented (Jefferson, 2020).

Furthermore, Harper and Porter (2012) acknowledged a scarcity within the Black community regarding receiving post-baccalaureate degrees. There is also a need for more Black male scholars to earn their doctoral degrees, discuss their success, and produce meaningful work to benefit the educational pipeline (Cuyjet, 2006; Harper & Porter, 2012). Furthermore, Jefferson (2020, p. 6) reminds us that Harper and Porter argue that Black men's success at the post-baccalaureate level needs deeper empirical examination. While there is a significant amount of research on access to higher education for Black males, research on their pathways to post-secondary education remains limited (Bauknight, 2020). Moreover, the research on the success factors of Black male students pursuing post-baccalaureate education is even more scarce, creating a gap in understanding how these students navigate and thrive in advanced academic environments.

The lack of data on Black males in a post-baccalaureate pathway makes it difficult to analyze a successful graduate's characteristics/traits/attributes. This study helped to find solutions to increase the success of Black males in post-baccalaureate settings. Institutions must become more proactive and diligent in treating Black males within higher education. Furthermore, leaders, faculty, and practitioners may be able to attain a greater understanding of the reasons how and why Black male graduate students are successful in graduate school.

Purpose of the Study

This study aimed to explore the experience of 16 Black male graduate students who completed their graduate program. Merriam (1998) proposed an essential interpretive narrative inquiry study that focused on how individuals comprehend their lived experiences and perceive what they share in their narratives. Researchers examined this group because Black male graduate students who have completed or are seeking a master's degree or higher within the past 5 years from various universities offer substantial and enriching insights on achieving a graduate degree or higher. By researching their experiences, they enhanced the tracking of advancement, success, and the hurdles these students faced while attending their universities.

This research attempted to target the success of Black males and other people of color, which will benefit educational policymakers and researchers. In addition, practitioners and faculty can contribute to basic and applied knowledge that will enable key stakeholders in education to better serve Black males in graduate school and beyond. The study explored the essence of the experience of achieving an academic goal of a post-baccalaureate degree.

This research study adds to the existing literature on the topic and expands the knowledge and understanding of Black male success, challenges to success, and recommendations for success. Information from this study enhances research literature and increases understanding of the phenomenon for scholars, community, undergraduate/graduate students, higher education faculty and staff, and other interested parties.

To address this gap, the researcher conducted a study that examined the experiences of 16 Black males who have successfully earned a graduate degree or higher from any post-baccalaureate school in the United States within the past 5 years.

Research Questions and Design

The following are some of the quintessential research questions addressed:

1. What are the characteristics/attributes/practices of Black males who completed a master's degree or higher within the past 5 years?
2. How does honest reflection with their academic degree program enable Black male graduate students to advance academically despite their obstacles?
3. How did/does your identity as a Black male affect(ed) your experiences in graduate school?

The qualitative approach of narrative inquiry has an emphasis on the lived experiences of 16 successful Black male graduate students within the past 5 years. More specifically, narrative inquiry encourages people to tell their stories by asking semi-structured questions that allows the data to be extracted from what participants stated. Clandinin explains it as "to enter conversations with the rest of our communities to develop a method—a way of talking and asking and answering and making sense—that will allow the narrative to flourish in this congenial moment for stories" (Pinnegar and Daynes, 2007, p. 1). The importance of viewing documents and listening to stories and meanings facilitates an understanding of the framework of the diverse educational engagement of Black men. Creswell (2003) states, "Life history is the study of an individual situated within the cultural context of his or her life" (p. 438).

Paying close attention to Black males' involvement, I encompassed open-ended questions in a semi-structured interview format and sought to understand participants' involvement. A key component to this qualitative study was that one of the main sources of the data collection method could be viewed in the form of interviews and journal entries. Imperative information on this subject matter was formulated by analyzing the triumphant Black males within higher education, along with their experiences with obtaining a graduate degree.

Moreover, triangulation of the semi-structured interview data was conducted by maintaining a journal and taking notes on different perspectives, views and understanding of the process. Survey (a pre and post interview study) and member checking ensured that the results were reliable and valid. Participants were given a copy of the data and transcript to check for accuracy and resemblance to their own experiences. With this method, I established the varieties of participation by Black males in their pursuit towards obtaining a graduate degree.

Study Significance

This study aimed to acknowledge and discuss the presence of Black males in graduate school and determine how involvement, other skills, traits, and critical race influence academic success and degree acquisition. According to Inouye (1989), "Although there is a considerable body of empirical research on undergraduate students, comparatively little is known about graduate and professional school students and their institutional environments" (p. 16).

Not enough is known from studies regarding how Black males express their lived experiences completing a post-secondary college or university degree (Bauknight, 2020). Most mainstream research has concentrated on Black males' failures in higher education, with only a tiny amount of attention paid to their successes (Pelzer, 2016). By collecting qualitative data on the participants' actual experiences, this study helps to close that gap. This book's research is unique in that it looks at the in-depth accounts of the narrative experience of Black males achieving an academic goal of a post-baccalaureate degree. This new body of research will optimize those numbers by highlighting positive situations and drawing lessons from the past as an inspirational living example. The research explored the dichotomy between education and opportunities.

Definition of Key Terms

Throughout the research there are terms that are necessary to define and understand to have perspective regarding the research and results. As technical terms can have different meanings depending on experience, culture, and viewpoint, it is important to have a worldwide meaning of certain words as they pertain to this research.

- Black. For this study, is used to describe the African American population: a person having origins in any of the black racial groups of Africa (Strmic-Pawl et. al., 2018). This includes, but is not limited to, anyone who self-identifies as African American, Caribbean Black, multiracial, or biracial in the U.S. Black population.

- Post-baccalaureate degree. Includes master's and doctoral programs, as well as professional doctoral programs in fields such as law, medicine, and higher education. Degree-granting institutions grant associate's or higher degrees and participate in Title IV federal financial aid programs (NCES, 2018).

- Success. Involvement includes activities such as the amount of time a student spends on academic pursuits, the use of technology, advising, and mentoring (Nwaokoro, 2010). According to Kim et al. (2010), "commonly held definitions include acceptable grade point average, retention toward a degree, and attainment of productive life skills" (p. 112). The pursuit of "student success is also linked to a plethora of desired student and personal development outcomes that confer benefits to individuals and society" (Kuh et. al., 2011, p. 8).

Delimitations and Limitations

The delimitation of this study was interviewing recent Black male graduate students who were enrolled in graduate level programs across the U.S. mainly southern states only. There may have been helpful data from previous graduates that would incorporate more people from diverse populations, but the aim of this study was to grasp the importance of increasing the retention rate/success of Black males currently, the before and after narrative that inspired or was a significant factor throughout their academic involvement during their graduate experience. Studies have shown that females and other races are succeeding in educational achievements at higher rates than Black males in education. This shortage of research needs to be readily available to the masses to further explain the need for Black males in the world of academics. Coincidentally, there is a shortage of information that is readily available regarding graduate students, even though there is a plethora of information available about undergraduate students.

Hypothetically speaking, there are a variety of boundaries and issues when talking about one population (Black Males). For instance, there are limitations in the study because a focus was placed on predominantly White institutions, Hispanic serving institutions, and historically Black colleges and universities. Why exclude the likes of community colleges and other institutions, such as tribal colleges and universities? A further boundary existed in the decision to focus on public and private 4-year colleges and universities and to exclude online universities and others.

One of the challenges faced was in the quest for Black males who met the research criteria. With a severe shortage of Black males completing post-baccalaureate degrees and the increased availability of online courses for students, there were limitations regarding selecting students to interview—those who were ready, willing and able versus those who had yet to graduate with their post-baccalaureate degree. After meeting with the Director of Research Studies and the faculty staff members of Student Affairs, it became clear that there were Black male students accessible and willing to participate in this research strategy. In fact, there were enough students who met the research criteria to qualify for good research. Finally, there was a limitation in interviewing participants who persisted and became college graduates. It would have been interesting to gain the perspectives of former Black male participants who did not persist and graduate from college.

Positionality Statement

I, the researcher, acknowledge and self-identify as a Black male who has completed a master's degree and a doctoral degree. My experiences as a student at a private institution, and as a student in the southern United States, may have made my understanding of the issue different. As a former graduate assistant for campus life, I'm fully aware that there is no I in team. One cannot do this academic journey alone—it takes a village to raise a child. Therefore, it is essential to gather multiple perspectives to see the entire picture.

By no means is this study suggesting that one race is greater than the other. Looking inside the classrooms, one can visibly see that there is a scarcity of Black males at the graduate level. Because I truly listened to their narratives and offered them the opportunity to share their experiences, while keeping my personal opinions out of it, I discovered that the participants were more ready to express their feelings and honest thoughts with me. I was able to mix professionalism with open and honest feedback, so the students trusted me with their feelings.

According to Holmes (2020), "a reflexive approach suggests that, rather than trying to eliminate their effects, researchers should acknowledge and disclose their selves in their work, aiming to understand their influence on and within the research process" (p. 3). Utilizing the university academic graduate writing center in addition to journaling allowed me to avoid my own personal perspective. Throughout this study a reflexive journal was kept that allowed emotions to be documented, so that I was aware and cautious of the way in which individuals were viewed in this study.

By being vigilant of biases, I am cognizant of their capability of influencing the research project. Perhaps this research will quench a thirst for knowledge for Black males, even at a young age, to look at the good in all things. This hunger was the foundation for the narrative that is being uncovered. Being able to have a lived experience of the anguish and disparities students are facing allowed me to have an insightful viewpoint and vision. What makes this study unique is that it delved deep into the areas of malfunction and offered a functioning approach. Through hearing about the experiences of the 16 Black males, one can see the multifaceted factors that are involved within the narrative inquiries.

The factors involved encompassed a hidden message that spoke volumes on the successful traits of individuals, rather than placing a microscope on their disparities. It is important that researchers have multiple lenses through which they operate outside of academia. These are the personal lenses that can stem from one's past and can be noted as the most predominant, such as those rooted in relationships with family, friends, and the community. Another is the justice lens, which is derived from the longing to ameliorate susceptible communities wrecked by nature and man's lack of energy to defend it. Finally, the caring lens originates from interest in the involvement of these students in reconstructing and revamping their lives through their scholastic ventures.

The implementation of my perceptiveness is contributory in the comprehension of what students are facing day in and day out after the post-baccalaureate life. Holmes (2020) states,

It is important for new researchers to note here that their positionality not only shapes their work but influences their interpretation, understanding, and, ultimately, their belief in the truthfulness and validity of other's research that they read or are exposed to. It also influences the importance given to the extent of belief in, and their understanding of the concept of positionality. (p. 3)

It is important to be aware of our own unintentional bias and to accept the implications that can bring into the research.

Concluding Thoughts

According to Wendling (2018), W. E. B. Du Bois's priority of a Black-centered academic ideology emphasized racial uplift, focusing on Black culture and the significance of seeking strength in economic, social and political communities was the priority of his Black-centered academic ideology: "Du Bois understood the higher education of an intellectual elite to be central to providing the cohesive, community-based environment necessary to ensure that the Black community maintained a strong cultural base from which to navigate and uplift society" (p. 285). If one were to truly take a deep dive into the world of higher education, they would see that Black males are marginalized. The statistics alone indicate the lack of enrollment and completion of Black males in graduate school. However, the educational pipeline has a history of negatively impacting Black male students, which contributes to high school dropout and low undergraduate enrollment and completion rates. Hence, the reference to a leaky pipeline (Heilig & Reddick, 2008).

Representation of black males is scarce, unfortunately, in an area where representation is needed the most, like college, a place away from home. Research shows there is an overabundance of attempts made to help offer a resolution to the disengagement of those students who ultimately abandon their academic journey. However, the truth is there are a variety of factors that can be the cause for the brutishly low rates of educational involvement, goal attainment, and matriculation of Black males.

This study took a further look into the way these individuals define their personal academic participation and their achievement for scholastic success at their selected graduate universities. The aim of the study was to listen to what participants had to say about their understanding of themselves as men, as well as what attracted them to and sustained them in diversity education. By addressing the research questions, insights were gained on how participants of the study were able to maneuver their obstacles and successfully eliminate barriers. Finding ways to structure a framework that would uphold the beneficial components of the student experience, student environments, and outcomes, academic achievements, and the number of Black males who earn a graduate degree or higher.

To reverse the shortage of Black males in graduate school there is a tremendous amount of action and research that is imperative if Black males are looking to become more marketable but also even more competitive in the business world, where certain higher paying positions require a graduate degree or higher. Education is something that no one can take away from you, something you have for the rest of your life.

According to Whiting (2006), there is still a need to increase the retention rate of American males, and further states that "it is my belief that a missing ingredient in closing the achievement gap is the lack of attention devoted to developing a positive image of African American males as scholars" (p. 228).

In addition, by creating awareness and starting a conversation about the issues that need attention with Black males in graduate school, the research will add to the stability of the students in the programs. According to Whiting (2006),

If we assert ourselves to see that an attempt must be made to close the achievement gap and to open the educational doors that have been consistently closed and/or locked, progress can and will be made. First, we must promote and nurture a scholarly ideology amongst Black males as early as academically possible. Despite years of learning to devalue education, Black adolescents can still be reached.

By reaching Black males in higher education, this study allowed me to inform educators as to what contributes to Black male success in graduate school. The study also aims to target educational policy makers, researchers, practitioners, and faculty who will have the opportunity to contribute to basic and applied knowledge that will enable key stakeholders in education to better serve Black males in graduate school and beyond. According to Bauknight (2020),

The success of Black males in higher education is important because mainstream research concerning Black males is negative and focuses on factors such as low graduation rates and being unsuccessful in college. The literature on black male achievement has often employed a deficit-informed perspective. Research employing a deficit-informed perspective contains an extraordinary amount of negative information concerning Black males and the Black male college experience. (Bauknight, 2020, p. 20)

This book offers a variety of relevant and current research focused on the lives and experiences of Black male graduate students, those attending Predominately White Institutions (PWI),

Hispanic Serving Institutions (HSI) and Historically Black Colleges and Universities (HBCU). Instructors, practitioners, educators, and principals of black young men, regardless of their race, ethnicity, or gender, can all profit from reading this book. Filled with thought-provoking concepts and real-life ideas geared towards the instillation of academic success and remodeling education, it seeks to change the lives of many.

Chapter 2
Literature Review

An understanding of the literature available is necessary to assess and increase the graduation and success rates of Black men as they embark on graduate school from various institutions of higher learning. The framework referenced within this chapter was coupled with various scholarly articles and peer-reviewed journals from multiple databases, original sources from prolific leaders in the world and the Black community with rich descriptions detailing the educational access provided to Black men, existing new literature on Black males, best practices, the Obama era, which lead to Black male mentorship, student involvement, and Critical Race Theory as it pertains to education. The research also helped to identify characteristics of successful Black male graduate candidates.

An extensive amount of research has been done examining males of color at the undergraduate level. The same or even more detail should be given to post-baccalaureate Black male students. In addition, attention must be given to the HBCUs, PWIs and HSIs in which these Black males garner access to graduate education. Are they creating awareness and filling in the gaps of literature to inspire Black males to secure a post-baccalaureate degree? The theoretical concepts from the study function as a way of contextualizing and framing how to increase the success, preparation, and recruitment of Black males in graduate school to achieve optimal levels of education. Throughout this chapter, references to numerous researchers from the existing literature on how it relates to Black males' aspirations for greatness will be explored.

Quality of Instruction

This study is interesting in that it borrows concepts from undergraduate student success being applied to graduate level student success. Vincent Tinto's publication of his model on student retention in 1975, inspired "the emergence of a theory-based spurred a proliferation of studies that now number in the thousands, making undergraduate retention one of the most studied areas in higher education as a field of study" (Berger et al., 2005, p. 11). The goal of this study was to increase discussion and dialogue and to establish a starting point, and to show there is a vital need to improve the retention rate of Blacks at the post-baccalaureate level, by learning from those who have paved and are paving the way. Howard et al. (2012) acknowledge that.

Throughout the history of the U.S., racialized groups have often had their experiences profoundly shaped by social imagery in ways that have created tremendous hardships in the quest for self-actualization and a healthy sense of self. The purpose of this literature is to shed light on the way Black males have been one of the primary victims of negative social imagery and how the remnants of these constructions continue to have contemporary influences, particularly when it comes to their schooling experiences in the U.S.

The goal of this work is to make an argument for the generation of new ideas, different conceptual frameworks, and innovative methods of inquiry that can be useful in dismantling negative imagery of Black males. It is our hope that these new approaches to studying Black males may play an important role in creating useful research, theory, and practices that will help to improve the schooling experiences and educational outcomes for Black males, who consistently find themselves at the bottom of most academic indices. (p. 99)

Educational Access for Blacks

Fortunately, there were black individuals who took control of the narrative surrounding what constituted a viable educational program for their communities. According to Brown and Ricard (2007), two prominent Black leaders, Booker T. Washington and W.E.B. Du Bois, played a central role in shaping the educational landscape for Black males. Their ideas had a profound impact on expanding access to education for black students:

"Over time, black colleges have merged these ideals into a dual mission of intellectual development combined with practical application. The synthesis of liberal arts and vocational courses in the curriculum of Black colleges and universities... has placed [HBCUs] at the forefront of higher education." (p. 121)

History of Access

Understanding the historical timeline of higher education for Black students, as well as the challenges they faced, is essential in grasping their experiences and educational pursuits. Despite significant obstacles, Black students have continuously demonstrated remarkable perseverance in their pursuit of education. These challenges also underscore the resilience Black students have shown in overcoming institutional resistance to their inclusion and success within American educational systems.

According to the Journal of Black Studies, Black male students' access to higher education has consistently been more limited compared to their white counterparts. This disparity can be traced back to the founding of institutions like Harvard University in the 1600s, which initially excluded Black students (Brooms & Davis, 2017). Between 1636 and 1820, 52 degree granting institutions were founded, all of which were predominantly white. It wasn't until the 1800s that Historically Black Colleges and Universities (HBCUs) began to emerge.

The first HBCUs began offering access to Black Americans in the mid- 1800s. Cheney State University in Pennsylvania, established in 1837, started as a preparatory school before transitioning to offer collegiate courses in the 1900s. Lincoln University, also in Pennsylvania, began accepting Black students in 1854, and Wilberforce University in Ohio, founded in 1856, was the first to be owned and controlled by Black administrators. However, it was Oberlin College in Ohio, founded in 1833, that was one of the first to admit Black students, in 1835, well before the establishment of many HBCUs. Oberlin College's early commitment to racial integration set an important precedent in the fight for access to higher education for Black Americans.

Before the Civil War and the abolition of slavery in 1865, institutionalized slavery and segregation made higher education largely inaccessible to black men. The founding of HBCUs in the post-Civil War period marked a pivotal first step toward providing Black students with formal access to higher education, though the struggle for educational equity would continue for decades.

The combination of slavery and segregation prior to the Civil War severely restricted Black Americans' educational opportunities. Though a few exceptions existed, such as Oberlin College in Ohio and Bowdoin College in Maine, African Americans were largely excluded from higher education. Abolitionists, missionaries, and progressive citizens worked tirelessly to break this pattern of discrimination, some quietly, while others actively established schools and churches in areas controlled by Union armies during the war to educate former slaves and their descendants (Brown & Ricard, 2007, p. 117).

Following the Civil War, the creation of hundreds of Black colleges and universities became a defining feature of Black educational access. The passage of Jim Crow laws in 1889, which mandated segregation in public institutions, reinforced the necessity for Black people to establish their own educational institutions. The 1890 Second Morrill Act, which allocated federal funds for Black colleges, often served as an economic tool for segregationists to control Black education, providing funding for schools that would remain separate from white institutions (PWIs).

By 1890, more than 200 institutions for black students had been established, largely due to the post-Reconstruction amendments (13th, 14th, and 15th Amendments) requiring states to provide public education for black Americans. The Second Morrill Act also extended federal support to schools enrolling black students, but it often further entrenched segregation, as it was used to fund schools that were separate from the predominantly white institutions (PWIs).

In 1895, a significant debate emerged between Booker T. Washington and W.E.B. Du Bois about the mission of HBCUs. Washington advocated for a focus on vocational training for the masses alongside liberal arts, while Du Bois believed in the intellectual development of an elite group—the "Talented Tenth" who would lead the Black community. Their differing perspectives helped shape the mission of HBCUs and remain influential in shaping the purpose of these institutions today (Arroyo & Gasman, 2014).

Despite legal advances such as the 1954 Brown v. Board of Education decision, which declared racial segregation in public schools unconstitutional, the road to integration was long and fraught with resistance. In 1963, 327 years after the founding of Harvard, Clemson University in South Carolina was one of the last major institutions to integrate. Federal support for black students through programs like the Second Morrill Act was often misused to create separate institutions, exacerbating segregation.

The creation of HBCUs was essential to the history of educational access for Black Americans. These institutions not only provided educational opportunities during segregation but also became central to the cultural and intellectual development of the Black community. In contrast to PWIs, many HBCUs adopted an open admissions policy that welcomed students of all backgrounds, reflecting the inclusive ideals of these institutions (Mathers, 2016).

However, challenges remain. The 1978 Regents of the University of California v. Bakke decision ruled that racial quotas in admissions were unconstitutional, but that race could still be used as a "plus" factor. This decision created a complex and sometimes contradictory landscape for college admissions, as institutions sought to comply with both the Brown and Bakke decisions. In the 1980s, Black enrollment in majority-white institutions peaked, but affirmative action policies and other factors have led many Black students to return to HBCUs, which continue to be vital in educating and uplifting the Black community (Stallion, 2013).

The struggle for equal access to education has evolved but remains deeply entrenched in American society. Despite centuries of systemic oppression, Black Americans have forged ahead, creating opportunities for themselves and future generations through HBCUs. Today, these institutions remain vital in fostering academic, cultural, and social advancements for Black students, continuing to serve as pillars of support, education, and empowerment.

Current Challenges

While in some countries the concept and practice of open-door admissions to colleges and universities would be considered natural, and maybe even progressive, in America it was viewed as a stigma by which to devalue HBCUs. According to Brown et al. (2004),

Black colleges literally reversed the tradition of social-class and academic exclusiveness that had always been characteristic of higher education. They invented the practice, if not the concept, of open enrollment. Its flexible admissions practices and academic standards are without precedent in higher education. This is, no doubt, a fundamental reason why Black colleges have been so widely criticized by leaders in higher education and why they have been largely ignored by the most prestigious honor societies. (p. 25)

Debates continue even today, claiming, in the spirit of humanity, that America adopts an open-door policy for access to institutions of learning to anyone who chooses to pursue higher education. Politicians and many others have debated making education free for anyone wishing to attend college or universities. According to Brown (2013),

The nation's higher education institutions might do well to emulate HBCUs by adopting principles and practices that meet students where they are first and then provide them with the spectrum of skills that will enable them to remain successful during and after college. (p. 126)

There has even been talk about making community college tuition-free, which would mimic the idea of meeting students where they are and providing them with a spectrum of skills. As William H. Gray, III, former president of the United Negro College Fund, has noted,

Historically Black Colleges and Universities play a critical role in American higher education. They produce a disproportionate number of African American baccalaureate recipients and are the undergraduate degree-of-origin for a disproportionate share of Ph.D.'s for Blacks. These institutions perform miracles in elevating disadvantaged youth to productive citizenship. If they did not exist, we would have to invent them. (Brown, 2013, p. 145)

Literature on Blacks in Education

The focal point of this study was to examine the success of Black males' pursuit of post- baccalaureate degrees. These historical difficulties and challenges serve as a gauge of how far Black males have progressed in terms of the main components now required to assure optimum performance for Black males furthering their education. When we analyze the most recent situational statistics involving percentages of Black students pursuing degrees at both HBCUs and PWIs at various levels of higher education, it becomes apparent that more attention needs to be given to student retention at the graduate level.

Statistics of HBCUs v. PWIs

Black students, particularly black men, have a lot of work to do, according to data from the National Center for Education Statistics (NCES). The numbers have remained modest over the years (see Table 1). According to data from Table 1, 66.8% of the total master's degrees were conferred on whites in 2018 postsecondary institutions, compared to 11.2% for Blacks. Even though the gap is closing, there was a 55.6% difference in 2018, compared to an 85.6% difference in 1976-1977, while the percentage of the white population with master's degrees was 90.6% to Blacks' 5%. Based on statistics alone, there have been major changes from 1976 to the current day.

However, HBCU institutions have seen a record high in enrollment. As the 2018 data from the National Center for Education Statistics (NCES) explains:

The number of HBCU students increased by 47 percent (from 223,000 to 327,000 students) between 1976 and 2010, then decreased by 15 percent (to 279,000 students) between 2010 and 2020 (forthcoming). In comparison, the number of students in all degree-granting institutions increased 91 percent (from 11 million to 21 million students) between 1976 and 2010, then decreased 10 percent (to 19 million students) between 2010

and 2020 (forthcoming). (NCES, 2018)

Table 1

Master's Degrees Conferred by Postsecondary Institutions, by Race/Ethnicity and Sex of Student: Selected Years, 1976-77 through 2017-18

Year and sex	Number of degrees conferred to U.S. citizens, permanent residents, and nonresident aliens								Percentage distribution of degrees conferred to U.S. citizens and permanent residents						
	Total	White	Black	His-panic	Asian/ Pacific Islander	American Indian/ Alaska Native	Two or more races[1]	Non-resi-dent alien	Total	White	Black	His-panic	Asian/ Pacific Islander	American Indian/ Alaska Native	Two or more races[1]
1	2	3	4	5	6	7	8	9	10	11	12	13	14	15	16
Males															
1976-77[2]	172,703	144,042	7,970	3,328	3,128	565	---	13,670	100.0	90.6	5.0	2.1	2.0	0.4	---
1980-81[3]	151,602	120,927	6,418	3,155	3,830	507	---	16,765	100.0	89.7	4.8	2.3	2.8	0.4	---
1990-91	160,842	117,993	6,201	4,017	6,765	495	---	25,371	100.0	87.1	4.6	3.0	5.0	0.4	---
1999-2000	196,129	131,221	11,642	7,738	11,299	845	---	33,384	100.0	80.6	7.2	4.8	6.9	0.5	---
2000-01	197,770	128,516	11,878	8,371	11,561	925	---	36,519	100.0	79.7	7.4	5.2	7.2	0.6	---
2003-04	233,056	146,369	15,027	10,929	14,551	1,137	---	45,043	100.0	77.9	8.0	5.8	7.7	0.6	---
2004-05	237,155	150,076	16,136	11,501	15,238	1,167	---	43,037	100.0	77.3	8.3	5.9	7.8	0.6	---
2005-06	241,701	153,696	17,388	11,738	16,037	1,253	---	41,589	100.0	76.8	8.7	5.9	8.0	0.6	---
2006-07	242,213	154,250	18,340	12,471	16,689	1,275	---	39,188	100.0	76.0	9.0	6.1	8.2	0.6	---
2007-08	250,203	157,622	18,759	13,166	17,480	1,294	---	41,882	100.0	75.7	9.0	6.3	8.4	0.6	---
2008-09	263,515	162,863	20,146	14,314	18,865	1,349	---	45,978	100.0	74.9	9.3	6.6	8.7	0.6	---
2009-10	275,317	170,243	22,121	15,554	19,423	1,419	---	46,557	100.0	74.4	9.7	6.8	8.5	0.6	---
2010-11	291,680	177,786	23,746	17,183	19,918	1,409	2,540	49,098	100.0	73.3	9.8	7.1	8.2	0.6	1.0
2011-12	302,484	183,222	25,284	18,632	20,751	1,298	3,518	49,778	100.0	72.5	10.0	7.4	8.2	0.5	1.4
2012-13	301,552	177,208	26,417	19,441	20,456	1,280	4,472	52,279	100.0	71.1	10.6	7.8	8.2	0.5	1.8
2013-14	302,846	173,303	26,608	20,565	19,955	1,219	4,890	56,306	100.0	70.3	10.8	8.3	8.1	0.5	2.0
2014-15	306,615	168,151	26,295	21,384	19,577	1,223	5,438	64,547	100.0	69.5	10.9	8.8	8.1	0.5	2.2
2015-16	320,574	166,161	27,024	22,749	20,071	1,229	6,129	77,211	100.0	68.3	11.1	9.3	8.2	0.5	2.5
2016-17	326,857	164,734	26,978	23,749	20,693	1,151	6,453	83,099	100.0	67.6	11.1	9.7	8.5	0.5	2.6
2017-18	326,870	164,714	27,552	25,255	21,273	1,076	6,658	80,342	100.0	66.8	11.2	10.2	8.6	0.4	2.7

[1] For years prior to 2010-11, the survey did not yet include the "Two or more races" category, and each student could be counted in only one race category.

[2] Excludes 387 males and 175 females whose racial/ethnic group was not available.

[3] Excludes 1,377 males and 179 females whose racial/ethnic group was not available.

NOTE: Data are for postsecondary institutions participating in Title IV federal financial aid programs. Race categories exclude persons of Hispanic ethnicity. For 1989-90 and later years, reported racial/ethnic distributions of students by level of degree, field of degree, and sex were used to estimate race/ethnicity for students whose race/ethnicity was not reported. Detail may not sum to totals because of rounding. Some data have been revised from previously published figures.

SOURCE: U.S. Department of Education, National Center for Education Statistics, Higher Education General Information Survey (HEGIS), "Degrees and Other Formal Awards Conferred" surveys, 1976-77 and 1980-81; Integrated Postsecondary Education Data System (IPEDS), "Completions Survey" (IPEDS-C:90-99); and IPEDS Fall 2000 through Fall 2018, Completions component. (This table was prepared October 2019.)

(NCES, (2018). U.S. Department of Education, Institute of Education Sciences, *National Center for Education Statistics*).

As we observe the numbers from 1976 to 2010, we find that student enrollment increased and then decreased between 2010 and 2020. We also see, however, that even though enrollment at HBCUs increased by 17% between 1976 and 2010, student enrollment decreased by 18%. This obviously implies that the students who were enrolled did not remain. According to the NCES (2018):

While black enrollment at HBCUs increased by 11 percent between 1976 and 2020, the total number of black students enrolled in all degree-granting postsecondary institutions more than doubled during this period. The percentage of black students enrolled at HBCUs fell from 18 percent in 1976 to 8 percent in 2014 and then increased to 9 percent in 2020. (NCES, 2018)

Between 2019 and 2020, HBCUs were awarded 48,200 degrees. Of the degrees conferred by HBCUs, only 6% counted for Doctorate degrees. Also, according to NCES (2018):

Of the degrees conferred by HBCUs, the majority (73 percent) were conferred to black students. Black students earned 44 percent of the 5,200 associate degrees, 79 percent of the 33,200 bachelor's degrees, 72 percent of the 7,000 master's degrees, and 59 percent of the 2,800 doctoral degrees conferred by HBCUs in 2019–20. At all levels, just over 2- thirds of degrees conferred to Black students were conferred to Black female students. (NCES, 2018)

The most recent data tells us that in the years 2017-2018, bachelor's degrees have fallen to 13% and master's degrees have fallen to 6%. Doctorate degree pursuits fell from 14% to 11%.

According to the NCES (2018),

Over time, the percentages of bachelor's and master's degrees conferred to Black students by HBCUs have decreased. For example, HBCUs conferred 35 percent of the bachelor's degrees and 21 percent of the master's degrees Black students earned in 1976– 77, compared with 13 and 6 percent, respectively, of bachelor's and master's degrees Black students earned in 2017–18. (NCES, 2018)

Additionally, the percentage of Black doctor's degree recipients from HBCUs was lower in 2017–18 (11%) than in 1976–77 (14%) (NCES, 2018) [See Appendix E for the relevant parts of the Doctor's degrees conferred by postsecondary institutions, by race/ethnicity and sex of student. Selected years,1976-77 through 2016-17).

The data from the (2018) NCES gives a snapshot of education as it relates to different ethnic races and genders. Over a span of 42 years, you can see the number of degrees conferred to U.S. citizens. Although it also demonstrates an increase of Black students who have received degrees, Black students' pursuit of higher degrees remains low when compared to their white counterparts.

In 1976, the overall number of white people who obtained degrees was 79,932 or 91.9%, whereas the total number of Black people who received degrees was 3,575 or 4.1%, a disparity of 87%. The table begins to show a progressive increase in Blacks; however, the white population percentage began to go down in 2006-07. Finally, in 2016-17 the total for white students was 107,455 (67%); the total for black students was 14,067 (8.8%), a 58.2% difference in the total number of degrees conferred to U.S. citizens today (NCES, 2019). (See Table 4 in Appendix E for the relevant data.) Doctoral degrees conferred by postsecondary institutions, by race/ethnicity and sex of the student: selected years, 1976-77 through 2016-17. The table indicates that white students were 94,225 (74%) in comparison to Black students at 9,371 (7.4%).)

Statistics on Doctoral Programs

During the presidential terms of President Barack Obama, from 2009 to 2016, there was a spike in interest and an influx of black men and women entering doctoral programs at American colleges and universities (see Appendix E for the relevant parts of the Doctoral degrees conferred by postsecondary institutions, by race/ethnicity and sex of student: Selected years, 1976-77 through 2016-17). This was a significant time in history for Black males, not only in education but also all over the world. It was a message of hope and self-image, reminding people that yes, we can, and we will make change. The grassroots movement was being heard, but it was also able to expand on existing opportunities and to create new opportunities.

NCES (2018) states that "of the 3.0 million post-baccalaureate students enrolled in fall 2017, some 1.6 million were White, 365,000 were Black, 275,000 were Hispanic, 215,000 were Asian/Pacific Islander, and

13,600 were American Indian/Alaska Native" (NCES, 2018). In addition, NCES (2018) further examined post-baccalaureate enrollment for the student population and found that post-baccalaureate enrollment for each racial/ethnic group was higher in 2017 than in 2000. For example, the percentage of post-baccalaureate students who were Black was higher in 2010 and 2017 (14% in both years) than in 2000 (9%) (NCES, 2018).

According to NCES (2018), "between 2000 and 2017, total post-baccalaureate enrollment increased by 39 percent (from 2.2 million to 3.0 million students). By 2028, post-baccalaureate enrollment is projected to increase to 3.1 million students" (NCES, 2018).

With black enrollment expected to increase, attention must be given to the retention of post-baccalaureate students. As this population grows, educators will be forced to accommodate these students in the classroom. The retention of these students would be greatly enhanced by an institution's ability to reach students where they are, as well as to create a clear and attainable path to get them where they need to be. According to Berger et al. (2005), an important distinction is that the concept of retention has evolved over time and so has the recognition that one size does not fit all in terms of retention rates and the policies and interventions needed to improve retention on any one campus. Hence, as the study of retention has developed, so has awareness that each institution must tailor retention to fit the specific needs of its students and the context of that environment. (p. 9)

Student achievement and academic success are based on a college's unique ability to design and include a diverse arrangement of classroom engagement with material that supports the student's interests. To be effective, these actions must be addressed in both HBCUs and PWIs institutions.

Best Practices

When looking at the realities of Black men's graduate recruitment, preparation, admissions, matriculation, persistence, retention, and likelihood of success, the literature in this section focuses on articulating the needs of the students of color, applying best practices, and proposing a set of best practice solutions for better engaging Black students on campus.

It is essential to look at best practices for retaining Black males in all educational institutions to uncover methods to duplicate in the future. "Black student retention in postsecondary institutions has continued to decline during the last decade at a 42% decline." (Baker, 2019, p. 4). To increase retention and minimize African American student dropout rates, PWIs developed programs focused on study skills training, mentoring, and tutoring. When compared to another group of African American students, participation in a support program had a significant impact on the retention of African American students (Baker, 2019; Johnson, 2013).

It is critical for Black males to take the lead in shaping the narrative about what is imperative to their ability to prosper in a higher education system that will provide purpose and propel them forward in their academic pursuits. Research paying keen attention to the success rate of Black male students at various HBCUs, PWIs and HSI institutions can teach methods to enhance best practices for everyone involved in education. Best solutions can increase the likelihood of everyone following best practices.

Howard et al. (2012) used a counter-storytelling method in a 2008 study involving the narratives of five black undergraduate males, which states,

In his research on African American males, [Tyrone] Howard made use of counter- storytelling to illuminate the ways Black males make sense of barriers they faced in their quest for academic achievement. He subsequently highlighted the importance of tapping into students' narratives to understand the internal processes that some Black males go through to excel in schools. (Howard et. al, p. 97)

This is pertinent to the current study method, which will be discussed later in Chapter 3. Nonetheless, Dr. Howard's 2008 study discovered value in the narratives of Black males and their contribution to knowledge, to understanding the needs and putting together a winning approach. Listening to others has a significant impact. To change the mainstream media's perception of Black males by studying successful students' techniques and listening to and acting on what they say:

As these studies have demonstrated, developing scholarship that makes use of Black males' voices has the potential to advance informed practices that begin to turnaround disturbing trends in the schooling experience of this population. We suggest that the incorporation of narratives voiced by marginalized people can also help to dismantle the dominant discourses surrounding race, class, and gender groups. These counter stories represent non-mainstream stories that can represent other truths, and other experiences that directly refute hegemony. (Howard et. al, p. 97)

Similarly, the positive impact of narratives from graduate students' best practice support programs can be attributed to the practice of seeing someone with whom you can connect with or who possibly looks like you and provide an opportunity to form constructive relationships with other Black faculty and students.

Furthermore, Quaye and Harper (2007) admit this factor, noting the condition of students and teachers, and state,

"Previous research emphasizes the importance of Black males' college experiences, including relationships with other Black students and Black faculty. It has been reported that the absence of these interactions greatly impacts students' academic achievement and well-being." (p. 138)

Keeping the challenge of boosting the success of Black males in higher education in mind, and to answer the study research questions, understanding relationships with students from similar backgrounds demonstrates that it benefits not only one's well-being, but also contributes to educational success.

Best practices include learning from what has worked in the past to help retain Black males in higher education institutions. Virginia Union's Vice President and Director, Dr.Strayhorn, a successful undergraduate model, believes that a sense of belonging is essential. It turns out that if you just give somebody some attention, and say "you matter", their performance will increase. We should all strive to mobilize ourselves and find out who is making the decisions within our communities. We should participate in programs that make a difference, such as the BAM (Becoming A Man) Organization in Chicago, which began with 400 members and now has well over 7,000 members. Being consistent and showing consistency in creating similar programs across the country that will make a difference in the world is important. Giving devoted attention to black male success and understanding that education is a good start in life encourages change.

More recently, Weissman (2021) explains what has been beneficial to doctoral students at UCLA as coming in as a cohort enabled students to "connect and create a sense of community, and that makes all the difference in the world." ... The literature has been clear that when students feel a sense of connection to a place and to other people, they tend to do well, at the graduate and undergraduate levels. (p. 10)

Mr. Edwards, one of the seven doctoral cohort members, discusses how his relationships and involvement with the other members of the cohort influenced his graduation experience. In his description of the effect of faculty and peer networks on engaging with PhD students, Mr. Edwards describes it as it worked. Students grab meals together and swap notes, sharing resources from their respective research areas, which has a "magnifying effect" on all their scholarship, Edwards said. But for him, it's not just about his peers but also the faculty. (Weissman, 2021, p. 10)

Dr. Howard continues, "We've come a long way, but there's still more work to be done." Cohort is a strategy or technique that should become the standard for graduate students who arrive as a group of people who have created a bond or are recognized as one. Dr. Howard elucidates:

He wants this cohort to be "the norm," not an "anomaly," We know what it takes. That doesn't mean that we're perfect, I think there's still a lot more work we can do, a lot more that we can be better at, but I think this model at least speaks to what can be done. (Weissman, 2021, p. 10)

By having everyone educate themselves, being the ultimate change, and insisting that those in control of making decisions include the Black male, these best practices promote and reverse the media stream. Best practices are always available and present, but the issue is that they are not being followed to uncover the truth and develop a pathway for success for Black male students.

The significance of notable accomplishments, examples of best practices from successful Black male graduate students, and research presented on this phenomenon by outstanding researchers was especially important. It is ideal to examine the undergraduate experience and apply best practices to the graduate experience. Listening to black scholars' narratives and insights, as well as other effective measures, can help everyone benefit from past experiences.

Furthermore, building on existing literature, including Dr. Tyrone Howard's (Black Male Institute) and Dr. Terrel Strayhorn's (Sense of Belonging). Statistics and research on the success rate of Black male students at various HBCUs, HSIs, and PWIs are retentively low. This study, on the other hand, will explain and make sense of the positive ways to navigate a post- baccalaureate degree while learning from scholars who have paved the way.

Black Mentorship

The Era of President Barack Obama

The presence of administrators and educators who are Black does much to boost the morale of students. It presents a reflection of the reality of the world which in and of itself acknowledges a respect for the contribution of Black people. Syed et al. (2011) discuss research that identifies mentors from similar backgrounds as particularly important to students of color because they represent prototypes that enable students to gain a sense of academic self-efficacy. On an emotional level, it may feel comforting to have the guidance of someone who has already solved some of the problems confronting one's own demographic group, and it may be less difficult to trust one's own than to trust someone who seems to resemble one's own (Blake-Beard et. al., 2011). Seeing a black man, Barack Obama, campaign for and win the presidency of the United States inspired millions of black men around the world to hope that their dreams might be realized as well. The same can be said when black students see images of Black administrators and educators on their college and university campuses. The value to black students of having black administrators, educators, and peer mentors is unequivocal when it comes to a student's engagement and morale. According to Black-Beard et al. (2011), Study on the mentoring experiences of 163 business school doctoral students of color found that graduate students of color reported receiving more psychosocial and instrumental support from, and being more comfortable with and satisfied with, mentors who were also people of color. (p. 627)

This point in the research will be critical as it specifically speaks to graduate mentorship relating to race. The mere sight of former President Barack Obama, a black man running for the presidential office and winning, was a vision that inspired other black men and women of all races to reach higher. It is imperative that we build a foundation of support and incentives to ensure black males' interest and engagement. According to Young (2010),

There have been articles, including one in the New York Times, that discuss the Obama Effect on test-taking scores. The Obama Effect is a term used to describe how Obama has positively affected certain aspects of our current society including the economy, politics, and education. The study consisted of 84 Blacks and 388 Whites in 2007, where they were administered a test of twenty questions concerning "survival" & "success", to see the effect on standardized test scores. On average, Whites answered twelve out of twenty questions correctly, whereas Blacks answered only 8.5 out of twenty correctly. Then again in 2008, this test was administered directly after President Obama's acceptance speech.

This time, the gap between the races was statistically narrow. Many people associate this phenomenon with a belief that Black people have been saying "we can" but now seeing the realities of this truth in Obama, are creating change in their own beliefs and motivation to academically succeed. (p. 13)

Does this mean, as many believe, that Obama's image is changing the perceptions that Blacks have about themselves? This research, and the Obama Effect, is concerned with its relationship to education. This factor gives credence to the concept that having more Black instructors and administrators in schools adds to the level of recruitment and retention, and comfort and inspiration of Black students. Witnessing a Black man achieving the highest office in the nation, which before him was unfathomable for Black males, lays the groundwork that anything is possible, and glass ceilings can be broken. President Obama's presence in the election has had an impact on African Americans, perhaps most especially on black males (Vaughn, 2015).

According to Vaughn (2015), There are several scholarly journals and books that discuss President Obama's rise to the presidency, his leadership skills, as well as issues of race. But for social mobility and the influx of graduate students, there are few. There are studies showing how former President Barack Obama had a significant impact on high school students, raising the level of standardized test taking and narrowing the achievement gap between black and white students. (p. 15)

The mentoring of Black male students by other Black males is essential to the success of Black males in higher education. When black students have positive role models it contributes to their learning environment (Palmer et al., 2010). To be successful, black students need to be able to identify with black faculty and staff who promote education (Palmer et al., 2010). Black students need successful role models they can identify with to promote academic competence and self-esteem (Grant-Thompson & Atkinson, 1997).

Lack of Mentorship

As with PWIs and HBCUs, there is a shortage of Black mentors across educational institutions (Sato et al., 2018). According to Brooms and Davis (2017), This qualitative study investigated the collegiate experiences of 59 Black males at three different historically White institutions. Specifically, we explore how these students construct meaning from their collegiate experiences and their efforts for educational success. As black males, they were confronted by a deficit perspective that often translated into lowered expectations of them across the college milieu—both academic and social—and posited them as outsiders on campus. (p. 187)

This perspective of scarcity has inadvertent consequences in the lack of representation of Black administrators and faculty. Black males are misunderstood and misrepresented by their white counterparts, and they are tossed into categories of deficit learning and subpar learning programs and engagement opportunities. This has served as a systemic disadvantage for Black males who otherwise would be able to compete fairly within a broader scope of opportunities. According to Brooms and Davis (2017),

It seems to reason that Black mentorship would assist in the matriculation of Black male students ... in response, the students articulated two critical components of their college experience that positively shaped their persistence efforts: (a) peer-to-peer bonding and associations with other Black males and (b) mentoring from Black faculty members. Findings suggest that these social networks and micro-communities both enhance and support Black males' persistence in college. (p. 187)

Other studies conducted examined the situational perceptions of Black and White mentors as well as the perceptions of Black students while engaging. Tuitt (2012) states that when it comes to the exploration of the phenomenon of mentoring in higher education, the research suggests that some Black graduate students enter classrooms taught by professors who are Black, like them, with the perception that Black faculty (a) are innocent until proven guilty, (b) will serve as role models who hold them to higher standards, and (c) will view Black students and be viewed by these same students as representatives of their race. The manuscript concludes by suggesting that Black professors must be aware of such perceptions and discover how to navigate this racial paradox if they are to successfully fulfill their responsibility to lift the souls of Black graduate students in the presence of their academic experience. (p. 186)

Although the paradigm of their perceptions needs to be acknowledged by the Black professors, who are more than likely also the mentors, that is essentially why Black male students are more successful with like-minded mentors. They understand, comprehend, and acknowledge implicit issues of the black community so they know how to help these men navigate through their issues, whatever they may be.

Theoretical Framework

The research questions were investigated through two theoretical frameworks. Alexander Astin's Student Involvement Theory and Critical Race Theory by Gloria Ladson-Billings and William Tate. Both are influential when analyzing student engagement and race in education. To increase the retention rates of Black males in graduate school, there must be an understanding of the challenges and processes these individuals endured. Astin's Student Involvement Theory combined with Critical Race Theory in Education provides key elements to understanding the success rate of Black males in higher education programs. According to Dancy (2012) and Strayhorn (2010), "the study of being a Black male on a college campus is complex, and it is in this complexity that it is studied." The 2-fold theoretical approach in Astin's Student Involvement Theory and Critical Race Theory was used as reference structures and preliminary ways of knowing.

Student Involvement/Engagement

The Astin Theory is a key component to implement in evaluating students' progress over the course of matriculation. One technique used in this study was to track and monitor the success stories of Black men so that further analysis could be made on the participants' involvement and how it impacted their environments. Astin (1993) offered several implications of his theory of student involvement for students, faculty members, and administrators.

Utilizing the student involvement theory, Alexander Astin states that the student receives what the student puts in. Focusing on the areas in which the retention rate can be increased opens the path for mentorship.

Healthy mentorship and advocacy promote the importance of these students staying persistent. By placing an emphasis on ability, the student must flourish in their academic community and more Black males will gravitate towards their personal niche in their school setting. Astin's Student Involvement Theory refers to the "I-E-O" model, the "I" stands for "input," which is the student's background and who they are—in this case, the personal characteristics of race and gender (e.g. black males) serve as the inputs. The "E" refers to environment, which is detailed as a higher education institution's setting and where the student decides which institution to attend. Lastly, the "O" stands for outcome. This references how the race and gender of a student (input) interacts with the university (environment) and what that interaction creates in the student's life and their lived experiences (outcome). Moreover, Alexander Astin's (1993) fifth assumption refers to involvement—the more involved a student is in their institution, the higher the level of academic achievement. Corresponding to Astin's Student Involvement Theory, the student's level of success is equal to the effort the student gives to their own achievements.

Research broadly suggests that Black males who are actively engaged in campus life gain more from the college experience and are more likely to succeed academically (Harper, 2012; Pascarella & Terenzini, 1991, 2005; Strayhorn, 2008b). Although there is a plethora of research that has examined the college experiences, engagement, and academic success of minority students, limited research exists specifically targeting the correlation between engagement factors and the academic success and college satisfaction of African American males (Harvey-Smith, 2002; Kimbrough & Harper, 2006; Outcalt & Skewes-Cox, 2002; Palmer et al., 2010). The study concluded that black male students who have a connection to faculty and staff on campus and are involved with campus life outside the classroom are more likely to graduate. Hague-Palmer, (2013) suggests that research is needed to address and incorporate academic and co-curricular initiatives, services and policies in the culture of higher education institutions that will enhance the college experience and ensure academic success, retention, and matriculation of Black males. This study will contribute to improving the number of successful Black males in higher education by examining participant involvement and engagement. This will have a beneficial impact on post-baccalaureate graduation rates and on increased graduate school enrollments.

Student Involvement. "You get out what you put in" may be trite, but it is undeniably true. Imagine how unsuccessful a student would be if he or she did not put out any effort or work. Alexander Astin states that the less involvement of the student inclines them to question their role as students, get less involved, or simply drop out.

According to Alexander Astin's (1984) interview, to understand the differences between college enrollment and future admissions, one must understand retention as a concept of involvement. There is a direct connection between individuals who are more prone to debt and unwilling to speak up and seek answers, whereas those who are more resilient will do everything it takes, regardless of the barriers. In reference to Levitz & et. al,(1999), Bean (1980) suggested that students who successfully integrate and are engaged in activities beyond the classroom tend to persist. (Levitz & et. al., 1999, p. 31).

Faculty Engagement. Taking a closer look at the Persistence Theory, Astin provides a multitude of implications of the theory of student involvement for not just the students but also for the administrators, faculty members, and students. This approach demonstrates that the load cannot be placed solely on the shoulders of the students. Students, faculty, and administrators take pride in becoming involved on their very own campus. Interestingly, when asked about the type of outcome goals to be sought, Astin replied,

One that comes directly out of the involvement concept is retention. One healthy thing that is happening on campuses now is the creation of retention committees that bring together fiscal people who are interested in retention because it reflects, to an extent, the culmination of their very efforts. (Richmond, 1986, p. 62)

When asked about the role of the theory of involvement as a guideline for developing students' values, Astin explained "We communicate values by the way we operate our institutions" (Richmond, 1986, p. 62).

Astin's approach includes implementing the cooperation of the entire university, from faculty to administrators all the way down to the students. Everyone played a significant part in bringing the involvement component into the university environment. More universities are beginning to see the power of involvement. Persistence and resilience, as well as effort both inside and outside of the classroom, are required.

Although this study aims to demonstrate the significance of Black student involvement within the theoretical framework of post-baccalaureate pursuits, it is also significant to study Critical Race Theory, which also provides layers as to how systematic acts of racial oppression have subverted the intent of Black students to attend and graduate from postbaccalaureate programs.

Critical Race Theory

Critical Race Theory is credited to Derrick Bell, Kimberle Crenshaw, Richard Delgado, Gloria Ladson-Billings, Mari Matsude, and Patricia Williams, who in the latter part of the 20th century contextualized race, racism, and power within economics, history, and individualized and group interests within legal studies (Delgado & Stefancic, 2012).

For the purpose of peeling back the layers of higher education, this study selected Critical Race Theory as a foundational framework. The purpose of this research is to identify the various factors that have influenced the current disposition of our society and its educational system to shed light on the residual impact it has had on Black men. In addition, providing others with an understanding of several underlying issues that have evolved into attitudes and situations that they are unaware of. Once people are aware they can come to grips with their feelings and thoughts, move beyond the details, rise above what was in the past and fully embrace their present.

Solórzano (1997) defines Critical Race Theory "as a framework or set of basic perspectives, methods, and pedagogy that seeks to identify, analyze, and transform those structural and cultural aspects of society that maintain the subordination and marginalization of "people of color"

Critical Race Theory originated in the discipline of law, such as in the U.S. Constitution, to transition former slaves equally into mainstream America. Critical Race Theory's switch to education pertaining to Black males was inevitable. When examining the tenets of Critical Race Theory, the marginalization of people of color is the focus, as it pulls from an underlying theme of breaking down the insistent system of white supremacy (Gilborn, 2005).

Derrick Bell (1992) outlines Critical Race Theory's six principles:

1. Acknowledges that racism is normal and endemic in U.S. society. Expect racism and oppression throughout institutions.
2. Skeptical about legal claims of neutrality, color-blindness, and objectivity. Instead, they articulate processes through which the political, economic, and social contexts are shaped by the longstanding racist dynamics of the United States.
3. Acknowledges that racism and oppression underscore social structures, thus differences between haves and have-nots (social stratification).

4. Counter-storytelling is a methodology to convey the experiences of people of color and display their differences from the dominant narrative.

5. Idea of Whiteness as property; it can be bartered, exchanged, or cashed in for other forms of capital (economic, social, cultural, etc.).

6. Seeks to eliminate racism and to address oppression.

This research attempts to see if Critical Race Theory can be applied to this issue with Black males in graduate school. Does race play a factor in the success of males in post- baccalaureate programs? The flexibility of finding someone like themselves, whether it is through a group or event they were exposed to, is important to encourage a sense of acceptance. Professors and administrators will see growth in each student if they welcome everyone with a sense of belonging. By channeling energy that is welcoming and understanding of diversity, professors can facilitate in expanding the representation of Black males in graduate school. "Maybe then these young men will have the opportunity to fulfill their potential" (Whiting, 2006, p. 227). In comparison, the exceptional Civil Rights leader W.E.B. Dubois (1903) states, "To be a poor man is hard, but to be a poor Race in a land of dollars is the very bottom of hardships" (p. 5).

Based on research from the literature (Gilborn, 2005; Selden, 1999; Solorzano, 1997), higher education practices reflect society's racist political system. This is important because Black students enter higher education to gain access to opportunities that would otherwise be out of reach, but what they face are the same challenges that are experienced by those not in higher education (Selden, 1999). Critical Race Theory, for the purposes of this study, aids in understanding systemic racism, which is imperative to overcoming oppression for Black males (Adams, 2018, p. 45). It is important that educational institutions reach beyond the status quo if a true discipline of change is to be encouraged for Black males.

Critical Race Theory in Education. Institutional racism refers to the intended or unintended consequences that emerge from the operation, procedures, rules, habits, culture, and symbols of a given organization or institution that negatively affect the marginalized group in relation to that of the dominant group. According to Myers (2001),

An assumption sometimes made by an institution's faculty and/or administration is that there is a lack of qualified Black applicants for academic positions; this despite the gradual increase in Black doctoral graduates and the mismatch between those graduates and the percentage of Black faculty."(p. 8)

Delgado and Stefancic (2012) assert that, "Racism is a common, normalized occurrence, not an outlier encounter, experienced by people of color in American society. Normative racism makes naming racism a challenge for people of color who confront day-to-day and systemic acts of racial oppression" (Delgado & Stefancic, 2012). As Blockett states, race can be espoused as

A fluid, social construct that allows a racially dominant group to manipulate subordinate groups to benefit racial supremacy and for economic, social, and psychological gain. A change in the inclusion and exclusion of racialized group's standing is based on the economic or psychological preservation needs of the dominant group, also known as material determinism. (p. 102)

Critical Race Theory theorists critique race-neutral policies and laws as part of a problematic liberalist ideology centered on individual meritocracy. Using Critical Race Theory as an analytic, Blockett et al. (2016) assume that racism is embedded within the educational environment and impacts the socialization of all doctoral students. As this project is specifically interested in the socialization and professionalization of doctoral students of color, particularly Black male students, Critical Race Theory provides a necessary lens to examine an asset-based approach to the literature reviewed in this book.

In studies such as this, researchers such as Griffin et al. (2014), driven by critical race theory, employ composite counter-storytelling to narrate the experiences of Black male faculty on traditionally white campuses. Situated at the intersection of race and gender, this study's composite counter-story is richly informed by 11 interviews with Black male faculty, alongside critical race scholarship that documents the omnipresence of Black ideology. Through the protagonist, Dr. Timesnow, a black male Assistant Professor, this study reflects on how his daily experiences incite racial battle fatigue, feed imposter syndrome, and circumvent an inclusive campus community (Griffin et al., 2014).

Furthermore, racism at traditionally PWIs may be a key contributor to the lack of strong mentorship and sponsorship for racial minority graduate students. In their discussion of white racism among white faculty, Scheurich and Young (2002) suggest that overt and covert racism at the individual level accompanies broader levels of racism existing within the institution and society. Overt racism refers to publicly conscious, harmful acts used against individuals or groups based on race. Covert racism refers to harmful acts used against others based on race that are not public. For example, even though a Black American doctoral student may be qualified to receive mentoring, a professor may consciously choose not to mentor the student because of racial biases. Scheurich and Young (2002) stated that "persons making covert, racially biased decisions do not explicitly broadcast their intentions; instead, they hide their biases and provide reasons that are acceptable within the discourse of the academy" (p. 223). Black male students must realize that racism is prevalent in American life and that "it is centered on the notion that racism is endemic in American life and exists in educational institutions in a myriad of forms. It is not individual but institutional or structural. The sole purpose is to end racial inequality." (Scheurich & Young, 2002, p. 223).

Higher Education. One cannot discuss W.E.B. Du Bois, without mentioning his most famous concept of black higher education, the idea of the Talented Tenth. Embedded in his advocacy for the public purpose of higher education, Du Bois believed that the most highly educated members of the black community, the Talented Tenth, were called to lead their communities out of social, political, and economic strife. "Through their 'knowledge of modern culture [they] could guide the American Negro to a higher civilization', assume leadership of the black community, and thereby challenge white supremacy, elevating black culture to its rightful place within the United States" (Welding, 2018, p. 287). Without such leadership from the Talented Tenth, Du Bois believed the black community would continue to suffer under white political and social control that did not prioritize the advancement of the black race (Welding, 2018).

Although the findings in this research serve to demonstrate where Black male students are in society, they also offer clarity as to the development of a system of education that was originally built for a selective group of white males. Furthermore, the literature of race factors in to give us a glimpse as to where we are as a nation. The measures necessary to increase the social and economic status of Black male scholars can be seen in the participants of the study's path through matriculation, toward a graduate degree, and beyond.

Student Involvement Theory, aligned with Critical Race Theory, commissions Black male students to challenge the status quo to effect positive change. This study explored the issues of Black males and higher educational success, guided by the research questions connected to Astin's Theory of Student Involvement and Critical Race Theory as it pertains to education.

Specific factors were discussed in the review of the literature. Ladson-Billings (2005) states that "students must develop and/or maintain cultural competence. She continues to state that "Students must develop a critical consciousness through which they challenge the status quo of the current social order" (p. 117).

Ladson-Billings (2016) explains cultural competence as:

Culturally relevant teachers understand that we exist in a complex, diverse, globally connected world, and that the world their students will enter as adults will be even more so. Thus, they comprehend the importance of helping students understand and appreciate their home culture while acquiring skills in additional cultures. But it is impossible for teachers to cultivate this competency in students if they themselves lack it. Far too many of our teachers have a mono-cultural experience and show little or no interest in learning about other experiences and cultures. (p. 36)

Ladson-Billings (1998) suggests that achieving cultural competence requires the student and the professor to be diverse in order to reach students in this dynamic globalized world. Ladson-Billings (2016) clarifies the definition of Critical Consciousness as follows:

This third component, or socio-political consciousness, speaks to the social and political reality of personal, community, national, and international civic life. To be able to function well in complex democracies, our teachers must help students make sense of these complexities. For students who come to school after witnessing multiple negative interactions of black people with law enforcement or hearing political leaders' rail against entire groups of people because of their home language or immigrant status, this can be confusing. Helping students make sense of these realities and rhetoric is what we must do to increase their engagement and help them see the relevance of schooling to everyday life. (p. 36) In 1987, Bell, a Critical Race theorist, named one of his books to describe the current plight of Black students by using a Biblical passage from Jeremiah, who mourned for his people's lack of deliverance saying, "The harvest is past, the summer is ended, and we are not saved" (Jer. 8:20). The insinuations from the title, "And We Are Not Saved: The Elusive Quest for Racial Justice", implies that the Black students who have made efforts for change still are in a place of little change. To continue the progress for change and equality, it is incumbent for Black male students in post-baccalaureate programs to be proactive in initiating incentives, mentorships, student involvement agendas, and networks that activate and maintain Black male engagement. Learning from what has worked in the past to help retain Blacks in higher education institutions will foreshadow what other institutions could do to accomplish higher rates. Some of those programs would include tutoring, mentoring, skills training, and support programs (Seidman et al., 2012, p. 11). According to research by Strayhorn, he uses the

Integrated Postsecondary Education Data System (IPEDS) and semi-structured interview data to provide a national portrait comparing predominantly White and historically Black public universities, as well as identify factors that influence the persistence and success of Black men in urban public universities. Findings suggest the importance of background traits, academic readiness, and the ways that urban public universities and society provide access, support systems, and close connections with communities for students. (Strayhorn, 2017, p. 1106)

These results suggest the importance of mentoring in the professional socialization of Black Americans on their academic journey. Doing so promises to expand educational and professional access in postsecondary settings. The utility of the illustrated findings should prove useful for both faculty and administrators interested in the engagement, retention (Strayhorn & Terrell, 2007), and attainment of at-risk or marginalized student groups.

Summary

Moving forward, the importance of mentoring in institutions and in professional arenas is critical to the successful socialization of Black Americans into both situations. Recreating academic programs to reflect a multi-racial and multicultural democracy calls for developing and strengthening mentoring opportunities within both undergraduate and graduate programs. Doing so promises to expand educational and professional access in postsecondary settings. The utility of this literature review should prove useful for both faculty and administrators interested in the engagement, retention (Strayhorn & Terrell, 2007), and attainment of at-risk or marginalized student groups.

This research and literature review were intended to influence further research in an optimistic and constructive manner, to create viable change in the ways we perceive and regard others academically and socially. The intention was to find and address patterns of history, analyze past and present statistics, and find best practices and active theories that comprehend how to initiate change in a positive way to increase the successes of the Black male in post- baccalaureate studies. Howard (2014) says,

Like Fanon, Tyrone Howard has set out to construct a new way of seeing and understanding Black males in American society. Yet, unlike others who have embraced the need to "save" Black males, seeks to do much more than raise achievement and increase graduation rates. He seeks to initiate a paradigm shift in the way Black men and boys are seen and understood ... without such a shift, a genuine change in outcomes and circumstances will not be possible. He has undertaken the Herculean task because he understands that the current image of the Black males—as an underachiever, a thug, criminal, a sexual deviant and predator, a shiftless father, and brainless athlete—is literally destroying Black men and boys. (p. xv).

Once this shift takes place within populations of our society, Black men can be seen for who they are, instead of preconceived notions of their characteristics or an insinuation of their worth. With equal representation of Black leaders as politicians, administrators, teachers, or mentors, Black men can aspire to achieve diverse positions of power and authority with confidence.

When it comes to Black people, the system does not always provide justice, and the same justice that is frequently provided to others in similar situations is required and must be provided to those Black male individuals. Understanding and not forgetting how Critical Race Theory plays a major part in the issue and why this refinement isn't given to these individuals is imperative. The point we strive to make with this meta-proposition is not that class and gender are insignificant, but rather, as Dr. Cornel West (2001) suggests, that "race matters," and, as Ladson-Billings & Tate (1995) insist, that "Blackness matters in more detailed ways" (Ladson-Billings & Tate, 1995, p. 52).

Critical Race Theory and Student Involvement Theory link the concept that one's environment and an individual's self-identity can play a role in graduating. Berger summarized what Astin (1999) stated by saying "differences in retention rates are a function not only of the type of environment provided by the institution but also a reflection as to how well that particular environment is designed to fit the needs of students enrolled at that institution" (Berger et al., 2005, p. 9).

The intent of this research was to ask the Black male participants about these perspectives and to articulate how and why these males have been successful. This will provide the key to replicate these findings and continue to make the Black male fruitful and prosperous. This study should add to the expanding number of studies that continue to identify ways to improve the overall success of Black male's graduate schooling experiences. It will also contribute to the body of literature on how to meet the challenges set forth by Howard (2014), who states:

I challenge scholars working on ensuring equitable educational opportunities for all students to consider the promise Black males offer to society as opposed to the stereotypes woven into the media and society. This is critical for Black males' educational experiences, but it also has ramifications for all other groups of students who have struggled with education and social marginalization. (p. 78)

Highlighting the successful ways a graduate student overcomes obstacles and makes it to the finish line is impactful. Listening to the graduate students' counter-stories plays an important part in redefining what it means to be Black, educated, and a male in the future. Due to others who have unique experiences and been in similar situations, help and comfort can be found in someone else who is in the same position or situation. By seeking opportunities to improve, expand, and create solutions for others who can learn from those experiences, it will assist them in becoming leaders and achieving their dreams and aspirations.

Chapter 3

Methodology

"The stories we tell literally make the world. If you want to change the world, you need to change your story. This truth applies to both individuals and institutions. "
— Michael Margolis, 2019

By gathering data directly from the sources of successful Black male post-baccalaureate graduates, we open the possibility of hearing stories that counter the traditional black male narrative of educational achievement. The opportunity to voice the narrative of the unique experiences of Black males by Black males provides a genuine and alternative perspective to the story that is typically told. Our voices are the measure of our presence as "the only thing that keeps us from floating off with the wind is our stories. They give us a name and put us in a place, allow us to keep in touch, they argue, they can help or heal a relationship" (Dwyer, 2017, p. 2). Because of the strength and power of a person's story, the method of narrative inquiry was chosen instead of any other qualitative or quantitative methods. Narrative inquiry gives us a front row seat into the minds and experiences of the storyteller. It offers perspectives that are embedded in social, cultural, and institutional practices and behaviors. According to Clandinin & Clifford (2016), Narrative inquiry examines human lives through the lens of a narrative, honoring lived experience as a source of important knowledge and understanding. In this concise volume, D. Jean Clandinin, one of the pioneers in using narrative as a research method, updates her classic formulation of narrative inquiry (with F. Michael Connelly), clarifying, extending, and refining the method based on an additional decade of work. A valuable feature is the inclusion of several exemplary cases with the author's critique and analysis of the work. The rise in interest in narrative inquiry in recent years makes this an essential guide for researchers and an excellent text for graduate courses in qualitative inquiry. (p. 17)

By hearing and analyzing these stories, a positive image can be extracted to allow individuals and institutions to see the Black male's truth from a different lens than might be typically told in the media, politics, or in stereotypes of Black males' success or failures. These narratives bring to the surface the ambiguities, complexities, difficulties, and uncertainties that impact the successful pathway to success. In this study, participants constructed their own narratives and offered insightful understandings that challenged prevailing assumptions about what it takes to earn a post-baccalaureate degree.

The narrative inquiry method also reflected on how student engagement within their academic degree program could have been created to foster a positive working environment for Black male graduate students to advance academically. This qualitative approach is anticipated to assist in the efforts of Black studies to move from a deficit-based focus to an asset-based framework and may be useful to educational researchers studying other marginalized populations. This approach can assist in answering what are the characteristics of Black males who completed a master's degree or higher within the past 5 years.

It became clear that it was necessary to include Autoethnography. Because of the complexities of this study, I brought stories to life by incorporating my own emotions and personal experiences in graduate education. I became completely immersed in the research, not only as a researcher, but also as the subject and narrator of the study. The majority of the 16 participants' experiences paralleled my experiences. In this study, I bring the reader closer to the subculture of the Black male experiences in graduate school by using autoethnography as a research methodology, along with narrative inquiry.

Autoethnography necessarily involves a great deal of reflection, introspection, and self-analysis. Because the stories were written in first person, I was positioned in such a way as to facilitate communication directly with the audience. Autoethnography is a research method that describes and interprets cultural texts, experiences, beliefs, and practices (ethno) using personal experience (auto). Auto ethnographers believe that personal experience is infused with political/ cultural norms and expectations, and they engage in rigorous self-reflection—dubbed reflexivity —to identify and interrogate the intersections between the self and social life. Auto ethnographers' primary goal is to depict "people in the process of figuring out what to do, how to live, and the meaning of their struggles" (Bochner & Ellis, 2006, p. 111).

First, because auto ethnographers focus on personal experience, they speak out against or provide alternatives to dominant, taken-for-granted, harmful cultural scripts, stories, and stereotypes (Boylorn, 2014). Auto ethnographers provide personal accounts of their experiences to supplement or fill gaps in existing research.

A second goal of autoethnography is to express insider knowledge of a cultural experience. This implies that the writer will be able to inform readers about aspects of cultural life that other researchers may not be aware of. A person who has directly experienced institutional oppression and/or cultural problems, such as racism, loss, or illness, can speak about these issues in ways that others with limited experience with these topics cannot. Insider knowledge does not imply that an auto ethnographer can articulate more truthful or accurate knowledge than outsiders, but rather that as authors, we can tell our stories in ways that others may not be able to tell them (Adams et al., 2017). In Chapter Four, I present the findings, characterizations, and major themes that emerged from the narratives of the 16 participants, along with parallel reflections, and do so by providing individual short narratives about each participant. The valuable data from the participants did create a community of similarities, which can be seen from their perspectives and experiences.

Research Design

When researching the experiences of Black males aspiring to obtain higher education degrees, both the participants and I must possess a keen aptitude to intuiting the unique subtleties and complexities that are key to the Black male experience. The data provided by participants has the potential to alter the way we perceive and interact with black males. Century-old stigmas can be minimized and an earnest resolve to be intentional about the success of Black male students can be achieved. According to Pepper and Wildy (2009),

Narrative accounts offer a powerful research strategy in educational leadership studies. They permit rich insights into the experiences of participants and are aligned with qualitatively oriented educational research. Narratives provide a means for participants' stories and experiences to be honored and given status. Data was gathered during semi-structured interviews with participants encouraged to 'tell their story' from each individual's unique perspective. (p. 19)

As this study attempts to answer the question of how Black males were successful in attaining a post-baccalaureate degree, a qualitative research design was utilized and involved collecting data through extensive interviews and the use of field notes to capture the researcher's observations of the phenomena under study

(Renz et al., 2018). The research problem as outlined in Chapter 1 further emphasizes how there is very little research on Black male graduate students' success. According to Denzin and Lincoln (2008), "qualitative research involves the study of the use and collection of a variety of empirical materials, descriptions of personal experiences, life stories, interviews, observations, history, and interactions, all to describe moments and meanings in individuals' lives" (p. 3).

Focusing on narrative inquiry embraces the storytelling aspects of individuals and gives value and a sense of connection to their stories. This methodological research utilizes the narrative inquiry approach to make meaning and to gain a better understanding of success factors beneficial to participants of the study who achieved post-baccalaureate success. Using strategies for qualitative content analysis, such as an interlinked approach to triangulation, as presented here:

Narrative inquiry, the study of experience as story, is first and foremost a way of thinking about experience. Narrative inquiry as a methodology entails a view of the phenomenon. Using narrative inquiry methodology is to adopt a particular view of experience as the phenomenon under study. (Renz et al., 2018, p. 824)

Moreover, with the narrative inquiry approach "these lived and told stories and the talk about the stories are one of the ways that we fill our world with meaning and enlist one another's assistance in building lives and communities" (Clandinin, 2007, p. 5). Furthermore, the 16 individual's experiences told through storytelling would ultimately increase the level of comprehension for Black males in pursuit of post-baccalaureate success. The research goal directs them to come to terms with the degree of difficulty to overcome and to develop and initiate a viable means to succeed in their educational pursuit.

Data Collection

This research primarily relies on three modes to collect data from participants: a survey, the participants personal philosophy statement, and the semi-structured individual interviews. The survey was completed first and included consent to participate in the research. Participants' experiences were surveyed, along with their characteristics and attributes that were vital to the data collection. Next, participants were asked to compose a personal philosophy of what made them personally successful at completing their post-baccalaureate degree, and what was a mantra they lived by or represented their life experiences. The participants' writings comprised their lived experiences throughout their program that successfully got them through. Finally, the semi-structured interviews were completed individually through a guided set of questions via Google Meet.

The results from all three of these activities were rich, with compelling descriptions beyond what was typically captured through standard structured interviews. The surveys were beneficial to show the digitized numbers and the themes that emerged from the characteristics of the participants. As Renz et al. (2018) outlined,

Data derived from these various materials requires a form of analysis of the content, focusing on written or spoken language as communication, to provide context and understanding of the message. These methods are time- and labor-intensive. With the advances in computerized text analysis software, the practice of combining methods to analyze qualitative data can assist the researcher in making large data sets more manageable and enhance the trustworthiness of the results. (Abstract)

The use of computer programs for filtering and analysis alleviated some of the additional interpretation that was necessary for this method of research. NVIVO was used to assist in the thematic coding of the data analysis. Each interview was transcribed individually once the interview was complete. For verification and accuracy purposes, Verbal Ink (Human Transcriber) and "Go Transcript" (Human Transcriber) were used, for an efficient and steadfast way to transcribe each interview. See Table 2 for an abbreviated set of interview questions that were utilized during the semi-structured interviews.

Individual Interviews

The semi-structured interviews were designed to collect data on such topics as barriers to student achievement and success when seeking a post-baccalaureate degree. Participants were asked additional questions about past and present help-seeking experiences. As participants detailed their experiences through a dyadic and semi-structured interview process, prompts were initiated to decipher significant data. Prompts pertinent to the research included questions about background, family history, geographical location, economic status, culture, influences, challenges, successes, conflict, expectations, and goals. Conducting a semi-structured interview assisted in engaging the interviewee to share their information spontaneously without concern for formality or pretense. As stated by Ryan et al. (2009),

The flexibility of the semi-standardized interview allows the interviewer to pursue a series of less structured questions and permits the exploration of spontaneous issues raised by the interviewee to be explored. The wording of the questions is flexible and facilitates different levels of language to be used and clarifications to be made by the interviewer. (p. 310)

Table 2

Abbreviated Set of Interview Questions on Student Engagement and Critical Race Theory

Student Engagement:	Critical Race:
1. Tell me a little about yourself and how you decided to attend graduate school.	1. How important is it for you to have a Black advisor or Black mentor?
2. Thinking back to when you first began your graduate program, what were your initial thoughts, observations, and impressions. Have they changed over time?	2. How does the ability to relate to a faculty member and/or to communicate about familiar interests affect your engagement as a Black male who completed graduate school, if at all?
3. How would you rate your academic program on a scale from 1-100? Why?	3. What do you feel are some challenges Black men face regularly?
4. What would you say is your highest achievement or highlight of your graduate career (thus far)?	4. How would you describe your family culture? Are there any traditions or philosophies you would like to share that you or your family members do?
5. What motivates you?	5. Speaking of culture, how would you define what it means to be "Black and Educated" or "Young, Gifted, and Black?" When people say these phrases what does that mean to you?
6. On the flip side, what would you say were your biggest challenges or struggles during your time in graduate school?	6. During your graduate academic program, how often did you experience the following feelings? (1) Anxiety; (2) Depression; (3) Helplessness; (4) Stress; (5) Homesickness; (6) Racial Fatigue?
7. There is some research that says students of color have unique experiences compared to their white counterparts. Would you agree or disagree with that and why? –Well, have you ever experienced racism at your academic institution?	7. When you did experience such feelings, how were you able to overcome them and remain committed to pursuing your graduate degree?
8. How do you describe your student engagement while in your graduate program?	8. Do you feel you belong in your graduate program? If yes, why? If not, explain why not?
9. Who or what resource did you turn to when you had academic questions?	9. Do/did you work while in school?
10. What were the barriers or difficulties you experienced inside and outside of the classroom?	10. How did you finance your education?
11. What about when you were dealing with personal matters, who did you turn to then?	11. How can higher education faculty and administrators work to increase enrollment of and the retention of Black males in graduate programs?
12. What was/is your support network? Were/ are they motivating?	12. What has been your approach to succeeding in graduate education? Meaning when an event occurred in your life during your graduate program that could be perceived as a setback, how did you rebound from it?
13. Does your support network help you handle the stresses of higher education?	13. How did graduate school prepare you for where you are in your life right now, if at all?
	14. How do you sustain that motivation to keep striving?
	15. Is there anything you would like to share with me that we have not addressed?

The goal of utilizing semi-structured interviews was to get the interviewee to engage comfortably and to promote substantial insight into their experiences. This was accomplished by engaging the interviewee's unstructured commentary.

The focus is on permitting the interviewee to tell his/ her own story rather than answering a series of structured questions. Underpinning the discovery interview is the principle that participants understand the world in varying subjective ways. Therefore, issues are explored from an individualistic perspective. A 'spine' of themes is devised by the interviewer to act as a framework to guide the interview process and reflect the interviewee's personal experiences of the topic in question. (Ryan et al., 2009, p. 311)

The exchange of information between two individuals with parallel objectives can offer rich insight into phenomena and systemic stigmas that have curtailed growth and quality experiences for Black males pursuing post-baccalaureate degrees. The dyadic interview offers an indispensable degree of data that demonstrates a measurable impact as to the interviewee's disposition and experience. According to Morgan et al., (2013),

This facilitates the collection of richer, more textured data from the participant than that obtained through formally structured, scheduled questions. At this stage, we should note that dyadic interviews are valuable for providing a measure of the depth and detail available in individual interviews, while they provide the interaction present in focus groups. (Abstract)

Finally, the interviews were conducted as follows: (a) interview of 60 to 90 minutes via Google Meets through the participant's personal laptop or workable devices; and (b) a post-interview 60 to 90-minute Google Meet session with the aid of the participant's personal laptop or mobile phone. The interviews were to interpret and intellectualize the insight of the 16 Black males. Gaining an in-depth analysis of the 16 Black males offered a qualitative method for data collection.

Field Texts

The data that was provided and shared was finally chosen during the process of gathering information, and this was a joint decision made by both the participants and me. According to Clandinin and Connelly (2000), "field text is shaped by researchers' selective interest or lack of interest, so the material gathered is interpretive" (p. 18). Pepper and Wildy (2009) further suggest that

Such texts are framed by the interpretive process of both researcher and participant, as participants interpret researcher comments just as their own comments are interpreted.... Similarly, participants selected the information they were willing to share. In writing field notes, we acknowledge our role as the initial filter in deciding which parts of the data to record as important and which to leave out. Throughout the process we remained mindful that the quality of the information obtained during an interview was largely dependent on us, the interviewers. As is customary for such research, we allocated all participants pseudonyms to ensure anonymity. (p. 19)

Field notes were handwritten in a small notebook as the interviews took place and were typed into a word document directly after the interview. Confidentiality was maintained in a specific field text folder. Utilizing field notes provided a complement to the audio-taped semi-structured interviews. Field notes allowed comments about impressions, environmental context, behaviors, and nonverbal cues that may not have been adequately captured through the audio recording. They provided important context to the interpretation of audio-taped data and helped recognize situational factors that were important during data analysis.

The Participants Survey

Next in the process was the online survey, which was utilized to gain more demographic information and descriptive insights into participants' experiences. The online survey comprised nine questions that lasted 5 to 10 minutes. SurveyMonkey was utilized to distribute the survey, administer the number of completed surveys, and collect and report all data. By using the online version, I was able to reach a greater number of participants simultaneously. Participants were also able to send the survey out to their colleagues, peers, and former students via email or text, allowing participants to complete the survey at a time that worked for their schedule.

The survey questions were:

1. What is your age?
2. What state do you reside in?
3. If employed, what state or U.S. territory do you currently work?
4. Which of the following categories best describes your employment status?
5. What is the highest level of school your mother completed or the highest degree she received?
6. What is the highest level of school your father completed or the highest degree he received?
7. What is the highest level of education you have completed?
8. What is your participant pseudonym name if used?
9. At what e-mail address would you like to be contacted?

Creating a survey that was compatible with tablets, smart phones, and computers was essential in ensuring the survey was accessible and formatted appropriately for all subjects, regardless of the device. I oversaw all data collection, data cleaning, data analysis, and any other tasks related to this study and its confidentiality.

Study Site, Sampling, and Recruitment

The proposed study was national in scope and not held to geographic boundaries. However, the study anticipated a predominance of Black male research participants from PWIs, HSIs and HBCUs mainly in the southern states, due to the larger percentage of Blacks residing in the southern United States. Purposive and snowball sampling were used. In studies that use semi-structured interviews that are analyzed using content analysis, sample size is often justified based on interviewing participants until data saturation is reached (Francis et al., 2010). The concept of data saturation was introduced into the field of qualitative research by Glaser and Strauss (1967) and refers to the point in data collection when no new additional data are found that further develop aspects of a conceptual category (Francis et. al., 2010). In this research, it was accepted that the level of data saturation was achieved with 16 post-baccalaureate graduates within the past 5 years. Failure to reach data saturation could have a negative impact on the ability to replicate the study and the validity.

During the recruitment process, snowball effect sampling for recruitment was used. According to Francis et. al. (2010), this method of sampling has several benefits for the research:

The chain referral process allows the researcher to reach populations that are difficult to sample when using other sampling methods. The process is cost-efficient and requires a smaller workforce compared to other sampling techniques. Furthermore, suggesting that when viewed critically, this popular sampling method can generate a unique type of social knowledge—knowledge which is emergent, political and interactional. (p. 3). This sampling process is powerful because it allows a network of participants to emerge based on the references that are given from others.

Content Analysis: Personal Philosophy

Participants were asked to e-mail me with a written personal statement pertaining to the individual participant's personal philosophy. The goal of compiling a personal philosophy was to read context and gain insight into who these participants are in terms of mindsets or their mantra's that may have helped them succeed throughout the process Clandinin and Connelly (2004) outline this as:

The goal of the narrative writer is to produce an ethical, honest interpretation of the data while being aware that other interpretations are possible. Creating narratives also involves tension centered on context. In any situation, context counts. Context is essential for making sense of any person, action or event. In writing narratives, the person in context is of prime interest, and the purpose is to make meaning of their experiences and to share understanding with readers. Such tensions are considered in crafting narratives and are viewed as interconnected rather than as separate and independent factors. (p. 20)

The focal point of this research was to produce candid interpretations of the data provided that reflects the experiences of Black males in seeking post-baccalaureate degrees, and to make meaning of their lived experience.

Study Participants

The participants in this study were self-identified as post-baccalaureate Black males who had completed a post-baccalaureate degree in the past 5 years. The participants had an understanding that they would be interviewed based on their experiences. According to Sutton & Austin (2015) "participants contribute data to research in a number of ways, such as through questionnaires, interviews, experiments, personal health records, narratives, focus groups, and direct observation" (p. 227). A total of 16 participants provided informed consent before contributing to the research. After consent and completion of the survey, as well as meeting the research criteria. That's when the study started to take its course with the interview process.

The participants were full of energy and were eager to share their lived experiences throughout graduate school. I gave the participants a chance to pick a date that will work for them to participate in the interview. According to De Laine (2000), "The agreement to participate in research bestows obligations on researchers to ensure that participants are treated in a manner that conforms to accepted ethical standards" (p.17). Every participant willingly and actively expressed their gratitude for being heard and valued. I had the upmost respect for each participant, throughout the process of being open and honest in a professional manner when dealing with the participants.

To maintain ethical and professional standards, participants were sourced through colleagues, professors, and social media sources. Explained by Given, (2008), "By working closely with an institutional review board and one's colleagues, the researcher can make sure that access to participants is academically and ethically sound" (p. 12). The study was able to follow the guidelines of the approved IRB and respected the participants schedule, availability and emotional welfare. Each individual participant was willing, able, and quite eager to participate in the research.

Data Analysis

In narrative inquiry, analyzing the data thoroughly is essential to ensure identified themes are accurate and truly representative of participants' narratives. Thus, the first step was to read, re-read, and immerse in the narratives from the individual, semi-structured interviews. Once the data was thematically coded, this process allowed open coding to identify themes and to write summaries of each participant. This involved identifying issues, patterns, and themes across the narratives. Key phrases from the interviews were underlined and highlighted, which created a codebook of sorts that identified repetitive words, topics, concepts, and ideas, called recurring regularities by Guba & Lincoln (1978). Data was then grouped with those that are related. After axial coding (Strauss & Corbin, 1990), themes were identified across the study. Documenting the process maximized clarity of the progression and illuminated understanding that what is claimed to be analyzed is being analyzed (Ryan & Bernard, 2003, p. 85). In the process of analyzing the narratives, themes and subthemes were discovered.

Themes and categorical language emerged from the data of the survey, the written document (personal philosophy), and the semi-structured interview, which was how the data was derived. According to Renz et. al, (2018),

Data analysis requires the researcher/s to review notes and begin to code data for categorization. Although software is available to assist with the coding process (e.g. ATLAS.ti), qualitative data analysis requires close reading of text, reflecting on data and writing down interpretations, and sequential text interpretations as examples. (p. 828)

Although this modern technology was progressive in concept, the data still required interpretation and reflection. In addition to the modes of data analysis, the software NVIVO, which creates codes and removes the need for me to create code names and themes, was used. According to Nowell et. al, (2017) explains that:

Lincoln and Guba (1985), to progress the research analysis, the software programs that are available do not analyze the data per se but rather make the data more manageable and easier to handle. These methods are often time- and labor-intensive as data are analyzed step by step, following extremely specific rules of procedure to assure trustworthiness of the study's methods and findings. (p. 3)

The thematic analysis was different from content analysis in that data is closely and carefully examined to identify themes and patterns. Moreover, content analysis provides a deeper understanding of categorizing and discussing the meaning of Black male's written personal philosophy. In addition to the philosophy statements, there was an analysis of interviews that were intellectually interpreted while a thematic analysis was carried out. This entailed coding all the data before analyzing and reviewing each key theme. Each theme was distinguished by deciphering the understanding of the participants' awareness as well as variations. According to Renz et. al., (2018),

The entire process of managing and analyzing qualitative data, if done properly, is both systematic and rigorous. However, with the advances in computerized text analysis software, the practice of combining methods to analyze qualitative data can assist the researcher in making large data sets more manageable and enhance the trustworthiness of the results. (p. 824-825)

In this study, it was imperative to manage the data in an organized way and to use analysis software to help explore the qualitative data that existed from the participants.

Validation Techniques and Researcher Bias

To show the validity of the research conducted, a validation technique was utilized to eliminate bias. That said, in conducting any type of research, it is not possible to attain complete validity and reliability (LeCompte & Goetz, 1982). Narrative, like other qualitative methods, relies on criteria other than validity, reliability, and generalizability (Connelly & Clandinin, 1990). Well-crafted narratives are identified as having an explanatory, invitational quality, with evidence of authenticity; that is, elements of adequacy and plausibility (Connelly & Clandinin, 1990). According to Renz et. al, 2018, the authors summarized that "Denzin (1970) suggested that the use of triangulation has the potential to increase the validity of the study, decrease researcher bias, and provide multiple perspectives of the phenomenon under study" (p. 826). The importance of triangulation was evident throughout the process, with the three methods used being 90 to 200-minute interviews, surveys, and personal philosophy statements.

According to Crimmins (2016), validating the participants who share their stories is crucial. The approach of a narrative inquiry into the lived experience of Black males and connecting the study of the theoretical frameworks of Astin Student Involvement and Gloria Billings-Ladson/William Tate Critical Race Theory were factors to consider throughout this study. Billings-Ladson/William Tate Critical Race Theory were factors to consider throughout this study. Trustworthiness of results is the bedrock of high-quality qualitative research.

Lincoln & Guba (1985), strategies to ensure trustworthiness using this method of qualitative text analysis include the use of diagrams to demonstrate an audit trail, triangulation to diminish the effects of researcher bias, and confirmability wherein procedures are clearly outlined for checking and rechecking data throughout the study (Shenton, 2004; Trochim, 2006). According to Krishna et al. (2010), "Biases can be defined as a systematic deviation from what would have been the most effective route to a goal because of commitment to another, particular tendency or inclination, especially one that prevents prejudiced consideration of a question" (p. 2).

Triangulation was achieved to substantiate the validity of the themes that emerged, and a variety of methods of data collection were utilized, such as the online survey, personal philosophy statement, and the semi-structured interview to capture different dimensions of the same phenomenon.

The process of member checking was also utilized to eliminate researcher bias. Participants were given a copy of the data and transcript to check for accuracy and resemblance to their own experiences. To achieve validation and credibility, member checking, also known as participant or respondent validation, a technique for exploring the credibility of results, was used. Data and results were returned to participants for fact checking (Birt, et. al., 2016). After the interview was complete, the themes and core ideals were extracted from the narrative inquiry interview of the participant. The summary of the interview was then given back to the contributor for validation of the correct meaning and abstraction of their information. However, as research ethics also addresses the integrity of the research activity, honesty, openness, and candid revelation of a study's strengths and limitations according to commonly held standards of practice are typical indicators of the integrity of the scholarship (Preissle, 2002). Being mindful of potential researcher bias and eliminating owned experiences was imperative to the veracity of the outcomes.

Conclusion

Not by consequence, but by choice, the way to succeed is to keep going and moving forward. Martin Luther King Jr. (1960), in his famous speech to Spelman College, said:

Keep moving, for it may well be that the greatest song has not yet been sung, the greatest book has not been written, the highest mountain has not been climbed. This is your Challenge! Reach out and grab it…but there is something we can learn from the broken grammar of that mother, that we must keep moving. If you can't fly, run; if you can't run, walk; if you can't walk, crawl; but by all means keep moving. (Blanton, 1960, p. 7)

From that profound speech, the theme "keep moving" is still relevant today. To keep the research moving in a positive upward way with attention and dedication, this study provided a positive solution to the issue of the lack of Black males who are successfully graduating with a post-baccalaureate degree.

Themes emerged amongst the participants that indicated which attributes/characteristics were necessary for a Black male to complete a post-baccalaureate degree. Participants' narratives were crucial in understanding their perspective of what worked and what assisted them to be a successful post-baccalaureate graduate. Although assumptions and speculations about what was specifically needed for the Black male population may automatically happen, data was needed to show what Black males believe they need to be successful. Ultimately, that is the only opinion and perspective that matters. Michael Margolis, an inspirational speaker, proclaimed, "The stories we tell literally make the world. If you want to change the world, you need to change your story. This truth applies to both individuals and institutions" (Maxwell, 2021, p. 181). If the stories about us are misunderstood, then it is up to us to tell a different story. This research not only encourages participants to give in-depth and honest answers, but it also provides an opportunity for institutions to also begin to tell a different story about their Black male population by telling their own story.

Narrative accounts are useful and educationally important because they bring theoretical ideas about the nature of human life as lived to bear on educational experience as lived (Connelly & Clandinin, 1990). "Narratives permit life-like accounts that focus on experience, hence their alignment with qualitatively oriented educational research. They provide a framework and context for making meaning of life situations" (Pepper & Wildy, 2009, p. 20).

In the end, it comes down to paying attention to details, to what study participants said, how they said it, and why they said it, and then making sense of what they said. From computer screen and phone interviews to transcriptions and data coding, from rigorously repeating the same process over and over to meticulously making meaning, connections, and relationships with existing literature and real-world data, the process is demanding when combining autoethnography and narrative inquiry. The following chapter will explain what emerged organically from the study's survey, philosophical statements and semi-structured interviews.

The data transcriptions are raw and unfiltered as the experiences of the participants. *Please be aware that the language you are about to see is explicit and not censored because it was how the participants felt. I know that most chapters do not begin with a participant quote, but this study required it.*

Chapter 4

Findings

When it comes to whitewashing, I think it really comes in two facets. On the white savior complex where it's like, "Hey, don't you see everything that's going on and how it's coming together to support the cause of Black Lives Matter?" I'm like, "You don't understand what I'm looking at," as well as whitewashing where it's like, "is it really that big of an issue or that big of a deal? Are you sure this is what you want to do? Like, do you not want to look at student activism in general?" There were a lot of times even when some of the language I was using, like I would say, "He was murdered." "Well, I think more killing, or we should soften this language for the audience." I'm like, I'm not softening my language because, as a Black man, I don't have a choice to be seen as softened and so why should I soften my language to appease those. "Well, the public service or whoever's reviewing this might not like that language or I feel that's very strong, and I feel that might seem as part of the problem and I don't think that's what you're trying to say." A lot of times it was also, "I think what you really mean is that—" "No, I meant what I meant."

— Study Participant Ray Participant Ray discusses how, as a Black man, he was perceived negatively, but also how he was expected to change others' perceptions by softening his language and whitewashing or diluting his ideals. Instead of being seen as he is and who he is, he was expected to inculcate Black males into the standard of a white male. Seeing other black mentors or successful students in the graduate programs not only lets us know we can achieve the same success, but we can do so as we are, educated black males. It is critical to have black representation in scholarly communities, as well as to be exposed to successful black mentors who share common experiences.

The research included stories of participants feeling as if their own Black life did not matter, or that Black representation in their graduate experience did not matter or hold value. For example, if there was a Black initiative or research on Black lives on campus, it would not receive the same level of attention and recognition as others, as participants stated in their interviews. The information was denigrated to make others feel at ease but did not accurately reflect what was going on. For instance, participant Chris stated how when he was President of Higher Education Strategic Planners Association (HESPA) and was responsible for inviting guest speakers, he noticed low interest or attendance on days when a black guest would be invited. On the other hand, when a white counterpart was a guest, the rooms would be full and students eager to learn from them.

To achieve a level of comprehension and meaning in what the participants' narratives describe and their experiences in the face of adversity, I will reflect and share perspectives and experiences as a participant observer who obtained a post-baccalaureate degree. By putting myself in the picture that the participants paint, my experiences related to those of other participants, some of which were quite similar, as well as providing some profound statements on characterizations and major themes. My reflections will be presented "side-by side," clearly differentiating what came out of the research and how my own experience relates to that.

Detailed descriptions and deep meaning will be further explained by the attempts to explore culture and convey stories via the participants' lenses in reference to my personal experiences with parallels and differences that enriched each narrative.

Various Ways of Knowing and Making Meaning

Chapter/Section Formatting Key

Voice	Formatting
Participants' Voices	Single Space, Block quotes, 12 size font: Times New Roman
Albert's Experience	1x1 graph in 12 size font: Times New Roman
Albert's Reflection	Subtitle then leads into 1x1 graph with 12 size font: Times New Roman
Albert Narrator of empirical research	12-point font: Times New Roman

In Chapter three, the choice of narrative inquiry combined with auto-ethnography was explained. Conducting 16 interviews with participants for a narrative inquiry method is rare, as it typically consists of 3-6 participants. The purpose of this study was to obtain multiple and varied participants' stories while also achieving some level of depth. While Black men who have earned a post-baccalaureate degree in recent years would appear to be a homogenous subpopulation, the reality is that multiple characteristics allowed the study to obtain richer and more in-depth data regarding this specific subpopulation. These characteristics include the type of degree earned, their academic degree program, geographical location, and diverse backgrounds and personalities.

The problem statement highlights the lack of literature on Black male graduate degree attainment, and the scarcity of positive imagery of Black males. It also examined each participant's contribution to knowledge and way of thinking, then compared them to the overall 16 participants. This led to a focus on what the participants were thinking and how participants' ideologies impacted their lives. This epistemological approach resulted in connections from the literature and mainstream media, revealing that the pipeline for Black males in higher education is abysmal, with extremely low participation.

Furthermore, the study purpose statement examines the Black male post-baccalaureate attainment in a nuanced way, which can be seen within the 16 participants. It is vital to inform educators about the necessary tools that contribute to Black male success in graduate school. The goal is to target policy makers in education, current and future researchers, practitioners, and faculty who will have the opportunity to commit to elemental and applied knowledge that will empower key stakeholders in education to better serve Black males in graduate school and beyond. The research questions were:

1. What are the characteristics/attributes/practices of Black males who completed a master's degree or higher within the past 5 years?

2. How does honest reflection with their academic degree program enable Black male graduate students to advance academically despite their obstacles?

3. How did/does your identity as a Black male affect(ed) your experiences in graduate school?

Participant Narratives

Participants defined themselves as individuals who identified as being Black. Although participants were born in all parts of the world, they still identified as being a Black male.

Participant narratives provided more in-depth and valuable information on what led these Black men to post-baccalaureate degrees. The biographies contain pertinent information about each participant's background, their family's educational attainment, and their educational history. In addition to participants' family background, peer influences, and mentors, life events that impacted their decision-making were included. The commonality of having a lot to be thankful for and practicing gratitude was embedded within their narratives.

Interestingly, a handful of the participants stated that they would go back to receive another higher education degree, even a post-doctorate degree, depending on opportunity. A percentage of the participants went on to receive double masters within their higher education programs. All 16 participants expressively shared the importance of graduate school and highlighted the notion of graduate school preparing them for where they are in their lives currently.

For the sake of documentation confidentiality, seven participants chose to use a pseudonym or alias name. The descriptors for the other nine participants were their first names. Each participant's narrative and how they told their story of their lived experiences served as narratives of how Black males are typically viewed in American society.

To gain a better understanding of the 16 participants before delving into the major findings. The section that follows emphasizes the participants' diversity. While participants came from all over the world, certain requirements varied depending on which post-baccalaureate degree they were pursuing.

Participant 1: Ray

Ray (age 25-34 years), the first interviewee, is from Dallas, Texas. His mother and father both attended college. His father received a graduate degree, but he is the first in his family to obtain a PhD degree. Ray had a very calm, confident and composed demeanor, and stated that he has brothers who look up to him. He holds a double master's degree—one an M.S. in College Student Personnel and Administration, and the other MA in Applied Research, Measurement and Evaluation from Central Arkansas University and Texas Commerce. Ray is one of the four participants who is nearing the end of his PhD program, which he is currently obtaining from the University of Louisiana State University. His current study is Educational Leadership and Research. He is currently employed as Assistant Director of Multicultural Affairs at the University of Arlington.

Ray shared various stories where he identified the educational environment of his graduate program as different and less developed than the environment of his undergraduate studies. As an undergraduate, he experienced black male mentorship and developed a relationship with his advisors who offered support. In his graduate program, he lacked Black male mentorship and had to navigate white spaces that he believes were not designed for him. Stress, anxiety, and homesickness were exacerbated by a lack of support and mentorship, with racial fatigue manifesting itself frequently both inside and outside the classroom. Ray revealed that he started a writing club with a group of friends and peers that he could count on at any time of day or night to help alleviate the stresses of higher education and personal issues. During the interview, Ray discussed how he prioritizes self-care, which includes understanding the psychological and intricate balance in his life. Ray believes that greatness is a state of mind and that you can use your past to influence a better tomorrow. He strives to engage, educate, and empower everyone he interacts with, including himself, for him to be the best version of himself. He said, "Things will not always be easy, so rest, if necessary, but don't quit." Ray claims that one of his most difficult challenges was not knowing what he didn't know:

I think one is knowing what I did not know. I'm seeing people do stuff, and I'm like, "What?" Am I supposed to be doing that? What are they doing? Figuring out—hey, I tell people all the time that I watch other people and then ask my friends, "Hey, can I see your CV or "Hey, tell me what you did your first year or your second year," so figuring out what I don't know and then figuring out how to do it. Then, being a Black male in higher education, especially in my past role, where my supervisor was white, people say she saw me as a threat. I don't know if that's true, but as a black male, which I am, her position was one of assessment. I was able to understand and do a lot of her job. That created boundaries, and it was like, "Well, listen, Ray; excuse me; now, let's do this.

Let's do that.

Participant 2: Bruce

Bruce (age 25-34 years) decided to use a pseudonym. He is from Greensboro Winston- Salem, North Carolina. His father received a GED. His mother went to college but received no degree and is currently a nurse. He is extremely impacted by the COVID-19 pandemic. He is the first in his family to go to graduate school. He said that he was not sure about going to college because he was the first person in his family to finish his degree and the first person in his family to get a master's degree. He earned a Master of Science (M.S.) in Organizational Development and Leadership from the University of the Incarnate Word. Previous jobs include Hall Director of Residential Life at North Carolina AT&T. He now lives and works in South Carolina in the same position at the College of Charleston. Bruce displayed reverence mixed with strong research, and shared professional stories from his experiences.

Bruce said that his mood shifted throughout his studies, from doubting his abilities to contrasting his self-worth, and his level of commitment to his behavioral patterns. Bruce experienced a significant shift in identity as he sought appropriate assistance and structured advice, which helped catapult him into further matriculation. Bruce experienced internal and external factors such as racial fatigue, anxiety, and depression/homesickness, both inside and outside of the program. Bruce didn't feel like he belonged at first because he was one of the youngest in class:

I was extremely nervous and anxious during my first year of graduate school because I was trying so hard to impress. Also, I was doing the school of professional studies, where I wasn't in class with a lot of people my age. I was the youngest in class most of the time. I was always told, "My daughters are your age," or "My son is your age." I was like, "Thank you; I am just trying to finish class." I thought I had to impress them because they were doing all these things in their careers, whereas my only job was Residence Life as a graduate assistant and going to school, whereas they were successful in the military and other ventures. I thought I had to try because I didn't feel like I belonged in those classes because I was so young. That was something that I had to fight. Through that first assignment, I helped clear that and chip that away.

Participant 3: Dr. Igbo

Dr. Igbo (age 35-44 years) is the participant's chosen alias name. His parents are from Africa, and both his mother and father went to college, and his father earned a graduate degree. Dr. Igbo is the first in his family to earn a PhD, which he recently received in Educational Policy Evaluation, Educational Evaluation, and Research from Arizona State University. He is married and has one son, whom he says was born while he was enrolled in the doctoral program. Dr. Igbo described how having a baby during his graduate program was a challenge in and of itself, but he still gives his wife a lot of credit for sticking by his side.

Dr. Igbo currently works as a professor at Minnesota St. Cloud State University, focusing on quantitative research investigating the intersection of higher education finance and access to higher education for underrepresented or minority students. During the study, Dr. Igbo graciously put time aside to do the interview as he was making a huge move from Arizona to Minnesota, indicating his eagerness to share his story. Dr. Igbo detailed that he has over 10 years of experience working with diverse populations in effective communication strategies, personal development, and behavior modification, while also conducting training for prospective students (parents) on costs related to higher education.

Dr. Igbo said that he had a Black therapist near the end of his program because he felt his life was difficult at the time and was able to overcome feelings of anxiety and stress, as well as racial fatigue. Although Dr. Igbo shared many of the same experiences as others, he brought unique skill sets, such as his determination to succeed and keen ability to write grants successfully. Dr. Igbo helped to explain the topic of academic funding, as well as the seemingly limitless possibilities and abundant resources available. He said that a colleague/peer helped him write and received more than $103,000 in grant money for a similar study.

Doing whatever it takes is the way Dr. Igbo enjoys life. However, during the interview, he expressed how the academy and writing standards were challenging for him. The obstacles of overcoming certain hurdles to earn his PhD were starting to become grueling:

Like, I don't know if you know, but when you read the article, like, the "high impact factor", which is how many people are going to actually read your article, it's going to be, like, three, maybe three and a half, you know? Like, you spend half a year, sometimes, to write a great article for three people to read. What the fuck is that? You know what I mean? That's completely stupid. I used to struggle with understanding my advisor, who was from South Korea, and I used to get mad. And I said, but I don't understand why we have to sit here and write this long-ass article for just three people to read, just to put it on our CV, and writing and just the academy, because the academy's bullshit, sometimes, because it's what they think they should value. So, if you do anything concerning an at-risk group or a group with which you identify, it's referred to as action research or activist research, which automatically minimizes, like, the Scientifics of what you know, which isn't a word, but the Scientifics of what you did. So, you don't ever want to be "caught" being a scholar activist, because, you know, you don't want to do that because you always want to be unbiased. So, the most difficult part was just getting past the people who kept asking why this was important to you and who were white, like, "What the fuck do you mean?

You don't see us dying out here in the street, and you don't see people choking the hell out of us? Like, that's why it's fuckin' important? So, having to justify, in a nice way, to this reviewer or to this editor or to this person in power that what you're researching is important because it can actually save lives, literally, is kind of like exhausting. And I think the other thing that I had problems with was just the writing; like, academic writing is just another archaic, you know, bullshit, just to say that you followed APA guidelines. It's just another way to kind of separate yourself.

Participant 4: Tre

Tre (age 25-34 years) was born in Georgia and raised in Houston, Texas. His parents both earned bachelor's degrees. He is the only male among his siblings, as he has two sisters. As the first person in his family to receive a graduate degree, he was filled with joy and pride as he described what it meant to him to receive his MBA in Business Administration and Management from the University of the Incarnate Word. Tre is now a football coach in Victoria, Texas. He believes that you must distinguish yourself and strive for the top, that the bottom is too crowded.

Tre's faith in God is evident in all aspects of his life. He spoke with certainty and confidence, as if he knew his own worth. He overcame adversity in his life, such as being shot as an innocent bystander. Tre expressed and described himself as self-motivated and dedicated to his craft, and he believes that life is a true blessing. During the interview, Tre recalled it being extremely difficult at one point in his studies, but he knew he had to finish what he started. He continues to believe that one must "Keep your energy up, don't let the fire go out; as long as you don't let it break you, you'll be fine."

During the interview, Tre described how he overcame other obstacles, such as being accused of plagiarizing/cheating on a class project. Tre explained how he was able to turn things around and pass the class with a grade of B+. His roadblocks strengthened him and prepared him for success. He disclosed a near-death experience that transformed his thinking. Having a strong mental state prepared him for the challenges he incurred.

A couple of weeks after the interview, Tre was involved in a serious car accident, causing bodily injuries. He disclosed another near-death experience that he described as being a motivational factor in his life. With the multiple challenges faced, Tre never lost his faith. His recovery is a testament to the saying, "Tough times don't last forever; however, tough people do." He fractured his right ankle and was left with numerous massive scars on his face. Tre placed a premium on triumph and perseverance. He discussed time management and balancing work and school. During the interview, Tre described his experience of maturing and setting himself apart from others. Detailing a thought-provoking moment as an MBA student, he said:

Man, just balancing the work. You know the class is 4 hours a day, 1 day a week. Since I was still a football coach on the side at the same time. So, it was just trying to balance their work and, you know, classroom time. Finding good time management was one of my biggest issues; I had to get better at it. It was challenging. Obviously, I got through it, took that time out, and completed the process that I needed to complete. But that was one of the things that I had to go through. You have to mature as a man and learn to manage your time better. Sometimes you may have to go study in the library, but some days you can't go out with friends or go out after work. You know, separate yourself and just go do the work you have to do for class. You just have to use that time where it will pay off at the end. It will be all good.

Participant 5: Bishop

Bishop (age 25-34 years) chose to use a pseudonym. His father completed high school, and his mother received an associate degree. He was the first male in his family to receive two master's degrees and have attended four different universities for his graduate studies. Before enrolling for PhD studies, Bishop attended Florida International University, where he obtained his Master of Science with a concentration in Higher Education Administration. He then chose to further his education at Cornell University, where he earned his Master of Arts in Human Development Psychology. He described how he spent a year at Iowa State University in the PhD program, Doctor of Philosophy in Higher Education Administration, before transferring to the University of Wisconsin, Madison, where he is now in his final year of a Doctor of Philosophy in Educational Leadership and Policy Analysis. Bishop discussed his activities and contributions to society as a Graduate Training Program (GTP) Equity Fellow.

Bishop has a Graduate Minor in Counseling Psychology, which allowed him to do a myriad of health work when he wasn't working on his academics. He brings a new perspective to the study, as he is currently investigating the experiences of youth of color in foster care and their transition to college degrees, access, retention, and success. Bishop mentioned that he wants to give back to the foster care community in some way, that he enjoys being a mentor to many of the youth in the community he serves, and that he does not want to disappoint the youth or the people around him. His sister has her doctorate in veterinary medicine, and his girlfriend just finished her program in psychiatry. Both are major inspirations and motivators who help him to keep striving. Bishop was genuine and honest when giving feedback on how he viewed himself, as well as how others viewed him as a threat at times. He stated that he is a big man, and that professors on campus ask him which sport he plays, or what was the score of the game. Aside from the barrier of everyone thinking that he is an athlete, Bishop is fortunate to be in a good, challenging program that also provides a great deal of support.

During the interview, Bishop mentioned two of his main struggles one of his struggles— one was that the educational opportunity came at a cost, while the other challenge was the scholarly writing requirements. Bishop described his circumstances:

I would say my two biggest were coming from a salaried gig to a stipend. I was getting paid pretty well, so coming out to a stipend meant that I had to change a lot of things that I had going on in my life. I couldn't go out and buy clothes and shoes and be like, "I'm going to take a trip here and take a trip there." I had to be more strategic in terms of buying clothes because I needed to buy clothes for the conference. If I'm traveling, I need to try to maneuver a way to get to these conferences and use that as my traveling time, so I'd say coming from a full-time position to a full-time student was a struggle... Then also, writing for me is a struggle.

Writing is just hard, to get to the journal level of writing. The papers are okay, but at the same time, they still need to be of a certain caliber, and you still need to have the correct grammar and all those different types of things. I just know I'm not a strong writer, so finding ways to just keep improving the language skills to get to that level where I could publish papers and people are wanting to read what I'm writing, because, again, it's full of content but it's also clear, I would say that's a big part for me.

Participant 6: Dr. Kobe

Dr. Kobe (age 35-44 years) was considerably like participant 3, Dr. Igbo, as they were both in the same age range, and Dr. Kobe also elected to use an alias. Dr. Kobe grew up in Youngstown, Ohio. His mother attended college but did not attain a degree; however, his father received an associate degree. Dr. Kobe explained how going to the larger Kent State University, where he received his master's and a PhD degree, was an adjustment from his undergraduate experience at Mount Union University. In addition, he has worked at the same place for over 15 years. Dr. Kobe received his Master's in Higher Education Administration, as well as his PhD in Higher Education/Higher Education Administration.

Changing and transitioning into a completely new situation, such as a job outside of higher education. Dr. Kobe explained how this was a job that was built from scratch, from the ground up, because his current position didn't exist. He recalled having to deal with the difficulties of balancing work, school, and family life. Dr. Kobe is now working as a Career Academy Liaison and Coordinator of Special Projects at Akron Children's Hospital. Prior to a new place of employment, Dr. Kobe experienced professional development within his graduate program and has demonstrated a history of working in the higher education industry. He displayed a strong sense of educational pride in his professional skills, such as event planning, higher education administration, program evaluation, and admissions. Dr. Kobe described the effect of having a black woman mentor late in his program as beneficial; his only wish was that she had come sooner.

Even though Dr. Kobe went through times of not feeling like he belonged, he showed how to keep a job for over 15 years, highlighting the characteristics of being a hard worker and showing longevity with commitment. A few weeks after the interview, Dr. Kobe informed the study that he now has his own business. Dr. Kobe described how his motivation to keep striving and thriving stemmed from his marriage and two kids and overcoming the challenges of balancing parenting, work and school life.

Dr. Kobe indicated a willingness to share his experiences as a doctoral student. He described areas in which he believed could have been more effective when dealing with faculty and other students. During the interview, Dr. Kobe explained a hard-hitting situation where he was not able to have thorough conversations about his topic with others, nor did he think that he was gaining the same connections as other students in the program:

I want to say that I think connecting with something I mentioned earlier, like being able to, especially early on, having that faculty or even fellow students be able to connect with my topic. Like I knew other students connected with other students or whatever else. I would talk to them loosely about my topic, though we weren't able to thoroughly talk about my topic. Kind of like those real, in-depth conversations and or whatever else about my topic. Again, like even the faculty, so like being able to like, really have those real, in-depth conversations until it's pretty much too late. late. But I think just being able to have those different conversations with people who look like me. Because, as I mentioned, especially going through my PhD program, being the only black male that's in those classes. So, no one else kind of knows like that experience kind of being able to go through that. That I was able to talk to, like, as a student or from a faculty perspective. So again, earlier in the process, like I mentioned about the two professors that I had for the online classes but liked for the in-person classes like that's not seeing or having like that visual representation of someone that kind of that looks like you like teaching that class. That you see and that you know like that it's possible like that's what I aspire to be like to be that doctor or whatever else. Or like having that visual representation. So, I will definitely say like that would be one of the hurdles or obstacles.

Participant 7: Dr. Samuel

Dr. Samuel (age 45-54 years) has a white father but still considers himself a black male despite the interracial status of his parents. His parents both received their GEDs. Dr. Samuel is married with children and, similar to Dr. Kobe, took a 10-year gap in between the master's program and their respective doctoral programs. The first generation to go to college, Dr. Samuel received his Master of Education (MEd) in College Student Personnel Administration. Dr.

Samuel was one of two participants who might have fallen out of the research criteria of completing a graduate degree within the past 5 years as he officially earned his Doctor of Education (EdD) in Higher Education/Higher Education Administration from the University of Texas at Austin in 2014. He also shared experiences of the school from which he transferred to Louisiana State University.

Dr. Samuel is currently a Senior Director for Admissions Programs at The University of Texas at Austin. He is a professional who is enthusiastic about higher education and is motivated to encourage, inform, and assist responsible individuals seeking a higher learning opportunity to better themselves and their families. Dr. Samuel assisted in developing the concept of affirmative action in society. The topic of affirmative action came up while speaking with Dr. Samuel about his dissertation topic, "How our law school admitted students without affirmative action for 6 years." Dr. Samuel shared historical insights as he recounted a story he heard from a judge in the 1960s. According to Dr. Samuel, it is extremely crucial for Black males in graduate school to have a Black advisor or mentor who looks like the student. During his graduate academic program, Dr. Samuel reported feelings of extreme anxiety and, at times, racial fatigue, similar to participants Ray, Bruce, and Dr. Igbo. More specifically, Dr. Samuel provided a variety of perspectives from both sides of the spectrum, as a student and as a member of administration. He shared insightful historical information and made wise connections to the present. Dr. Samuel has been at the same institution, as well as his same place of employment, for over 21 years, emphasizing the qualities of consistency and longevity.

During the interview, Dr. Samuel discussed an unwelcome comment he received from a nurse while in school as a pre-med student that changed his perspective on medical school and inspired him to do what he does today:

Because when I was a pre-med student at UT Biology, I had a lady completely, disenfranchise my thoughts and my beliefs, and I mean myself, but she came to speak to our pre-med group, an African American pre-med group. She was a Caucasian lady and was a nurse, I believe. She was our guest speaker. She went around the room and asked people quietly before it started, she was like, "What's your name?" Blah, blah, blah. She said, "What do you want to be?" I said, "I want to be a medical doctor." She's like, okay. She's like, "What's your GPA?" I told her it was a two-point something. She said, "Oh, "You'll never be a medical doctor with that GPA.' She completely ruined me for the rest of my life. I didn't believe in myself, but I didn't know that I could go find a lower tier medical school or dental school. I didn't know any of that. That's one of the main reasons I love doing what I do now.

Participant 8: Tim

Tim (age 18-24 years) elected to use a pseudonym. Tim is from Memphis, Tennessee, where both parents attended school; his father received a bachelor's degree. Tim received an MBA from Texas A&M University and had a great understanding of the obstacles that came along with completing his graduate degree. He mentioned a few times that he did not have a support system in his 1st year as a graduate student. Tim's financial hurdles motivated him to want to move up in his field. Tim felt that having a mindset of how you show up depends on your amount of success. At times Tim felt like other professors who were not Black did not care about him.

Tim mentally shifted from believing he was not good enough to believing he needed to work harder to get where he wanted to go. He spent the majority of his life as one of, if not the only, Black males in his graduate classes, which took a mental toll on him. Outside factors such as balancing work, school, and family seemed impossible at one point, and he reported frequent feelings of stress, anxiety, depression, and, on occasion, homesickness. Tim was going through very similar feelings to other participants during their graduate program. He mentioned that faith and involvement in the Black Grad Student Association, in addition to close relationships with roommates and upper-older classmates, were tremendously beneficial in graduate school. Tim gave insight on his experiences with alienation/isolation and how to successfully overcome such barriers. Positive self-talk and affirmations, such as telling himself he could do it, had a positive impact on his success.

He was passionate and motivated about getting more students into college and graduate programs who were Black and resembled him. He believed that a white faculty member might not really see the importance of that, especially if that wasn't their field of interest. He believes other black faculty members can help serve as a support system and help connect ideas. Tim shared a moment where he believed it was difficult to learn and to be himself when attempting to interact with his cohort and faculty:

I would say definitely being a minority in my cohort. My program is focused a lot on your experiences and sharing those, but it's a lot of group work. But if you're surrounded by people you don't want to work with and you don't think anyone cares about you, then that really impacts your learning and how you see things. So, I will definitely say my cohort would probably be my biggest challenge. Texas A&M University, where I earned my master's degree... It is a large, predominately white institution, and I thought since I graduated from Mississippi State and conquered that, it will be easy going at A&M, but it's a whole different beast because it's so much larger and there are so few people of color there. Another challenge that I didn't learn until towards the end of my first year is that it's harder to make friends as you grow older and as you move to different places. And I wasn't prepared for that. And I had a really strong network and a strong group of friends at undergrad. But this was my first time being in a new place, having to make all new friends all over again.

Participant 9: Chris

Chris (age 18-24 years) was one of the youngest of the 16 participants. He is from Rock Hill, South Carolina, where he attended Coastal Carolina University for his undergraduate experience. Both parents attended college, and his father received his graduate degree. Chris is currently in the last semester of a graduate program at Louisiana State University, seeking his Master of Arts in Higher Education Administration and Student Affairs. Currently residing in Louisiana, he is employed as an intern for Transfer Student Programs and is an active member of the community. He is President of the Higher Education Strategic Planners Association (HESPA).

Chris believes in inspiring and empowering people to live their highest vision in a context of love and joy. Chris explains that "it's our job as higher education and student affairs professionals to guide and challenge any student we come across to become the best version of themselves that they can." Becoming the best version of himself, Chris highlighted balancing life with time management, and the importance of events happening at all times of the day. Furthermore, Chris discussed throughout the interview the awkward looks he received when walking into his first graduate class, which was different but similar to Ray's experience. When Ray referred Chris to participate in the study, Chris demonstrated the successful process of snowball recruitment.

Furthermore, as the only one of one or two black males in his class, Chris put a spotlight on connections with many of the participants. Chris, like Tim, would write positive messages to himself on his bathroom mirror. Chris shared narratives on reaching out to different faculty members and peers. He stressed the importance of his parents' support when he needed it the most. He believes in setting up your platform and getting yourself out there.

During the interview, Chris shared his thoughts on his major challenges and how he had to find a way to keep it moving. Although Chris said he arrived at graduate school with the right attitude, he described the barrier of making proper connections with faculty, professors, and other students. Chris described his situation:

I would say my biggest challenge would just be, you know, I would say just reaching out. I'm a big person in the sense that if something happens, say, while I'm working on something or working on a project, and I get stressed, I don't let it be known. I see it as a sign of weakness sometimes for me to actually reach out and, you know, talk with people. A challenge for me is getting support from cohort supervisors or people in the career center where I work by just letting them know that I'm having a hard time. But the big challenge remained. I was saying that was definitely a big challenge for me my first semester to, as I actually did, reach out to people in the office and let them know, like, how I was feeling. Why I was thinking about leaving LSU would transfer, and it took a lot. I had to swallow my pride and just let them know. I don't know if this is for me. I doubt myself a lot. I hate it. I hate when I do it. I don't know why that's the way I am.

This is how I am. I don't know. What is this? It just happens a lot with me. Now, I doubt myself a lot more when it comes to different things. I doubted myself the first semester when, basically, classes and workload started coming. I was like, "How am I going to do this?" I have these 15-page papers due in a week or two. And I'm just like, "It is what it is. I can't write this.

Participant 10: Jeff

Jeff (age 25-34 years) is from Houston, Texas. Both parents achieved graduate degrees, and he was destined to earn two master's degrees. The first graduate degree he obtained was from Trinity University in San Antonio, Texas, in Business Administration. His second master's degree was from the University of the Incarnate Word in Broadcasting & Communications in 2013. Similar to Dr. Samuel, he could have fallen outside the research criteria of graduating within the past 5 years. However, his experience was relatable, and he had impressive places of employment. Jeff is currently a sports anchor in Austin, Texas. His personality was very entertaining and energetic.

Jeff is big on utilitarian approaches and detailed throughout the interview his belief that you are how you treat people. During his interview, he discussed how he serves as an example for other black men and how he has benefited from seeing people like himself in positions of power. He discussed his approach in graduate school to reaching his full potential while also having the opportunity to fail or make mistakes. His faith and utopian belief systems catapulted him to success. Jeff, like Dr. Samuel, Dr. Igbo, and Dr. Kobe, is married with a baby girl, which he said motivated him tremendously and helped alleviate his very frequent levels of stress created in and out of the classroom. Jeff is the type of person who is always on the go. He conducted the interview from his car, which was parked as he dropped his daughter off at day care. Jeff demonstrated mobility and determination by stating that he is always on the move. He explained that everyone has a bad day, and you won't be down for long. His work ethic is unmistakable, as he believes that good things come to those who work hard and treat others with respect.

During his interview, Jeff discussed the possibility of helping others and providing a handout to those in need. He was primarily concerned with being a morally upright and good person in general. Jeff believes that with everyone's help, America can grow and progress. He quoted Teddy Roosevelt, saying, "Believe you can, and you're halfway there." Jeff believes that students are shaping their perceptions of what a black man can be and that they will change their minds once they get to know him. He claims to be fully engaged in his studies and believes that you get out what you put in. Jeff discussed how it was no sleep and all work most of the time:

I mean, I guess the hours, but it's like who kind of wants it and who really wants it." It's hard; yeah, you are putting in crazy hours. I remember there was like a 2-year stretch during my second masters experience where I would wake up at 5:30 or 6:00 in the morning, work out, and then I would go teach from 8:00 or so until 4:30. And then I would either go intern or go to grad school after that. Then, you know, go home, write a few papers, grade a few papers, get four hours of sleep, wake up, and do it again. And it is a grind, but it is what separates you from the people who aren't willing to put it into work.

Participant 11: Dr. Taylor

Dr. Taylor (age 25-34 years) is from Houston, Texas. Both his parents received graduate degrees. Dr. Taylor's father works as a superintendent, in which a school was named in his honor. He mentioned that he has four brothers and that they are extremely close. He mentioned their involvement in sports, as well as his experience as a quarterback at Texas A&M. Dr. Taylor earned a Doctor of Physical Therapy from the University of the Incarnate Word. In addition, Dr. Taylor is a Fellow of the American Academy of Orthopaedical and Manual Physical Therapists and a member of the American Academy of Physical Medicine and Rehabilitation. He currently works as Director of The American Orthopedic and Sports Medicine.

Dr. Taylor was open and felt comfortable sharing. He mentioned that he went through a lot of test-taking anxiety throughout his graduate program. Dr. Taylor discussed how he had difficult long and full days at certain times during his graduate program. His mission was to never get burnt out and to practice time management skills. Like many of the other participants, he used resounding willpower to reach his goals. He was another great example of the snowball effect/recruitment process—Jeff referred Dr. Taylor to participate in this study. Growing up with his father as a positive role model in the home, Dr. Taylor, similar to Jeff, knew he wanted to have an advanced degree in some shape or form. Dr. Taylor emphasized the importance of students knowing their history and where they come from. Dr. Taylor has exuded confidence since first grade, referring to himself as a boss, if not a CEO.

He was always impressed by his father's success, the joy and happiness that he expressed when he said that his father received his Doctorate at the age of 26. Taylor's narrative included conversations about how he went through the pipeline of education and access to resources.

Using quotes from historical public figures such as W.E.B. Dubois, Frederick Douglass, and Martin Luther King Jr., Dr. Taylor believes that it is critical to keep giving your all. It was also critical of the fact that he had a black mentor. Furthermore, family is very important to him. Learning about his family history and ancestors has been important to him throughout his life. It was critical for him to see people who looked like him in positions of power. However, Dr. Taylor discussed his experiences in graduate school and how he was unprepared for the long hours that were required:

During my graduate program, I'm going to say that the hardest thing for me was being in long classes. Graduate school is so long. It's a full day. Excuse me. I wasn't prepared for the eight-to-five school gig. Trying to stay on track, to make the best use of my time, and to avoid becoming burned out was difficult for me. I took on the role in my class of being the guy that runs around and pumps everyone up; I got school awards. I got the Spirit Award twice. I thought I was cheesy at first, but that's what I did. I had people say, "That's probably why you didn't pass your test because you were always running around trying to pump all those up." I just did the best I could. I'm just not going to let people into my mind; I must stay moving. I have to keep going. It's all these things for me, just trying to find that balance between work and life. That was pretty challenging.

Participant 12: Dr. Langston

Dr. Langston (age 25-34 years). Both his parents went to school and his mother earned a graduate degree. Langston had the pleasure of attending three different universities and was one of the participants who attended an HBCU as an undergraduate. Dr. Langston was proud of his alma mater, North Carolina AT&T experience. He also attended Ohio State and earned an M.A. in Adapted Physical Education. Furthermore, he was admitted to The University of Texas at Austin and earned his PhD in Curriculum & Instruction: Physical Education. Dr. Langston currently serves as a tenured professor at The University of Texas at San Antonio (UTSA) within the College of Education and Human Development. His research areas include Physical Education and Teacher Education in the context of Black communities and the intersection of race, sports, and education.

Dr. Langston expressed his gateway of publishing his work as attainable. He personifies a different way of thinking, that situations that to some people that can be viewed as obstacles were, he sees those same areas as opportunities where he can thrive and understand what it means to care for students and find the joy within graduate school. When Dr. Langston experienced the loss of his mother, it was extremely hard on him, however it motivated him to want to achieve new heights in her honor. He currently teaches courses that prepare physical educators to become instructors at the secondary level, net games, and individuals with disabilities. Dr. Langston's esteemed narrative was vital to straightening out the key components of mentorship, peers and the idea of publishing to expand your skill set and marketability.

Dr. Langston has a great sense of humor and an optimistic intelligent mind frame. In his interview, he explained how he dealt with the small microaggressions he might have faced at his institutions. The HBCU experience has equipped him for the real world. Black students' experiences at their HBCUs were affirming, instead of always comparing themselves to the white experience. He also enjoyed learning that there is value in a professor telling you your paper is not ready yet.

More recently, when not teaching, Dr. Langston invites colleagues and professionals to events hosted via LinkedIn and through Zoom. Dr. Langston, a tenured professor, finds time to host events on a variety of topics, including "Presidents of Universities" conversations, "Blacks in Higher Education," and "Financial Services Goals," to name a few, with over 600 attendees. I was able to attend one of these and found it to be an inspiring and knowledgeable resource.

During the interview, Dr. Langston discussed the differences in experiences he has had with North Carolina AT&T, Ohio State, and now Texas, where he claims to have found happiness:

This was the biggest, I think, at the time. It was the biggest in the country. Like how you go to school with sixty thousand students. So, I might have been overwhelmed when I first got here coming from AT&T because it was just so big. But then, by the time I got to Texas, it was like, "Oh, Texas is not that big, even though it is, you know? I mean, it was just normal, and it was cold and dreary. And then you get to Texas, where it's 60 degrees in December. So, I think my perceptions changed in terms of, like, when I got in there, I was really happy that I went to Ohio State. You know, man. The Ohio State! And then I got there, like, man. These people are unhappy, and there's lots of, you know, toxicity here. And when I get a PhD I'm going to be happy. And then when I got to Texas, I was really happy, and I stayed that way. Like it didn't dissipate.

Participant 13: Papi

Papi (age 25-34 years) decided to use an alias, much like many of the other participants within this study. Papi is from Texas. Both parents have earned their bachelor's degrees. Papi received his Master of Business Administration and Management degree from the University of the Incarnate Word. He explained how he played football during his master's program and how he dearly missed the unity and connections with other teammates. Papi decided to take a big leap to the University of Iowa, where he is in his 2nd year of a PhD program in Business. Unfortunately, the feelings of depression and stress from curriculum and outside factors such as the COVID-19 pandemic, mixed with the Black Lives Matter movement, became a commonality among most of the 16 participants, and he felt like he has/had no help.

Papi showcased the importance of interacting with those having shared experiences as peers and having mentorship as a reliable support system. He stressed the importance of impactful and understanding professors who challenged him to become the best that he could be. Papi explained how his capstone project was insightful because he undertook original research regarding skills commonly desired by MBA graduates. Papi recalled his working title: "Skills Desired of MBA Graduates: A Qualitative Analysis of MBA-Level Job Postings." Papi analyzed and reported the employment trends of 1000+ graduate alumni who participated in the coordination and execution of several events including a week-long conference showcasing faculty and student-led research. Hundreds of incoming graduate students were involved in new student orientation, and career-focused panel discussions featuring a university Provost, elected state official, and C-level executive provided a plethora of opportunities.

Papi described one of his most difficult challenges as connecting what he was learning in the classroom to what we would be doing once he graduated. He discussed the importance of networking and connecting with peers in order to thrive in life. Papi believes he has no one to turn to for help, and as such he described the challenges he has faced so far in his graduate career:

Yeah, I will say that was probably it, like trying to balance the time between football and grad school. And then, when I was in graduate school, when I was doing my MBA program, because I didn't have a plan, I wasn't someone; in fact, I worked at USAA and was just getting this degree to help me get promoted. I didn't really have a direction for what I was learning or where I would like it to be applied until I got to the capstone courses, and then there was like one qualitative research class. We were designing studies for companies atomic vehicles, but until I get a direction that uses that work, I think one of the biggest challenges was not really having a way to connect what we were learning in the classroom to what we will be doing once we graduate... Well, you know, out here. I would say that the biggest thing here is, is that like it doesn't feel I have help. I don't know if I can't speak for other students, but it just seems like the advice I'm getting from my advisors isn't really helping that much. Which is probably the reason why I don't like my time here. And I'm sure that that doesn't help. What this is like, I don't know. Sometimes the stuff they tell me just doesn't really seem to be working, so yeah. You got that. That's just me. Yeah. I would like some better kind of help.

Participant 14: Johari, JD

Johari (25-34 years) was born in New York; however, he moved to Texas with his family when he was younger and received his education there. His father's highest level of education is a bachelor's degree, while his mother has a graduate degree and was a member of the military.

When reflecting on his own academic journey, he credits his parents for their support as well as his real-world experiences for shaping his world view. Throughout the interview, he discussed how his interactions with other international students at the University of the Incarnate Word prepared him for his time at an HBCU. Johari attended TSU, Thurgood Marshall School of Law and graduated Cum Laude from Texas Southern University. His university enlightened his HBCU experience, which he described as life changing. Johari was 21 years old when he enrolled in the Law School program. He described his run-in with the law outside of the classroom, which he was concerned would prevent him from furthering his education.

Johari was personable and very honest with his responses, a truthful individual concerned with the well-being of others. When Johari gave an update on being sworn in at the Alabama Courthouse, he expressed great joy. His happiness can be viewed as a victory and a reward for all that he had to endure. This update highlighted his ascension and dedication to matriculation, a truly heroic story of free will and never giving up. Furthermore, Johari, like Dr. Langston, takes pride in the fact that he attended an HBCU. He believes that his institution took the necessary time and provided assistance in ways that made unimaginable connections possible. He emphasized that no matter what one is going through, they must be able to find joy in whatever they must do.

According to Johari, the struggle to blend in with others and dress professionally was at times overwhelming and difficult. Johari expressed his displeasure with his inability to present himself as his true self during law school. Despite his feelings of not being himself, he managed to show up to work every day in a suit and tie. Johari described his experiences as a law student in terms of how he showed up to classes and events:

Throughout my school years, especially at my law school, you know, I got to the point where I would realize... Oh, I can't be Joe. I can't be me. These folks don't get to see that. I have to come in here with a suit. I have to come in here with a tie. I've got to say got to, instead of "gotta." I've got it. I've got to really be on my Ps and Qs and act like them because they're not going to accept me for being me. I can't come in here and say, "Man, I think this is the problem. We need to go about it this way or that way. People want to hear their vernacular. You know what I'm saying? And they want to see you looking like them. They want to see you, you know, attacking things their way.

Participant 15: Tayo

Tayo (age 25-34 years) was born in Paris, and his family is from Nigeria. Surprisingly, the name Tayo means Warrior. He has lived in five different countries and four different continents and takes great pride in the culture of the land. His parents both received their bachelors, and his father received a graduate degree. He is the oldest of three brothers. Tayo is currently living and thinking in an "empire state of mind." He is very empowering, and he uses his leadership and involvement skills for the greater good of society. Tayo earned a Master of Business Administration (MBA) degree in Marketing, Communication, and Media Management from Fordham University in New York. Tayo stated that he was a Social Chair and Student Advisory Council Project Leader at Fordham Graduate School of Business. He is currently a consultant, an author, and a public speaker. There is a real resiliency to his story. He is the author of a book titled *Use Your Difference to Make a Difference*. Tayo's work mainly focuses on cross-cultural studies, class culture, and communication, and he has a fervor for diversity, equity, and inclusion.

Tayo provided an eminent way to view diversity on a global scale. He shared knowledge and different ways of reinventing oneself during the COVID-19 global pandemic. He drew attention to a troubling issue occurring in Nigeria, a country where he once lived, which he explained as SARS, or police brutality against the people of Nigeria.

In combination with the obscure actions within his SARS story, he spoke of feelings of anxiety, depression, stress, and racial fatigue that were very frequently due to the internal and external factors in the classroom. Tayo felt it was critical to focus on the success enablers that contributed to his personal development. A true beneficiary of assistance, he recognizes that it takes a village to raise a child. Tayo demonstrated self-motivation and independent thinking. He explained how his father had the highest education in the family, and how one of the most motivating factors for him was to become like his father. He stated that Nigeria has a joke for the future, that you are either an "Engineer, Doctor, or Educator."

To earn his master's degree, Tayo had to overcome anxiety as well as country requirements. Tayo describes his difficulties in obtaining the necessary paperwork, as well as his time proving to himself that he is capable of eventually achieving success:

It was the fact that I'm from Nigeria, a lot of companies don't sponsor visas for international students. And so, I have this thing where, you know, I don't, I guess I don't sound like a typical Nigerian. A lot of people always make all these assumptions. But when it comes down to the passports, you know that, you know, companies have interesting policies and also would say, sorry, we don't sponsor. Oh, if you were American, would it? I had to work really hard to get a specific type of visa that allows me more flexibility. They call it the O-1 visa. So, it's a thing they say it's a visa for aliens with extraordinary abilities or something that stands out to describe it. And it's a you know, it's a lot of money you pay for it. You're not guaranteed. Right. Because the government requires you to meet three criteria: you have to have done work that's recognized nationally, and you have to have, you know, lots of letters of recommendation from reputable, reputable people. And then people say that your work has to be something that only you can do. Other people can't do that. So that was the toughest part was the need to prove myself, even though I knew I could do it.

Participant 16: Michael

Michael (age 35-44 years) chose to use a pseudonym. Michael was born in Philadelphia, interestingly the same day the Berlin Wall came down, which he mentioned as a fun fact. He is part of a blended military family. Michael served in the Navy. His mother and father attended school; however, he is the first in his family to receive a master's degree and will be the first to obtain a doctoral degree as well. Michael received his Master of Science Management (MSM) in the field of project management from Strayer Online University in Texas. His asynchronous and online experience was positive and provided him the opportunity to explain himself on paper. However, he felt it took away from his social connections within the community/classroom settings. He is currently in the final year of his doctorate program studying Philosophy and Organizational Leadership. He is enrolled in a program at the University of the Incarnate Word. Michael worked as a Project Coordinator at UTSA (University of Texas at San Antonio). Unfortunately, on the same day, both he and his mentor were terminated from their place of employment due to the COVID-19 pandemic.

Michael's expectations as a graduate student were beginning to align. His impediment to communicating effectively with staff and faculty was obvious. The difficulty of meeting certain expectations came into existence. Michael realized that, at the end of the day, it all came down to compromise:

My biggest challenge and struggles with being a graduate student are ensuring I'm effectively communicating with my faculty and staff. One of the challenges I felt was because of the difference in lived experiences with other faculty members, it's really difficult to just communicate what I'm asking you to do... An example would be when I failed, she was just like, "I'm here to help. How can I help?" My go-to answer is, "Well, I would really like the help when, instead of providing criticism, you help me solidify it and "Make it work more than what can be changed." ... That was simply saying, 'Well, here's my idea. As a student and also as a service customer, here's how we can better change or work with this idea. When it comes to faculty engagement, the thought process of, let's change a portion of this to clearly reflect their understanding... Then I feel like that's where the tension and frictional stress of trying to meet those expectations come into play. When it comes to dealing with the others, like student-to-student engagement, one of the barriers are also part of that experience aspect. I learned through inspiration, more than learned experience, and where our history of understanding is, experience is the product of doing something that was once a positive reward versus the inspiration of saying, It's taking the situation, seeing what exists, and what can be done about it, so it's envisioning and having that difference in philosophy really becomes challenging, but then, at the end, it's coming.

Summary of Participant Narratives

These 16 black men, who have completed or are nearing completion of a post-baccalaureate degree, provided a profound version of themselves. Each participant also expressed their uniqueness through the settings and backgrounds of various posters and pictures that were present during the semi-structured interviews in their homes. Each participant was applauded for having a functional internet connection and proper lighting to effectively communicate throughout the interview.

Certainly, the participants had several similar characteristics and experiences in common.

Feelings of sense of belonging were frequently mixed with feelings of stress, anxiety, and depression, which explains the importance of mental health and self-identity characteristics of intrinsic motivation. Participants were transparent, authentic, real, and honest; they displayed vulnerability about their graduate process and the challenges and successes that occurred within their graduate environment. To gain a better understanding of the participants' experiences with graduation and the degree requirement plan, the following will be explained.

Differentiation of Graduate Degree Requirements

Even among the participants categorized and described in the same fashion, there were notable differences in their graduate specialized concentration field. The participants' post-baccalaureate credentials include master's and doctorate degrees, such as professional degrees, Juris Doctorate (J.D.), and Doctor of Physical Therapy (DPT) degrees. Although all graduate education is not the same, there are common experiences between the differentiating degrees.

Participants with an MBA master's degree had to pass an entrance exam, as well as typically 2 years to complete the requirements for their degree. There were specific concentrations of degrees such as Master of Arts, or Master of Science. For example, Tim stated that his process for graduating and earning an MBA was:

So many, I would say, are graduating. For me, it was a tough time, even to the finish line.

So, I just finished this past May. So, I finished at the start of the pandemic. You know. So, to be able to say that I finished my graduate program, my program requires us to do two internships and take an elective. And I really feel like I took advantage of that. And I really grew inside and out. And I was able to graduate with a lot of experiences that people in my cohort were jealous about. But it's because I was this intentional about it.

Participants with a doctorate degree, PhD, had to apply to get into the program, complete the required coursework, ascertain a topic on which to begin research, and finally defend the dissertation and publish the research. This process typically takes 5 to 6 years, with the second half devoted to research. According to Dr. Samuel, it was different at his school, as he explained:

Here, we had a class called the qualifying exam class. It's different in different schools, so you had to register for a class, and it basically taught you to write your literature review. That was one of the things it did, because you have to do a literature review before applying for your proposal, having your proposal, and defending your proposal to advance to the next level.

Albert's Experiences

Personally, after 9 years, I have completed my doctoral program, and I can tell you right now that it takes time and commitment from all members of your community. Even in my own experience, I began the dissertation process with a role model and sponsor in the form of a Black female committee member.

Specific degrees conferred were Doctorate of Education (EdD), Doctor of Philosophy in Education (PhD), and a Doctor of Physical Therapy (DPT). As for the DPT degree, physical therapists are doctors, but they're not physicians. They undergo additional schooling as required for their specific professional practice just like any dentist, nurse, doctor, surgeon, optometrist, orthodontist, or therapist. More specifically, according to Dr. Taylor:

I'm not sure if it's something I do to myself. If I were to be honest, I had a hard time with my board exam. It actually took me a year to get my board. In order to practice. I had a doctorate degree, but in order to practice as a licensed physical therapist, you have to pass your boards. I took that test, probably three or four times, and it got to the point where I said, "No, it's not the content. I have the knowledge. It's literally this test.

Struggling to pass the board exam was an impactful barrier Dr. Taylor had to overcome that was different from the other participants. Even though it's not a board exam, the single participant who received a Juris

Doctorate degree (JD) had to pass the LSAT entrance test, as well as complete the 3-year coursework. Finally, the bar had to be passed in the state in which they will professionally represent clients. Participant Johari JD, explained the different experiences in graduate school:

In graduate school, the biggest struggle is money. OK. As always, the name of the game but especially for law school. Your first year, you're not allowed to work at all. It was against the rules. Second and 3rd year you work in but your trying to intern to work in your fields. People don't pay interns for real like big giving. You know, a $500 here and a

$1000 there that don't do anything for your stomach. You know, so there is always money trying to figure out how you ever pay for books, pay for rent, eat, or have Ramen noodles for dinner every day. We figured out a long time ago that you have to learn how to finesse.

Despite his financial difficulties and inability to work, Johari managed to eke out a living. He described the reality of not working and how he was able to survive on a limited supply by being careful about what he could afford for dinner and day-to-day living. Nonetheless, Johari shared valuable information about his experiences as a law student. His and other participants' experiences demonstrate practices that aim to assist people in forming better relationships, overcoming oppressive foundational identities, understanding the differences in post-baccalaureate education, and coping better with life's contingencies and difficulties.

Although the 16 were very diverse, there was still a close relationship in how they all succeeded. There are factual differences, in particular, when it comes to different fields of study and levels of educational attainment. For instance, the five who earned the MBA discussed how, even though it was a struggle, it was a beautiful outcome. The four participants who were working on their PhDs had various reactions and ways in which they dealt with the prospect of pursuing a PhD. They were confident, happy, rich, and unbothered, as opposed to those who had completed and earned, and who had gone through the grid iron. Most were happily married, had children, and lived in a nice house. They have been in their current positions for at least 14 years. There has been an evolution, either from a higher-paying job or from the realization that they were reaping the benefits of their efforts. The relationship was handed off and entered the system, walking unapologetically in their greatness.

Even though participants who had earned their PhD degree shared some of the same sentiments, those who were still in the pursuit of their PhD program placed a strong emphasis on racial fatigue, high anxiety, and the ability to work full-time but mostly part-time jobs. Mental health awareness, as well as diversity and inclusion, were all-powerful. For the one participant who had yet to receive his master's degree, unity among all and having your close friends and peers around you were important because he suffered from homesickness and the fact that no one looked like him in class most of the time.

Philosophical Statements

Each of the 16 participants wrote a first-person self-reflective philosophical statement to convey positive narratives on how their mottos or mantras were used in everyday life, which aided in the participants' progress toward their degrees. The participants' philosophical statements are filled with what they believe and provided either quotes or positive information that was useful in fully understanding who they truly are. Participant statements included advice from family members and even distinguished educators and historical figures. (A complete list of the 16 participants' Philosophical Statements can be found in Appendix F.)

Their statements were compelling and concise. They reiterated that it is not what you think, but how you think, that matters. Powerful and meaningful philosophical statements were interwoven, clarifying and describing ways to make meaning and the ways data collected was connected to the characterizations and the three major themes. It was important to see what might have helped participants overcome barriers that were not known to them initially, and what was the philosophy or motto that got them through the rigid process. For example, Kobe wrote in his philosophical statement:

My philosophy is that education is one path to making a better future for yourself. Education is a way in which someone can write their own narrative for their life and not let it be determined by their family or the zip code they are growing up in.

Albert's Reflection 1: Write your own story

I believe what participant Kobe was saying is that you should not let yourself play the victim; become the victor. Be intentional about what you want and deliberate about your future. Be open-minded, work hard, and investigate; also, question others. Questioning is a way to get to the truth. Ask for help when you need it and lend help when you can, know that the ones that need help will not always easily tell you that they need help. It's the trust and value aspect that goes into fostering and developing healthy relationships with everyone. Do not let someone else write your story; be who you are and want to be.

Definition of Characterizations

Understanding the data in a comprehensible manner encompassed a multitude of tasks, starting with an analytical approach to the data as information was being composed and then interpreting the identifiable data of information into prevalent characterizations, resulting in 10 characterizations or categories. As mentioned in chapter 3, I re-read the transcripts and watched the interviews many times to remember the main message that helped each participant individually and then as a whole. For academic reasons, I discovered the most used phrases and synthesized them to describe the participants' experiences in a truthful and respectful manner that represented their true sentiments and connection to their graduate experience.

Faith (Spirituality; Higher Power)

The first characterization, Faith (spirituality; higher power), is one that believes in a higher power, the almighty Lord. Understanding how to maintain faith in the face of adversity was paramount. Jeff defines what it means to believe in a higher power:

I mean, I don't want to get, I guess, too churchy on you, but what motivates me is trying to find a way to maximize my potential. I feel like God put us all here with a certain amount of potential. And if we don't get close to realizing our potential in as many aspects of life as we can, we're wasting. And it's like insulting, you know. So, what motivates me is the fact that I'm blessed, man. I'm blessed with an opportunity to be an intelligent, educated, and well-rounded young man. And so, if I'm not showing that off, every single day, in every single way, it's like a slap in the face to me. I've got to max this thing out.

Jeff was speaking about how you show up and show out; don't just be there for the sake of being there but always give it your all and put your best foot forward. He expressed the idea of realizing one's full potential for the greater good of humanity. Throughout the study, the emergence of faith (spirituality; higher power) was also noticeable in most of the participants' experiences. The idea of believing in something bigger than themselves motivated most of the participants to continue succeeding. Dr. Kobe discussed details from his similar study, as well as why he persisted:

So, these are experiences that students have as they are going through their doctoral program. So, like the first, there is self-awareness. So, there's self-awareness; this includes everything from having faith to believing in a higher being. Persistence, being able to persist through their program.

Dr. Kobe explained his deep understanding and relationship with a higher power, which allowed both the participants in his study and him to continue with their graduate programs. Most of the participants were not super religious people; however, they do have faith. In a similar fashion, Tim reiterated the importance of faith:

So, I'm not a super religious or spiritual person, but I am, you know, I do believe in the faith. And so, I prayed and asked God to let me know. I wanted to go out less. I felt like he told me to come to Texas. And it has been a growing and learning experience. But this turned out to be a really great experience. And so, I see why he wanted me to come here. So that is a little bit about me and how I ended up coming to grad school.

Tim described how he prayed to God to show him the answers and where he should go. He described his development in faith as a "growing experience." Ray, however, was extremely passionate about God and believed that aligning with strong spiritual leaders was a key factor in what provided him with stability and a solid moral guide. He described himself as an "old school Baptist," adding, "so finding that right Baptist church that gives me all the inspiration…. On Sunday, I'll need an organist. That's all I need to hear some days." They felt a spiritual guidance to fear no one but God. They also felt an anointing from a higher being with a higher cause directing them..

Albert's Reflection 2: The Need for Faith & The Holy Spirit

The term "faith (spirituality; higher power)" can be used to mean the belief system that forms the basis of the conviction that God is in charge. Exceptional abilities to fear no one except God, but they felt anointed by a greater being for a higher purpose.

Albert's Experience:

I was raised in a spiritual family. My great-grandfather was a preacher, and my mother and father regularly took us to church. According to my grandmother, the praying warrior of the family, who has long been a churchgoer, she wishes to "hand the mantle" to me. During the last years of my PhD coursework program, a professor I looked up to basically advised me I should drop out of college, which is a testimonial I have never shared before. If I had followed his advice, I might not be in the position I am in now. A word to the wise: never let anything or anyone convince you otherwise.

To fully grasp the meaning of the characterization "faith" (spirituality; higher power), most participants stated that they believed in God in some form or fashion. Most of the participants owned their faith and explained how they always had praying people around them. Some mentioned praying mothers, and other individuals would pray and believe not only when things were going well, but also when things were going poorly. Remarkably, nearly 95% of participants mentioned faith and belief in a higher power as the foundation for achieving post-baccalaureate degrees.

First in Class

The second characterization, First in Class, refers to being first in their family to be in a postbaccalaureate program, being the only Black male in their class or program, and setting a first-class example to others. Participant Tim describes his experience as follows:

My younger cousins look up to me, you know, because I got a college degree. I had a great undergrad experience, but I also went there and got a master's, which shows them that they too can do it. And, you know, the family prayers and the family support, you know, do go a long way. I could just spend all day talking about it. It feels great. You know, I think there was a time for me when I wasn't sure if I would go to college, let alone get a master's. I got two degrees—not one, but two—from two different great universities. And there was once a time when I didn't know if I was going to go to college. I'm a first-generation and low SES [socioeconomic status] student.

Here, Tim explains how he was a first-generation graduate student and how that pressure to be the first in his family motivated him to keep going once he was there—not only to make his parents and family proud, but also to show and lead his younger family members, even extended family members, that there was a way to accomplish these goals.

> ## Albert's Reflection 3: Turning into a Reality
> For him and his family, the "facade" of getting a degree was now a steadfast reality. Once it is a reality, it helps Black men appreciate their experiences even more.

Furthermore, participant Dr. Taylor described how he has grown accustomed to certain realities and the way people progress in the South, particularly Texas: He explains

There were 52 of us, 52 or 53 in the class, and maybe a little bit more than half were female. I could be wrong. Don't quote me on that. As far as people of color versus-- If I was to guess, I would say there are three Black males in our class and we had one biracial female. She's Black and Hispanic, I believe, which is, I wouldn't necessarily say a shock but I went to Texas A&M With the exception of the football team-- from where I grew up, being one and the only Black male in the classroom is not something that's new to me. It's something that I'm used to.

Here, Dr. Taylor showcased the rarity of being a Black man pursuing a post-baccalaureate degree. In his case, not only was it a statistical fact, but he also embraced the unique opportunity to be different and prove his value within the educational system.

Like Tim and Dr. Taylor, Participant Dr. Kobe mentions what aided him in his success and the challenges one might encounter for being a first-generation, low-income student or possibly the first to go through the process:

I would say that like the main support was from peers and then on some topics or some questions that had to be the faculty. Because like my immediate family thinking about like my dad, my brother, sister, and maybe my cousins and all those different things like they weren't able to offer that academic support. Like they were able to offer emotional support, they were able to offer encouragement for different things of that nature. But they wouldn't be able to answer any questions about comps or dissertation or a theory or this or that or whatever else. So, then I know that's sometimes like that could be a challenge for – I mean periodically it was a challenge for me as well. II know that can be a challenge for many people going through their doctoral program. Especially if they're first generation or even low income.

Here, Dr. Kobe gave one of many examples of how a first-generation student can have, but overcome, shortcomings due to his family's lack of experience with higher education.

Albert's Reflection 4: Long-Term Connections

Although family, regardless of their experience, is imperative for the emotional and mental support to endure the process, it also requires the student to make connections in order to get the sustainability that is needed to finish the program academically.

Albert's Experience

I completely understand Dr. Taylor and others because, in my experience as a graduate student, there were always one or two, and never more than three, Black people in my class. I was the first person on both my mother's and father's sides of the family to earn a PhD. Like Tim, I enjoy going back to my family and spreading wisdom while also showing them what I've learned and the connections I've made to the real world. We are a source of inspiration and tremendous energy that feeds off of one another. I'm not going to disappoint anyone.

To provide a full understanding of the meaning of the characterization First in Class, many of the participants stated that they were the first in their immediate families to earn a master's or a doctorate degree. A large portion of the participants own their "only-ness" of being the only black person in the class. Interestingly, nearly 88% of the participants were first-generation graduate students, the first males in their families to obtain such degrees.

Other Mothering

The third characterization, Other Mothering, was not planned; it just sort of happened. From a woman of color professor or assistant assisting students in navigating their coursework to a woman of color's passion for assisting students in succeeding not only in school but also in life. A few of the participants mentioned the bonds and relationships that were formed, as well as the positive ways in which success was fostered with the assistance of women of color. Participant Chris described how his relationship with his boss was a working formula:

My supervisor. Luckily, she's a black woman. I can honestly say I could be honest with her. I'm like, "Hey, I said I feel out of place, you know?" You know, I'm getting taught by white professors who teach with 90 percent white women, you know. And then when we have these different conversations that challenge the conversations about race, it's like they don't talk, but I'm the one mainly talking. I've seen that a lot in this program, too.

Chris speaks about how he was able to be honest and have tough conversations with his supervisor that he could not normally have with his professors. In a similar instance to Chris and as the other participants that indicated other-mother examples, Ray said that a black woman helped him to open up and to succeed. Ray stated that he has two master's degrees and is pursuing a doctorate degree, which success can be attributed to his two black female mentors:

I have two master's degrees and will graduate with a doctorate degree because of a black woman who is my mentor. My PhD is in educational research, with a focus on higher education. I'm taking a lot of statistics classes. There's a lady named Dr. O. (her pseudonymous name) She's now the associate vice provost. She latches on to all the black women and men and is like, "Hey, you need to get this degree; this is going to set you straight. This stuff will make you look different from others." She was like, "Hey, you higher-education people all need to start getting published. You all aren't doing this; this is what you all need to do. to do, like, "Let me take you all and get you right.

Ray was also able to get guidance and advice from a Black woman on what graduate students should be doing at the graduate level. He describes how Dr. O, his mentor, was able to latch on to him, as she does to all the university's black women and men. In addition to advising him on which degree he should pursue to distinguish himself from others, she aided him as he advanced in his career. Bruce, like the other participants, Ray and Chris, had the good fortune of having a Black woman as a supervisor; in his case, she was the Dean of Campus Life:

It was Dr. X [his Pseudonym name] That was one of the things, was that I was like, "I don't know where to get my hair cut," and she probably could have been like, "Why are you asking me this?" I don't think that's what she was going to say, but you never know how people could say things or feel about things. That was something I expressed to her, and she was able to help me out in that process. It goes on to helping at least one person in one positive way, even if it was something small like showing them that you would like to help them get a haircut.

Bruce was able to get a solid recommendation on where to get a good haircut in the city. He gave an example of how Dr. X helped him in a positive way and discussed how she was able to assist him during the processes.

To further clarify the meaning of the characterization of Other Mothering as it pertains to the academy, research has shown that women of color typically possess mothering qualities that go above and beyond the institutional design, having candor, openness, and a sincere desire to assist others. Many participants described their connections with women of color. Surprisingly, nearly 12 of the 16 participants considered their involvement with other female professors or faculty to be an asset in obtaining a post-baccalaureate degree.

Full Graduate Scholarship or Parental Funding

The fourth characterization was the concept of full graduate scholarship or parental funding, which essentially meant tuition funds. When it came to paying for tuition and expenses, participants were able to be economically creative. Some of the participants received loans or

Albert's Experience

Following the participants' examples of other-mothering, I reflected on my own graduate experience, where, like Dr. Kobe, there were two Black female faculty members, one of whom was a dean and the other a part-time professor, who aided me in my efforts to complete the Doctoral Program. I had the opportunity to take the "Practicum" course near the end of my coursework. Dr. X (a pseudonym) was the Dean of the University of Residential Life at the time. She created a position for me and hired me as a graduate assistant after I finished the practicum. Here, I learned valuable techniques for dealing with myself in professional and higher educational settings. She allowed me to join her at school board meetings. She would let me tag along with her to faculty meetings and events, and she would also invite me to a variety of leadership conferences, both in and out of town. For me, things started to fall into place. I had a job and was making money. In fact, my first black female part-time professor arrived later to help me with my dissertation process. She would advise me to research and outline first, then write and fully explain myself so that anyone reviewing my work does not have to question me later. She would always tell me to "be yourself," and she assisted me in compartmentalizing the process of earning a doctorate degree. Furthermore, if I had any questions or concerns about the process, she would always respond quickly to my texts and e-mails. Her availability and accessibility were clearly critical to how I made sense of my own progress. She was crucial in assisting me with the recruitment of the 16 participants for the study. She instructed me and prepared me for a proper, semi-structured interview. I would practice my proposal with her until I felt comfortable presenting it to the entire committee. Weekly meetings would be scheduled during the dissertation writing process. If one of us was ever down, or if I was having writer's block, we would send each other motivational quotes or Bible verses to cheer each other up. From my perspective, I didn't want to let her or myself down in any way. were able to earn scholarships or graduate assistantships/stipends, which covered a portion of their tuition. The study acknowledged that a small number of participants received financial assistance from their parents, as some were fortunate enough to benefit from their parents' military service. For example, Chris describes how his mother initially assisted him with tuition:

So, with the Graduate School and my assistantship, they handled a bit more of the tuition, which was helpful. Sorry, I had to pay like a thousand out of pocket. I will say that for my first semester, my mom covered that. She did pay it, like my mom is big on me not worrying about those payments yet just because she knows I don't have that full-time job yet. Like she just wants me to, you know, do my work, get a job, and then go on to the real world and do it. So yeah, she definitely took care of that first payment. I told her I'm taking care of her my second year; I've been working all summer to get a little bit more independent. Let me take care of this payment. You did enough. Jeff also described receiving financial assistance from his mother to cover tuition and his experiences growing up with a brother:

I came from a family where a lot of people have a lot of degrees. And so, what my grandparents did is they told their kids, as long as you're advancing your education in a timely manner, we're going to pay for it. And so, they did that for all of my mom ['s degrees] and for all of my uncles [degrees]. So, that is what my mom told my little brother and I that as long as you're advancing your education, we're going to pay for it. And so that obviously doesn't mean you can take 8 years to get your undergrad, but if you're going from your undergrad in a timely manner to graduate. And then, if you go on from a masters to like idea to a different kind of masters my mother was willing to pay.

Not all the participants were able to receive parental assistance. Tre discussed having to take out loans and how his loans will be paid back one day:

I'm still in the hole; I'm buried deep in student loans. But I feel like, you know, it'll pay off. You know, I'd say that I'm always positive with myself. Now that I've got a salaried job, I'm making a good salary—really good money. So, you know, I was starting to feel the other side of it. Everything is starting to come around. I'll start paying off those loans. They are going to be gone. So, it's going to be alright.

Tre explained how he was able to pay for graduate school. He described how he still has a large amount of student debt, but his new job has given him a positive outlook because he now has the opportunity to begin paying off the student debt. Tre was discussing correlation, as were a few of the other participants, in order to obtain funding for graduate school.

Ray, like Tre and the other participants, described what it took for him to attend Louisiana State University:

It's been really just loans, minimum loans, the mortgages, using my paycheck to support my brothers, and sometimes, tuition assistance. LSU pays for six hours of tuition only, but I had to pay out-of-state fees and all that other stuff still.

Albert's Experience

Participants Ray & Tre reminds me of the fact that I also took out a fair share of student loans for funding. Even though I was not fortunate enough to have my parents pay for my academic tuition at any level, they were able to help me navigate through the processes of scholarships, FASFA, and loan applications Jeff and Chris's situation mirrored my experience. as it relates to funding. However, my mom's assistance in applying for colleges, grants, and loans, as well as finding creative ways for me to attend the best colleges in South Texas (Trinity University and Incarnate Word University), both of which cost over $50,000 per year, was invaluable. When I saw the price, I never gave up; if I wanted something, I found a way to get it. If I don't have the entire amount, I'll start with a portion of it and then piece it all together until it's complete. My parents taught me that winners find a way. It's not so much how you start as it is how you finish. For my MBA program at UIW, I received a scholarship for my football team participation, and my PhD funding came from loans and FASFA with minor scholarships as it relates to funding. However, my mom's assistance in applying for colleges, grants, and loans, as well as finding creative ways for me to attend the best colleges in South Texas (Trinity University and Incarnate Word University), both of which cost over $50,000 per year, was invaluable. When I saw the price, I never gave up; if I wanted something, I found a way to get it. If I don't have the entire amount, I'll start with a portion of it and then piece it all together until it's complete. My parents taught me that winners find a way. It's not so much how you start as it is how you finish. For my MBA program at UIW, I received a scholarship for my football team participation, and my PhD funding came from loans and FASFA with minor scholarships.

Full Graduate Scholarship or Parental Funding is the scholarship received from or paid for by parents. The vast majority of participants were able to obtain some form of financial assistance on their own, while a few were able to obtain parent assistance. It's fortunate to have parents who are fruitful enough to pay for their son's education, which in turn helped them to be motivated to finish their degrees. Finding ways to get tuition paid for seemed impossible to some, but by taking the necessary steps, they were able to do so. Admittedly, the participants discussed how difficult it was to balance school and work at times.

Parental Educational Level

The fifth Characterization was Parental Educational Level, which means that the degree attainment of their parents or household was very important in the participants' pursuit of their goals. Some believe that because their parents did it first, they were able to do the same or even better. In his written philosophical statement, Johari emphasized the importance of family and the realization that we must do this for future generations. He wrote:

As a family member who has matriculated within higher education, it is important to understand that they set the foundation for generations to come and I am proud to have a family who helped to pave the way. "The revolution will not be televised." Gil Scott Heron.

It is critical to carry on the work of our forefathers and mothers. They were the ones who made it possible for us to know it was possible to achieve the highest level of education. Tre talked about not conforming to the norm and striving for higher goals, not being satisfied with a single degree:

My philosophy statement is to strive for the top because the bottom is too crowded, it just is just that you got to separate yourself. The norm was in our first family. It was, I go to high school and get your diploma and then people started going to college and started educating themselves, us, a little bit about bacs (Baccalaureate) degrees. So, I want to challenge myself to get a master's degree. Both of my parents had their bachelor's degree. I feel like that was the norm. I don't want to be the norm, nothing against them. But I want to set a bar for my family and my kids, hey, you know, my dad did is so they can achieve something higher than me

Tre spoke to the other side of this characterization of Parental Education Level. Here are examples of some of the participants' mindsets shifting from seeing their parents as motivators to wanting to achieve more than they have seen. There's an understanding that knowing your parents can do it gives permission to go out there and achieve your dreams. Vice versa when Dr. Taylor highlighted the importance of seeing his family members, especially his father, set the educational foundation:

My dad, seeing him do it, seeing my brothers do it, the people I worked with, seeing my bosses do that, that's something that's just continuing to keep me to push. I'm always reading books. I'm always trying to help to grow. I just believe in growth and being better. That's just how it keeps me going.

Albert's Experiences

My mother has a bachelor's degree in interdisciplinary studies and a master's degree in creative writing, and my father has a B.S. degree in Political Science from UCLA. Their child- rearing practices demonstrate the importance of early childhood education in the home. My father used to make me pick 10 words from the dictionary and write a sentence in my own words about each one. Who knew that practice would come in handy today? My mother is currently assisting me in practicing techniques such as using notes as a guide when presenting and rarely looking down when presenting. She instructs me to choose someone in the room and make eye contact with them. It only takes one person to understand or favor you. Speak to them as if they are your friends, and don't be afraid because they are different and have important titles. The educational foundational system that worked for me instilled discipline and education in me, transforming me into a lifelong learner who is fascinated by new words.

To make sense of the characterization of Parental Educational Level, among the 16 participants, the parents matter because either the participants aspired to be like their parents or dreamed of reaching higher than their parents' educational level. Many participants described how their parents' upbringing influenced their decisions to pursue specific goals to ensure that families and generations are wealthy rather than poor.

Interestingly, all the parents went to school; however, as previously stated, most of the participants are the first in their family to earn a post-baccalaureate degree.

Upward Mobility

The sixth characterization was Upward Mobility, which can be explained by moving up in society. One should be in a better socioeconomic position in living the American Dream and enjoy the fruits of their labor, or to put it another way, earn more money with more degrees.

Dr. Langston describes a hypothetical situation in which graduate students were not broke, to gain an understanding of salary increases as education increases:

I think being broke is our biggest challenge, really think about this even in your own experience. Right. So, you are at work right now. In addition to being a grad student. Right. You have this certainty from work. What if you had your salary from work to be a grad student. And all you had to do was to be a grad student? That would be awesome right?

Dr. Langston proposed a hypothetical scenario in which students are paid to be a graduate student and can focus solely on their graduate studies, thus getting past the most difficult barrier of being broke as a graduate student.

In many ways, the characterization of upward mobility and striving for higher goals was shared by most of the participants. Participants described how they had received and would continue to receive assistance from others. Tim wrote in his written philosophy statement:

A key lesson learned from my mom that still sticks with me today is, "a closed mouth won't get fed." I took that and combined it with the importance of mentorship. Together the two have allowed me to be successful and have led me to where I am now. No successful person has gotten where they are without the help of someone else and in my opinion, the best form of help is mentorship. Throughout my journey, I have had great mentors who have poured into and supported me.

Tim explained how, throughout his journey, he had learned the value of mentorship and how not closing your mouth can help you move up the ladder of success. Key lessons learned from his mother, as well as mentorship, were critical. Closed lips will only get you so far. Tim described learning to open his mouth and express his needs, or better yet, going out and getting what he needed.

Dr. Samuel used humor to explain why he continues to progress in graduate school to earn more degrees and a higher salary:

It's funny, the way I started with the master's degree as to how I ended up at the PhD level. I did the master's degree, mainly to further my education and move up in the world. I was working in financial aid, so I figured if I had more credentials behind my name, I could move up faster, better, and easier. Whereas I said, I was working full time in the financial aid office when I started the master's degree program. I enjoyed it, I went part time, of course, I'll say only two classes per semester, and by the time, instead of 2 years, it took me 3 years…By the time I took one of my last classes, one of my professors was a full time staff member at UT, and he was telling us he was about to retire. He said, "I'm going to retire from being a CBO." He was the Chief Business Officer at UT. He's making well over six figures. He said, "I'm going to retire from being a CBO," he only taught one class per semester in our program…He said, "I'm going to retire from being a CBO, and I'm going to come to the higher ed program and teach one class a semester, and I'll do that for about 3 years, and then, I'll completely retire." In my mind, I was like, "I want to be you when I grow up." [chuckles] Because I was like, "Okay, you're going to retire from UT, and you're going to work part time." That's like two checks, you get the retirement check, you're going to be teaching, you only teach one class a week, it's about 10 people per class, probably, going to be making $60,000 to $70,000 while you're doing that. I wanted to do that…That was the main reason I decided to do a PhD, was again, the same reason I did a masters was to move up, but it would also allow me to become a professor, if I wanted to teach in higher ed.

Dr. Samuel described the main reason for continuing with graduate studies. He explained how having a master's degree allowed him to advance. He learned from another about the opportunity to teach one class per week and potentially earn that sum of money to achieve the goal of becoming a Chief Business Officer and receiving retirement checks, emphasizing upward mobility.

Ray, like the other participants and Dr. Samuel, spoke about the importance of education and the benefits it could provide for him and his family. Ray used a quote to explain the impact if he chose not to continue moving forward:

I just think there's a quote that says, "Education is the passport to tomorrow, for the future belongs to those who prepare for it today." That's by Malcolm X. That's one of my favorite things. That's what I'm preparing for. I'm getting my stamps on my passport for a better tomorrow, and that's through my education.

I'm trying to also prepare others and let other people see a world that they probably would not have ever been able to see by someone else. I'm just hoping to keep moving forward and just rest if I must, but I can't quit because if I quit, it's going to impact so many others.

Ray described striving for success through education to have a better tomorrow. He believes that education prepares others and allows people to see a world that they would not have been able to see otherwise. He emphasized the difference that education can make in someone's life, and their desire to get more out of life.

The characterization of Upward Mobility is the ability or capability of advancing to a higher social or economic position, the underlying factor that many participants persisted in; the desire to obtain a higher-paying and more distinguished position. Most participants expressed a desire to advance economically, to be able to purchase a home, and to live a happy and peaceful life. Surprisingly, many participants explained how one of their goals was to make a difference in the world while also maximizing their full wealth potential.

Diversity and Inclusion

The seventh characterization, Diversity and Inclusion, means to be open to and accept other differences. However, race, ethnicity, gender, gender identity, sexual orientation, age, social class, physical abilities or attributes, religious or ethical value systems, national origin, and political beliefs are all examples of diversity. Participants explained how they were diverse and open to new ideas during their time as post-baccalaureate students. Throughout the interview, Jeff defined diversity as what it meant to bring different life experiences and perspectives with you wherever you went, even by saying:

"You know, women have different experiences than men. People who are raised in certain religions have different experiences in other religions. Certain sexual orientations have different experiences than others. When you're in the minority, you're going to experience life differently. You see life through a different lens. And that doesn't change just because you're in grad school. But you've just got to bring your perspective to school, bring your perspective to work, and let your perspectives help you improve wherever you are."

Jeff explained how we have differences in religion and sex, and different experiences that we all have, and how that is just the way life is. He also talked about being a minority and being able to look at a variety of perspectives or outlooks on how you show up in society.

Michael, like most of the participants, was able to define what it meant to have diversity and inclusion. He described the concept of understanding and just thinking humanistically and also what to take away when there is a difference between really seeing different stereotypes. He explained:

An example that I thought about, that I was saying, if I wanted to speak about how diversity and inclusion really came into play, but it was also a lived experience which was not even at the time when I was even thinking about college was 2002. I was in the military and I was in my tech school. I wasn't able to drive, so I had to rely on others to provide me a ride. A local marine base was offering to show a free movie, which was "Black Hawk Down". I decided to go, I enjoyed the movie and then I came back to my command, but thinking about it now, I was like, "I'm watching a movie about military tactics, like an action movie in an auditorium full of marines who are about to live this experience just after 9/11. Now, exactly, so you can see it's like these people are about to watch their life unfold and potentially have other consequences for our freedoms.

Looking around, it went from, now I don't just see people, I don't just see uniforms, but I see names, I see people's faces, I see that these people are human beings. That really brought in that understanding of just thinking humanistically, that really takes away that there's a difference between really seeing those stereotypes.

That's when I say, "Okay, you know what? Those stereotypes can be challenged," because I have this lived experience of seeing whether they were Black, white, or wherever state they're from, wherever their heritage is, is that when you go towards a mission and you're seeing people very like-minded who can see this outcome happening, then it becomes more of a clear understanding. That's when you started knocking down barriers, having those tough conversations. Like I said, bringing that experience into a classroom and without specifically saying, "Oh, I just went to a movie and had a life-altering or life-awakening moment back almost 20 years ago." It resonates when you see that difference, that diversity in the classroom as well, today.

Michael spoke of putting a face to a name, and the importance of caring for mankind and ethnic groups. Everyone has a purpose to fulfill, to do it in harmony and peace; to strive for equality amongst all, to be free and to be included; military experience related to real world experiences. Diversity has a variety of educational benefits, including increased cultural and racial awareness, improved critical thinking, higher levels of community service, and a more educated citizenry, to name a few. However, other components, such as equity and inclusion, are critical to fulfilling diversity's promise to higher education in general.

Inclusion, which is frequently linked to diversity, is critical for all members of a campus community, but it is especially critical for historically underrepresented and marginalized students. Understanding what it takes to be inclusive and diverse requires not only a group of Black people, but all racial and ethnic groups involved, as Johari, JD, stated:

There is little diversity. I still believe, you know, that HBCUs have more diversity. Though there are larger pieces of diversity, I think there are more depictions of African Americans and African American culture. And a lot of times African Americans forget that diversity isn't just about us. You know what I'm saying. And I mean, you know, at UIW [Incarnate Word University]. There are so many different types of ethnic groups there that it's crazy. It was just a small percentage of us because it was a Hispanic and international serving institution. It's mostly about sports, but what you don't see are the different types of people like you see at a UIW or University of Houston, like you see at an HBCU.

To thoroughly grasp the meaning of the characterization Diversity and Inclusion, the participants felt it was critical to have unity among all people and for them to be represented. Everyone must collaborate and recognize the value of representation. All matters of unity and representation should unite as one, as one love and one peace. Participants frequently expressed how they were able to relate to others who did not come from the same background as themselves, despite living in an environment with a scarcity of black people. Noticeably, more than half of the participants emphasized the importance of being inclusive and demonstrating diversity both in and outside of the classroom.

Awareness of Systemic Racism

The eighth characterization, Awareness of Systemic Racism, was used to generate knowledge about how participants explained racism through the concept of microaggressions or less blatant racism. Whether it was a Hispanic student wearing blackface, or a handful of the participants complaining about being accused of plagiarizing or receiving a D for an assignment from professors from different backgrounds than their own. Some participants expressed nuances that they did not encounter but witnessed, as Dr. Langston explained:

So I think that was a moment. And then I was like at Ohio State that there were there were some subtleties that like you kind of had to look at. Right. So, I don't know if I did experience it, but I witnessed it. So, in the doc program I was in, it was a physical education, teacher education. Also, adaptive P.E. Right. And the methods classes, the teaching methods, classes where you're actually teaching people how to teach are the vanguard classes their the top class skills class where it's like teams sports war games and all of that stuff, or where data courses where you teach the REC courses. This is for the students. They need their P.E. electives there. They're not so much heralded. They're not going to get you jobs or the market. So, all the white faculty, their students got access to those classes that were more likely to get you hired. Those things were mostly white and Asian. So, if you were Latino, or Black, you didn't get access to those classes.

Dr. Langston explained how some issues that are not so visible were still regarded as microaggressions or racism in relation to the concept of limited resources for Blacks. To further clarify how participants made sense of awareness of systemic racism, Dr. Igbo described what it was like to experience institutionalized and covert racism in the Midwest and South:

All right, so, in the South, you know how you have this; like, in the South, you know the people say and look at you, like, "Don't come across this street," right, you know what I'm saying. Like, this is straight-out overt, like, this is the racism we know: you don't cross that street, they don't cross the street. Where, in the Midwest and kind of the other places, it's more institutionalized, and it's more covert. Okay, so, and institutions of higher education, if you don't know what it looks like, then you don't understand that it's racism, right. So, a lot of the racism is based on institutional policies that have been in place for hundreds of years that are enforced by state and local agencies. So even if the president wanted to change policy, he couldn't, right? Or they do the racism through colorblind ideology, which is, "I don't see color, so, therefore, our—" I can give you a perfect example. The president, who is a smart dude, bomb, intelligent, I would love to have a 15-minute conversation with him, because I feel like he's also on a whole other level. But he made a statement that said that we don't need multicultural student services on campus, because the campus itself is a safe place. That's good, like, in theory, that's good, right? But the problem is that you've got a bunch of racist-ass motherfuckers that come to campus with their own ideologies and, therefore, enforce racism and other policies through their positions that make the campus unsafe. So when a student or a staff member or a person of color experiences a racist experience, they don't know where to go, "Where do I go?" Because there's no multicultural services, okay, there's no real black people here, you know, and I'm not even going to front even out here sometimes, the white people treat you better than the Latinx people and the indigenous people, and sometimes the Asian people. They treat you like trash. They treat you worse than a white person ever could... You know, like, I have never experienced so much racism from other groups who are not white [laughs], you know what I'm saying? Like, what the hell is that? And that's some of that, you know, I kind of said—the term I use is, all right, so, my mentor had a quote one time: he was, like, the insidiousness or the greatness, you know, interchangeably, of racism is that you don't have to be white to perpetuate it. And then the other thing I tell students, for them to understand, for those who are, like, and I tell them, "You can't see me through the eyes of your oppressor, because you're looking at me through how the system says a black man should be, when that's not how I am," right?

Dr. Igbo described his experiences by identifying the various forms of racism and how it could come from anyone and everyone from a variety of ethnic groups of people. Dr. Igbo was treated unfairly as a result of structural or institutional policies and practices that were embedded and established in Dr. Igbo's institutions. He defined it as distinct from overt discrimination in that the black male is portrayed individually in relation to what the system expects.

The characterization Awareness of Systemic Racism incidents that the participants encountered or witnessed is indicated in Bruce describing an incident involving a Hispanic student on campus who was dressed in black face. Bruce described his encounter with the situation, which left him uncomfortable:

There was an incident of blackface on campus. I won't say this is the exact quote, but I believe I remember somebody saying, "Well, they were Hispanic, so it's okay for them to do that." No, that's not how that works. We talked about the history of blackface and the BSU and ASO asked me to come speak. Not necessarily knowing that I'm an administrator as well, but as a graduate student... I spoke about the history of blackface, where it came from, and what it did. It was on television, it was on the San Antonio news, and they didn't understand—not they, not this academic population, or the faculty and staff—the ramifications of blackface and where it came from, what it did to people. They just saw it as a no-no. I was like, Well, kids are being kids." I was like, "No, it's not just a no-no. It's a malicious attack." Even though they didn't intend for it to be malicious, the impact was.

Bruce explained the blackface incident and how it was not taken seriously, as well as why others were playing with it. Even though it may not have appeared racist or unfair to others, the connection relationship considered by Bruce was not well received. In the same way that the other participants were aware of systemic racism, Johari, JD, may have encountered racism on a systemic (structural, institutional) level. According to Johari, his teacher did not call him by his name the entire semester and gave him a D+ as a letter grade despite the fact that he was a good student with good grades most of the time. He described the situation:

So, my last year of the fall, this lady gave me a D-plus in writing. Everybody at school knew I didn't get a D in my life. Even if I was telling somebody I got a C or less, they wouldn't believe it. And they know me. This lady wouldn't call me by my name for the entire class or any of the black students. She found a nickname for all of us. She could remember all of the Hispanic and the closer to white-looking student's names, she would recall. Oh, that's this boy and that boy. That's right. That's my TSU girl. That's my boy. Like all of us, were boys and girls, though... And I had told her multiple times, you know, my name is Johari, or Joe, or something. And, you know, she just refused for the entire class. She was rude to me. She would always look and skip over my raised hand. And she would tell me, oh, you talk every class I want to go and get all the other hands first and come back to you. Whenever I had questions or stuff, just very, very rude. The last day she asks everybody about how they felt about the class. I clearly let her know that I was treated unfairly. I felt like, you know, you called me and everybody else by boy or girl name this whole semester. She was just really rude and gave me a D, knowing I did good work.

Johari described a situation in which he was aware of systemic racism and how it influenced his experience as a Law student in one of his fall semester classes. Even though he was able to express his feelings to his professor at the end, he still believes there were inequities or inequality in how he and other black students were treated. Furthermore, to even further elaborate on participants' awareness of systemic racism, Chris' experience with another professor is significant. Chris described how he hasn't directly observed racism; however, he described how a situation in which he and another Black woman classmate were called out for plagiarizing on an assignment that may have been considered an injustice or simply not right action. Chris explained:

If I did, I never noticed. Just because no I didn't pay attention to it, I will say I did get a little hint of it from one of my professors. So, I thought she was being a little racist when it came to me and another black student because we were the only blacks in her class, which was a law class in higher education. Like me this one, you know, black women, we are very knowledgeable on different subjects. When it came to law, and I think she was intimidated by that because it used to be me and her being a black woman talking.

And then, you know, white women as well in the class. And there was this one assignment that I know I did great on. You know, I did everything correctly; I had my sources put in directly. And all of a sudden, she says, I had plagiarized, and I say, OK, how did you know I know what plagiarism is? Oh, I didn't do that... And then I asked one of my white counterparts because I was curious what their comments were. And I looked at their paper, and I was like, "Oh, it kind of looks like you were harboring along the same lines as mine." Like, it doesn't look, you know, much off from mine. But she didn't get plagiarized. But I did. And the other black women did, that might have been racist. That was very interesting to me when it came to that professor.

Chris described a situation in which he became aware of systemic racism after turning in an assignment and having it signaled out. Although more evidence of actual plagiarism may be required, Chris felt cheated by his professor when he noticed he and another black classmate were the only ones who were mentioned for plagiarizing for an assignment.

Albert's Experiences

Chris and the other participants prompted me to reflect on my experiences in my master's and Doctoral programs. There were two incidents in my past that could be considered a racist experience as well. During my master's program, I received a C in a Master class taught by a white male professor fresh from the University of Texas. He gave me a D on a final report while giving the rest of the class B (+) and A's. We had a diverse group of international students in the class, and this Asian group stood out to me; they struggled to communicate in English and present their ideas when it came time to present. I'm not sure which aspect of their research was articulate enough to receive a grade, but they proudly informed me that they had received a (B+). Another potentially racist incident occurred when my advisor (a White Female) at the time, who was also the professor of the class "Intro to Research," gave me a C for the course. It's worth noting that she was also my mentor at the time. She stated several times of her disapproval with her feedback that she did not agree with my topic, which was "Increasing Black Mentorships" within the educational system. We discussed the institution's requirements, which state that if a student receives two (C)s, he may be withdrawn from the program. More importantly, after receiving that C, I had to retake the course, which affected my eligibility for financial aid. Fortunately, I retook the course with a different professor and received an A, which clearly showed it wasn't the paper or the content, but rather her own opinion of disapproval which she was grading the paper on. Granted, I am aware there are always aspects I could be better at, I am also aware that there was no merit for that professor to give me that grade. I believed there was still a chance to earn a passing grade of at least a B.

To gain a full understanding of the characterization Awareness of Systemic Racism, participants felt discriminated against in some way, from comments to facial expressions, because they were the only Black male in the class to be singled out. While most participants stated that they did not experience racism firsthand, the participants saw inequity or inequality that made sense of the characterization of a situation that was considered racist. Surprisingly, many participants mentioned the injustices of today's world leaking into the institution in how they show up to class every day.

Paying it Forward

The ninth characterization, the concept of Paying it Forward, entails keeping the momentum going and reaching out to those who may require assistance. Repaying someone not only with money, but also with an act of kindness, to better oneself and rise above one's circumstances. Participants mention countless times that they have had to pay it forward. Dr. Igbo shared his thoughts on his experiences assisting others in need:

I literally dedicated my life to helping my community. So, I literally worked with at risk students. So, on campus, I work with African American men to make sure they get recruited, retained, and make sure they graduate through, like, holistic programming, teaching them about themselves, making sure they have all the resources, being that campus liaison.

Dr. Igbo felt the burden of researching constantly and tirelessly to get it right to help at-risk students of color see the value in the education pipeline. It was almost as if the adage "win the battle but lose the war" applied here. It will be a difficult battle, but someone must do it.

Bishop discussed his experience and the motivating factors for reaching out to and uplifting youth, particularly those in foster care. He said:

My focus is looking at the transition of individuals of color who've been in foster care to and through post-secondary education. When I'm not doing higher ed work, I work with foster care youth. I do a lot of mental health work and things like that. It started when I was in Florida, I was working at a group home, that I would take these massive higher education books to the group home, and kids were like, "What're you doing? What is that?" Then we started talking about school, and then like, "Yes, I thought about college, but there's nobody in my immediate circle that could talk to me about that. I talked to my social worker, and they just said, that's not really the route that you're going to go." I was like, "Dang." Then I started picking up on those different types of things. That's what I'm studying right now: the experiences of, particularly youth of color, and their experience in foster care and their transition to college degrees. Basically, access, retention, and success are what I'm focused on.

Bishop gave an example of Paying it Forward here in how he was able to show the kids in the group home college books and how to gain access to college resources. He mentioned how he would share stories about why he chose college and why he continued to pursue higher education as a leader or someone they looked up to. Most of the participants expressed a desire to make a difference in the lives of young people. Ray described how he was a part of something bigger than himself, and how he aspired to do and be better as someone who truly makes a difference in the world. He said:

Understanding everything that I went through, it motivated me. It was my grade. It was preparing me for something bigger and better than I could even imagine. Also, my family. I'm doing this now, like I said, I'm trying to break generational curses. I'm trying to be an example for I have two little brothers; one is 7 and the other is 14. It's like, "Hey, your option is you can go to college. I know what you're going through; I know where you're raised and stuff like that, but the first thing you don't have to see anymore is a jail if you don't want to go there." offer this understanding, I tell people that I'm big on my ancestors. I'm big on my history. I know my history. I tell people if you know your history, you have to do better. Too many people died and went through hell that I don't have to go through. I have a debt that can never be repaid. A little piece of repaying my debt back is getting my education and showing others that "Hey, let's get this together" and motivating them as well. Going back and making sure I'm active in my community and not just running away from it.

In this context, Ray emphasized leaving a Legacy, which is a component of Paying it Forward, recognizing that there are various paths one can take in life to increase opportunities and create upward mobility. Staying grounded is his goal and, in service to a greater purpose, he believes, is one way he stays motivated. He felt it was important to know his family history to truly appreciate what it took to get to this very moment where he could prosper. Ray's encouragement for a brighter future for the youth and others. Ray embodies that characteristic of Paying it Forward as he shows that he is one who cares about family, history, friends, and the community. Not only does he want his education to have an impact on his own life, but he is motivated by the fact that it will also create a brighter future with better days for all around him.

Albert's Experience

Bishop, Dr. Igbo, Ray and the other participants discussed their perspectives on paying it forward. It reminded me of my journey from where I am now to where I came from, and it has been a true honor to work as a Guest Teacher for Clark County and the Humble School District, teaching elementary and middle school students. The model of success for the youth begins with leadership and accountability. Doing everything with a positive attitude and demonstrating to them that Black men can be teachers. I've begun to work with the Special Education Departments and resources. I have seen, even in a short amount of time that I spend with students, that the students look up to me. I am cognizant that I maintain a positive and upbeat attitude as I'm proud to be a role model. I was asked to be a Leader of the 100 Black Men of Las Vegas through the school, where we would meet every Saturday from 10 a.m. to 2 p.m. As a way of giving back, we would introduce and distribute information books on college resources, financial independence, and dealing with mental health issues. Only by being the best person, I know how to become, can I truly repay people by sharing and passing down my knowledge and resources with students and other classmates. Throughout my graduate studies, I was always there for a classmate or a professor. If a student needed assistance with the new technology system or submitting an assignment, I was available. Not only as a student, but even after, I plan to continue to Pay It Forward by networking with the Black Male community as a member of the "Brothers of the Academy" and "Trio," where we discuss how the higher education system is now dealing with current issues.

The definition of Paying it Forward is repaying the favor, reaching out, and assisting others. Participants described instances in which kindness to oneself was demonstrated by being kind to others. Most of the participants performed acts of kindness in the community as well as in and out of the classroom. Almost every single participant stated that paying it forward had helped them advance further in their respective graduate programs. Astonishingly, participants found satisfaction and happiness in being able to give back and pay forward, as well as to earn post- baccalaureate degrees.

Mental Health/Awareness

The tenth and final characterization, Mental Health/Awareness, is concerned with one's personal issues and how one deals with them. Participants emphasized the importance of being aware of one's mental state and not becoming overwhelmed by one's surroundings and work. A handful of participants described how they dealt with difficult times such as anxiety, depression, and racial fatigue, as well as isolation and homesickness. In this example, Dr. Kobe discussed the importance of self-care for progress:

I talked about this in my answer like having a personal development self-care. Because people will even talk about like how they during their program they – like they stopped playing video games because they really need to have the balance, and they really needed to be able to focus.

Self-care was an example given by Dr. Kobe of when distracting behaviors had to be stopped permanently or even temporarily at times to maintain focus. In a related manner, many of the participants discussed the importance of mental health awareness and taking time to reflect, heal and try to recover from the Black Lives Matter issues. Dr. Igbo described the importance of mental health awareness and seeking help from a Black counselor as follows:

Personal matters, man, like, towards the end, I had to get me a counselor. Like, I just straight up went and got a counselor. Like, my wife, she looked at me and she was, like, "Listen, go get you listen my wife does so much and voiced my concerns, and she was, like, she basically hit me with, "I can't be all for you, so you need to go find you a counselor." She was, like, you know, like, she hit me with some real knowledge, and then I went and found a counselor. So, whoever if you write this in the paper, be, like, if you are going to do this journey, get a black counselor that understands the academy and living the experiences of being black. Because it's not like, when I saw George Floyd being murdered, that my life stopped, or me being a student stopped, right? I was feeling that shit, trying to write a paper. I was trying to write my dissertation, like, I was, like, "Yo "there was just days, sometimes, that I just had to, like, "I can't write nothing, because I feel like I'm going to fucking lose it." So, I think I had to get me a counselor that actually just helped me process some of the things I was feeling, some of the things that was going on, and being a husband, being a father, things going on in my community, you know, things going on as I think one of the things he told me was, like, "You know, you're going through a lot, and it's not all your responsibility."

His wife advised Dr. Igbo, telling him to see a counselor. Because of the stress of academic writing, and feeling the effects of Black lives being taken, he couldn't write anything some days and felt like he was starting to lose everything. While attempting not to take on all the responsibility for trying to overcome everyone's problems, he felt the weight both outside and inside the classroom, and outside events were beginning to influence his inside-the-class assignments.

Tayo, like most participants dealing with mental health self-awareness, was descriptive of his personal feelings of panic and anxiety when it came to dealing with education and the real world. Tayo described what had happened to him physically and emotionally during his time as a graduate student by stating

Yeah, I have anxiety. I sometimes I get panic attacks, too. So, I've certainly built it multiple times and each time because of racial tension. Or it could be with that from class. Or it could be classwork. It could be the class rebels involved...Yes. Had serious anxiety knowing if I was going to get a good grade based on something or knowing if I was going to meet a time when only I could take time off for holiday, that wasn't then anxiety walking on campus sometimes. I went to school in a very conservative neighborhood. Initially, I thought no; it was Lynchburg, Virginia. It was during the Obama years, and I didn't feel anxiety until then, and then I started getting looks when people were walking around... Well, first of all, I put a name to it, and I started telling myself that it was not a weakness because No, it isn't. I'm the oldest of three boys. And one of the things is that they don't show any emotion. And I'm very, very emotional. But I add that internal struggle all the time. And so it kept happening. It was because I was having a panic attack. That's why it happened. And like, OK, I have to do this; I need to understand what's happening to my body because I don't know where this is coming from. And so, as I started to really sit there and look at it, it became clear that I never processed many traumatic things. And so that was the first step... But something that happened to me first, I did physically feel like I couldn't breathe. And then I was like, "Okay, all right, work on this." This was my first step. But I wouldn't encourage that from any of this...Yeah, I did. It was back a year. My chest was beating, and I couldn't sleep. I couldn't stand up. I couldn't. I was just walking all over the place and I felt like I was claustrophobic.

Here, Tayo described his state of psychological and emotional distress, stating that it was difficult for him to breathe at times. His mental health appeared to be suffering because of all the stress.

In addition to the participants' emotional well-being, Tim and the rest of the world were experiencing a pandemic. Tim described a turning point in his graduate school experience during the interview:

Life is hard, but you can do it. And it's something I really learned. I try to keep that in mind even during this quarantine. COVID season. Your mindset impacts a lot of how you show up. And so, my mentor told me my first semester, you need to reflect on who you are, who you want to be, and what you're got to do to be better. And I reflected and I did those things. And that was my turning point from my grad school experience.

Tim shared his advice on Mental Health Awareness and how he was able to make a shift amid the stressors of the education experience and the global pandemic. Recognizing that his mindset had a significant impact on how he presented himself, he claimed that by making time for self- reflection, he was able to reach a breakthrough. The notion that the mind is a terrible thing to squander plays a role in mental health.

The definition of Mental Health/Awareness is consciousness and understanding of mental fatigue and dealing with academic stress, in addition to dealing with the trials and tribulations of daily life. It was necessary to conduct a self-evaluation or self-check on oneself to continue or strive to succeed. Many participants believed that the topic of mental awareness deserves more attention. Interestingly, a few participants described how they used professional therapy to help them progress through their graduate programs.

Summary of Key Findings of Characterizations

- 15 out of 16 participants were fully employed or working full time during their graduate studies. The major congruency of the participants was the recurrence of employment during the graduate program and working currently. The theme Employment Viability Trumps All recurred, as each participant described how they made themselves available to work long hours to survive and still be able to manage a full academic course load.

- There were 14 participants who mentioned they were first generation college graduate students, meaning they were the first of their families to receive graduate degrees. The education level of parents and the age of the participants were revealed. Most of the participants' fathers had completed the highest degree within the household, and this was the case 70% of the time.

- Participants explained this interesting finding by it being one of their motivating factors that helped them succeed. This led to the discovery that the participants have/had a parent in the household who had received a college degree. In addition to this as motivation, it was the help of participants' upper-class students, friends, and family that was stated was the intrinsic motivation that truly should not go unnoticed. Regardless of a parent's highest level of educational attainment, participants were motivated and/or encouraged to continue their graduate education.

- This study consisted of 16 Black males from various locations and varying ages. Still, the congruency in age was noticeable. Sixty-eight percent of the participants were from the age group 25-34. The online survey displayed national numbers that are congruent with education today. According to Bialik and Fry (2019), the Pew Research Center indicates that "approximately three-quarters of full-time post-baccalaureate students at public institutions were under age 30, with 37 percent under age 25 and 37 percent ages 25 to 29" (p. 1).

The consistency of interesting findings that were shared by all 16 participants was remarkable. Each participant contributed to the creation of a diverse and all-encompassing sample size. Allowing each participant to reflect on their lived experiences while revealing their truths to me was beneficial in understanding participants' everyday experiences of their reality, and information shared and disclosed. The interviewee and I both benefited from the research because they contributed knowledge to help complete the interview properly.

Three Major Themes

After looking at the descriptive statistics of the participants, conducting their interviews, obtaining their narratives and characterizations and gaining insight into how they view themselves and the world through philosophical statements, the study developed three major themes. These themes and characterizations interweave to describe the experiences of 16 Black men in completing their post-baccalaureate degree. To fully understand the connections and relationships to each theme, excerpts from the participants will represent each finding (see Figure 1).

Figure 1

Successful Black Males with Post-Baccalaureate Degrees Model

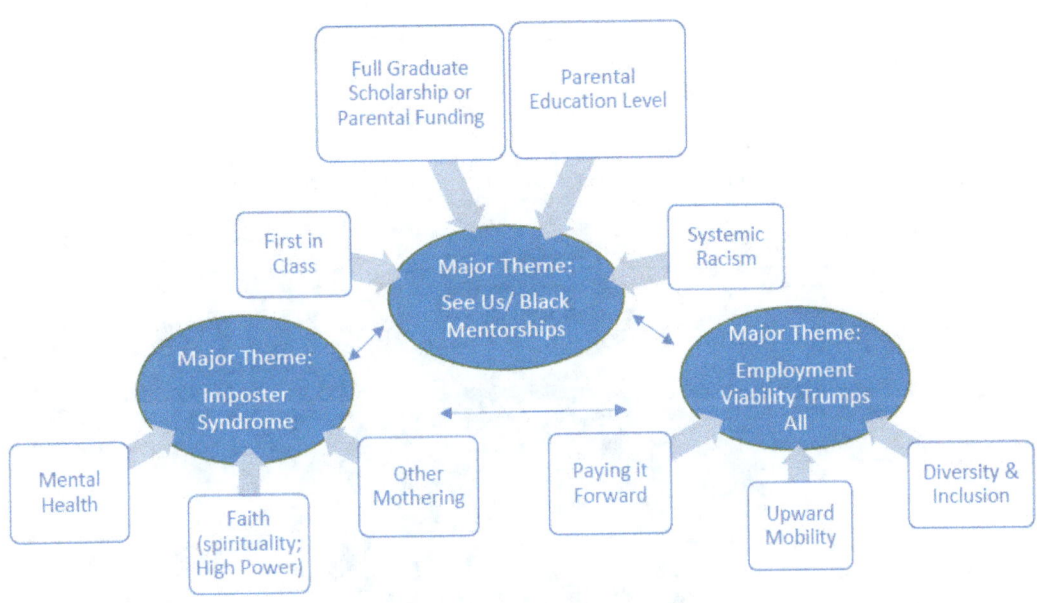

Note. Emerging characterizations by major themes.

Displayed in Figure 1 are the three major themes of the study. Although the participants in this study noted 10 original characterizations of involvement that they felt were significant to the study, the three major themes common to most of the participants that emerged were Imposter Syndrome, Employment Viability Trumps All, and Black Immersion.

Through the utilization of the coding process presented by Clarke and Braun (2006) and by incorporating the process of line-by-line interpretation, we found that three main themes have a success model that allows each term to be understood and stand alone for importance. These concerns are given in the order of the number of participants who expressed these major themes as well as the frequency of words used to define the three major themes.

To provide a visual model and to describe the process of graduate education, the Model of Successful Black Males with a Post-baccalaureate Degree (SBMPD) is a model for encouraging Black male's post-baccalaureate to improve outcomes in higher education settings. This model is an illustration of the 16 participant narratives, which are, in a sense, a synthesis of the participants' experiences as graduate students. For explanatory purposes, the Model is taken as a whole and individually explained in three parts that work together as one to generate and understand various ways of making meaning.

The connections between the 10 characterizations would be fully explained in each prospective section of the model, in retrospect of the three major themes. The next section shows how the three major themes have three to four characterizations merging into one major theme. The SBMPD lays out a road map for individuals and institutions to follow to ensure Black men's post-baccalaureate success. SBMPD examined Black men's successful post- baccalaureate completion to fill a gap in the literature that focused exclusively on post-baccalaureate education.

Figure 2

Major Themes of Black Immersion

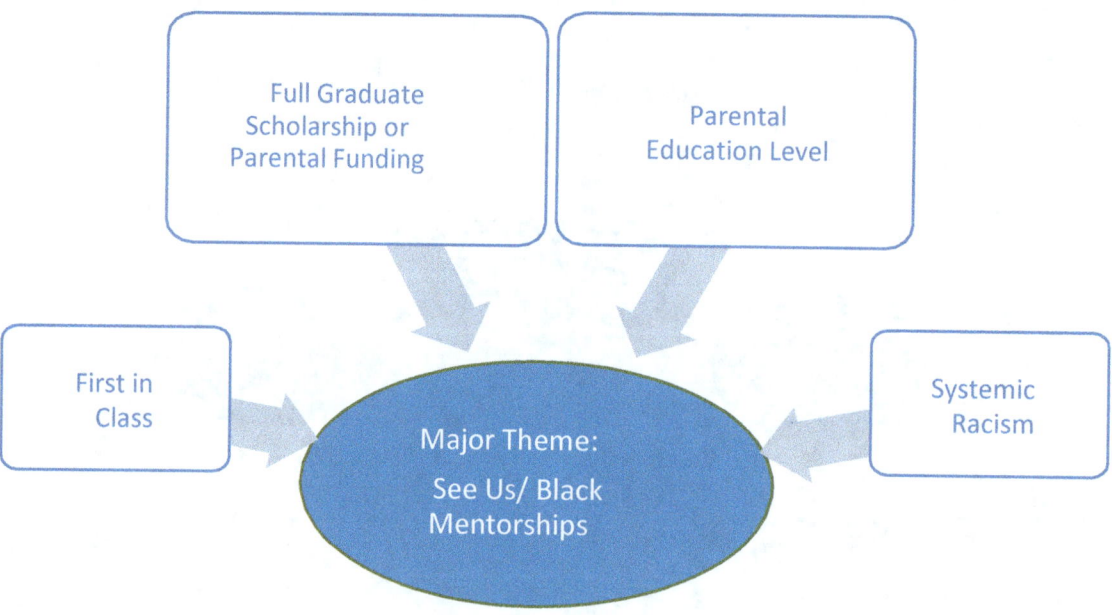

The most prominent theme to emerge was "Black Immersion," which 16 out of the 16 participants found significant to their success in higher education. The Black Immersion theme can be described and characterized by two components. Four of the 10 characterizations fall under the theme Black Immersion: First in Class, Parent Educational Level, Full Graduate Funding, and Awareness of Systemic Racism.

The first component is summarized as "See Us." Often, we hear people say, "I don't see color." While this phrase is intended to seemingly create an atmosphere free of bias, it does the opposite. The participants want to be seen for their originality. They don't want to be cast in a barrel of apples defined by the lifestyles common to the masses that are derived from societal norms which may or may not be relevant to them. Pertinent here is the quest to be acknowledged as the individual they are, as represented by their skill set, philosophies, beliefs and lifestyles.

This is the first component of Black Immersion – the idea of being seen, or "See Us" (Black males) as who we are. This is where the characterizations of Full Graduate Funding and Awareness of Systemic Racism correlate to the notion of needing to be seen, as in to be seen as an equal with the same opportunities as their white counterparts. The successful participants had a commonality of Full Graduate Funding, but in the general population of Black Males, that is not the norm. This is one factor that makes them succeed in completing their degrees. This factor shows the need to increase funding for all Black males to increase the success rates. The other characterization of the Awareness of Systemic Racism left the participants with the perception that they were not seen for who they were, that their ideas and voices were not heard, and that their opportunities were limited due to the fact of them being a Black male. Their experiences of racism made the participants' desire to be seen as who they really are increase even more.

Although we all want to be seen, these Black males said that they felt they were misunderstood, misinterpreted, or just plain judged based on their race, which in turn made them want to fight harder to make a difference and show a different version of a Black male than what others might have expected. This led them to their success.

Examples of the participants' need to be seen were characterized in Full Parental Funding and Awareness of Systemic Racism. The participants acknowledged that Full Parental Funding was an aspect that may not have been given to everyone but was an influence on their success.

Astoundingly, nearly 60% of the participants were able to receive a scholarship or have their parents fully fund their graduate education. Johari explained how financial funding of education can be a relief of stressors if the student has it, or an extensive burden if the student doesn't have it:

First, it's just more affordable for the second about, you know, a lot of them [white counterparts] just have a more comfortable position and have a more comfortable position financially, mentally. They're all wrapped up in each other. And, you know, when I got into financial trouble. The trouble that troubles, you know, and other things in my life, but it's easier to come to class. And there are no African Americans. Minority students are worried about their kids. They're worried about their financials. They're worried about, you know, all this other stuff that goes on. And there's just a lot of it. And so, it's hard for us to keep the same focus.

Although Johari did not have full parental funding, he was able to find ways to financially sustain himself through his 1st year of law school, even though he was unable to work. If students are not able to find a way to finance their educational and personal needs, then they are not able to continue their education and obtain their degrees. Although this is true for all students, the likeliness that there is full parental funding or even resources to find solutions is more limited for Black males compared to their white counterparts.

The participants unanimously agreed that black males have different experiences than their white counterparts. Their experiences are distinct and distinctive to black culture. The difficult tale of the black male experience includes hidden factors which Chris explained:

We definitely have very different experiences than our white counterparts, you know, especially this thinking about, you know, when you walk into that classroom and you know, it's a different right than their white counterparts and white people are for as loss….And white people are like, oh hi, didn't know you were going to be here. It's just an awkward, awkward moment, that awkward silence that happens when you're walking or the awkward stares you get out there. That's a big thing, you know, especially when it comes to what's going on in the world today. What happens when you try to have those conversations with these white counterparts? And like in my multicultural council course, right now we're having those difficult conversations that are facilitated by a white professor. And I asked them why the white students couldn't participate, and as white colleagues in my class, they were quiet about this type of interview or type of question discussion that we're having. So that's a big difference. They don't know what it feels like to be, you know, black in America or black at a PWI like this. That's a big difference that I've seen, especially with what's gone on a day.

Chris explained how, not only is the Black Male experience never acknowledged, but even when it is a topic of conversation, the conversation is meek because white counterparts rarely know how to embrace the topic or are fearful of saying the wrong thing. Sometimes the educational systems have systemic racism embedded into them that is not even acknowledged. Bruce conveyed how the educational system is also centered around white counterparts:

I think that is possibly one of the most important pieces is having someone that has done that. It's hard, in a sense, to not have that because I think the education system is centered around Whiteness, in a sense, or centric ideas, and that you may not necessarily always speak about a Malcolm X, or other Black figures within history that have done similar roles. Then, also, they may lead you to resources that can help you cite more Black information, as opposed to having to rework it around a set of data that was a lot more white people, or something like that, or that didn't look like you. You had to tailor your data around that, to 'How will Black people--?' When the study was done on this. I think they will have more resources, and what not, to do there so I think that's very important. Especially if you're diving in something, like how you're diving into what your thesis is. I didn't really do that as much in mine, but it was still important, to me, to have somebody like that. It would be very important to me.

Systemic racism is not an idea to be agreed or disagreed upon. It can be deeply woven into society and culture or it can be simple ideas that stem from racism that are still embedded in policies. Dr. Samuel described an experience of systemic racism, but also how he overcame it to triumph:

I agree, because there probably was this barrier, but when you mentioned that, I just can't remember it, because it was so long ago. I still have it, I think African Americans have it, I have it as a professional. I forget our term, the higher ed term that we came up with, but we don't belong. We call it the imposter syndrome. I'm sure that came up every now and again, but I probably, I taught myself, and I had others who told me, who encouraged me that you do belong, you are worthy, you should be here, especially, when I did my dissertation, because I did my dissertation on, basically, how our law school handle-- We had to admit students without affirmative action for about 6 years...I interviewed some alumni from the '60s, and there was this one judge who told me, he said, "Without a doubt, if it wasn't for affirmative action, I wouldn't have been admitted to Texas law, I would have never gotten into law school." He said, "I'll tell you this: affirmative action didn't make A's in the class; affirmative action didn't walk across that stage and get that diploma." [laughs]... That's all I needed to hear. He said, "Affirmative action didn't make a 3.9 GPA." I was like, "That's right." We write those papers; we get those grades on those papers. I finished with a 3.97, I said, "Nobody did that but me." We just needed a shot; we just needed a chance.

The second component to Black Immersion is the need for Black Representation in Mentorships within the post-baccalaureate programs. The participants conveyed that their experiences of mentorship within their universities and colleges mattered. The outcome was that, when they were mentored by fellow black professors, colleagues or students, they were quicker to have success in following through with their post-baccalaureate program. Others who did not specifically have a black mentorship felt that, if they did have that support, it could have eliminated barriers, shortened hardships, and would have been a personal inspiration to see themselves in the success of others with whom they had similarities. Black Mentorships Mattered and had a significant effect on their success.

Participants needed to surround themselves with other black successors, a positive network, and opportunities that they may not have thought were possible because they saw black role models in positions of leadership. Having black representation in the mentorships consistently allowed the participants to commit themselves to personify the type of people others looked up to and emulated. During the study, 100% of the participants detailed an experience or a feeling regarding the need to have Black representation present during their post-baccalaureate degree journey. The need for black mentorship stemmed from the characterization of First in Class. Meaning, not only are they sometimes the only Black male in their course so they are one of a kind or first in the class, but it also means that these Black males create an additional burden on themselves to be successful so that they don't fall into the mold that society is expecting them to. In this instance, it would mean failing out of post-baccalaureate school. Since this is such a strong motivation for these students, not only do they succeed, but they become first in their class among rank and success of completion. Ray shared a metaphor he used regarding explaining the Black Male experience. He explained that he would be giving a presentation about being Young, Gifted, and Black where he said

Ironically, I have a presentation on Young, Gifted, and Black in a few weeks. When I think of Blackness, I think of amazing, I think of awesomeness, I think of even though we've gone through so much hardship, so much suffering, torment, that we still rise. I think of Maya Angelou and, a lot of times, also The Rose and the Concrete work, which is a metaphor for Black people. We're the rose that broke through the concrete.

He described himself as not only a rose that grew and prospered, but one that accomplished all those tasks in spite of there being concrete around him at times, which he broke through. Ray believed this of all successful Black males, which is why when he sees another Black Mentor it brings a different level of respect, and he understands the struggles that were endured and the concrete that had to be broken.

Michael describes what it was like to be near another black male and how it helped him with his graduate experience by

Having that connection of just walking through the halls and saying, "Hey, Dr. Anderson." I'm not just saying we're just two African males, just two people who are passionate about education, but we're also saying, you know what? We're able to have just that sit-down communication. We did a few times, even though academic excellence and academic affairs are completely two separate entities, we still had that proximity, and I learned from my project management in my graduate program was that osmosis learning exists, where you're going to learn from the people you're around, just by being in the same vicinity.

For Michael, having a sounding board like himself, or even just seeing and being in proximity to like-minded individuals, built his confidence. Chris explained the significance of seeing others who appeared like him by saying:

I will say now going into graduate school, very important, you know, especially going into graduate school. You know, I had a predominantly white institution. I want to see more people like me. I want to be able to go to a supervisor that looks like me, so I don't have to hold back or feel like I have to hold back and, you know, getting their advice, you got different papers on me right now regarding, you know, black students. Like one of my classes I had to do a literature review on black mental health. I'm at a predominately white institution. I did. I did get feedback from both our black professionals and the paper and everything. And it opened some of their eyes. You know, I had to present it as well, give a positive presentation. You know, some white, white, white professors came in. And it was ever very intrigued, very intrigued with it. They ran straight. So that was definitely rewarding.

Chris clarified his perception that it's important for people to see themselves in other successful people. When mentored by other black professionals, his ideas were not only accepted but shared with all the professors and faculty. To have more successful Black men in post-baccalaureate programs, more successful Black men need to be visible to incoming Black men who have a desire to complete those same achievements.

Bishop describes how he made decisions about graduate schools based on Black Mentorship availability. It's very important, man. It's super important to me. Every program I applied to, I had to have a person of color. I applied to seven or eight programs and got into four. Four or five, I can't remember, but all of them were black advisors. I felt like without a Black advisor, I would be setting myself up for failure because I think I needed someone who I can really talk to about the program but also talk to them as a person of color.

For Bishop, not only seeing other black men was important, but also seeing other women of color was also beneficial in his inspirations. Even if you "look" alike but do not have similar life experiences or upbringing, then it's also very difficult to envision success in their shoes. It's crucial to see others who are similar, but to also hear about their backgrounds to share common life experiences. Those factors influenced him to choose a program where he felt like he could be himself, but at the same time still get the guidance without the judgement.

Tre gave his perspective of what he believes it would mean to have a Black Mentor, since he did not have that opportunity at his institution:

I think to be honest, I think it's extremely important because, you know, as black males, as black people in general, we can relate to certain things. You know, other races they can't, you know, and this is just a reality, a factor in things. So, you know, it is not. No, no. Shame on that race. And like I say, I had my adviser was white and he was a great adviser. But to say if that I had a black adviser, that was there. I feel like we can relate more so that I can, you know, can get closer to him.

Another characterization of Black Mentorship is acknowledging that, from the demographic statistics that were gathered in the survey, it was evident that the Parental Level of Education became a factor of success. The level of education correlated to the success of the participants in part since the parent became an automatic mentor. Therefore, when the participants saw their parents were successful in education, they were equipped growing up to understand they could also achieve those same accomplishments.

The two components of See Us and Black Mentorship Matters combined create the idea of Black Immersion. Not only do Black male students need Black mentors so they can see themselves in the success of others, but they also need to be seen as themselves by the students, faculty, and staff. Universities and colleges would benefit in the success of Black males by creating an immersive culture for Black males to be successful by seeing and being seen as successful Black males.

Figure 3

Major Theme of Employment Viability Trumps All

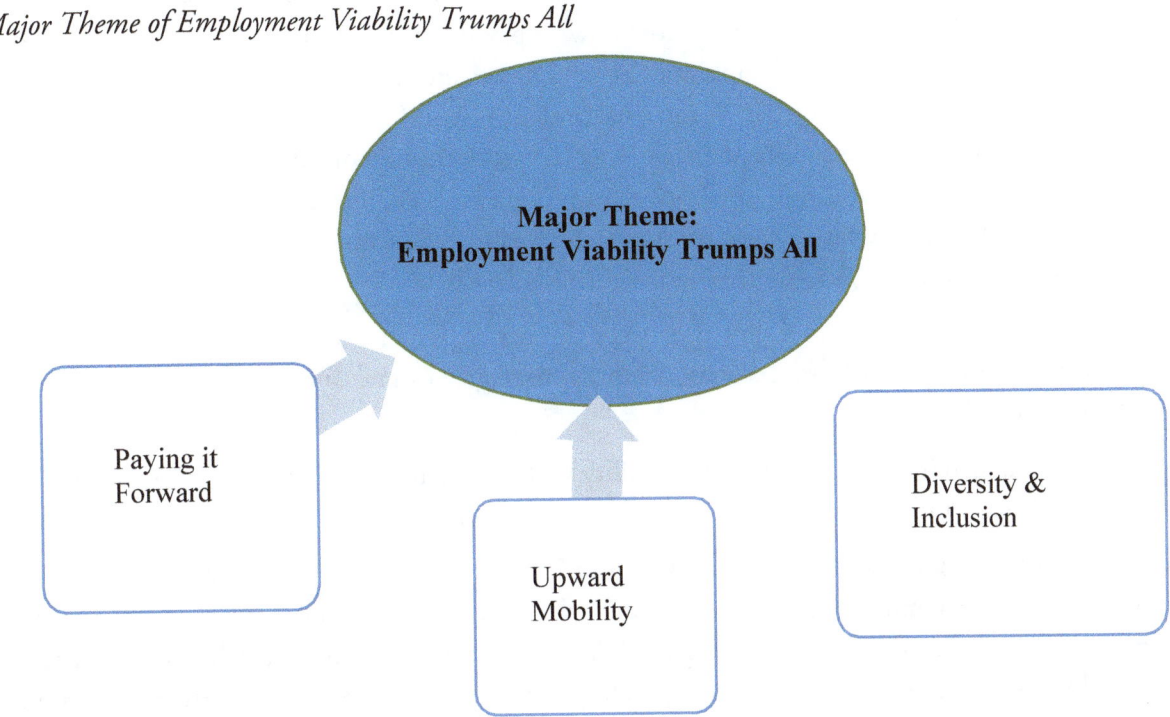

The second factor, 15 out of 16 interviewees cited as essential, was Employment Viability Trumps All. With the word employment meaning "the condition of having paid work" and viability meaning "the ability to live, grow, and develop or the ability to succeed or be sustained," the term Employment Viability means having the ability to sustain, live, and develop by the means of having paid work (Merriam-Webster, n.d.). Employment Viability Trumps All, the importance of having a job or income for participants to be able to complete and succeed with their degree. The importance and significance of being considered for work while doing graduate studies was astronomical. Ninety-four percent of the participants either worked full-time or part-time to provide for everyday means. The work required the participants to show adaptability and the right amount of social competence while working long, flexible hours.

The paramount reason for educating oneself is to secure higher paying careers in the workforce. Students who are oblivious to educators seldom are the recipients of ongoing employment referrals or recommendation opportunities. Educators who devalue the contributions and abilities of students often invest very little energy in being supportive of the students' process and/or learning experience.

The three characterizations of Employment Viability Trumps All are Upward Mobility, Paying it Forward, and Diversity and Inclusion. Employment promotes independence and personal achievement. Not only is employment an apparent want, but it is also a need to be vital and can grow. Without the basic needs of food, water, and shelter being met, it is difficult to enter the next level of growth, whether academic or personal. For some of the participants, it wasn't a choice; it was a need to work.

Employment Trumps All is the need for money to survive. Tayo's experience led him to thrive both in and out of the classroom, which embodies the characterization of Upward Mobility. However, without his employment opportunity he would have had to drop out:

Well, it was a combination. So, with that in mind, my dad offered to help, which is great. And then at some point when he couldn't help anymore, I had to figure out how to make money. So, I remember writing a letter to the dean and said, "Look, I don't know how to pay for this semester. So, this is what I've done in school. If there's anything that I could apply for, let me know. And then, is there any way I can work off the rest of it? So, I didn't know until the day of my final semester. And I received a scholarship for $5,000. And then I was able to work off the rest of the debt. So, I would work throughout the day, which I think was a 40-hour work week every week in addition to school. And so, I said, "Well, if you are able to be a teacher assistant and do this, we'll consider that part of your tuition. But I had to get creative because, you know, I worked my way through my program.

Tayo was able to gain upward mobility after receiving his degree due to his accomplishment, but he also had some upward mobility in the process of ascertaining his degree by creating an opportunity for himself due to his financial hardships.

Dr. Samuel explained how having Upward Mobility with future and potential employment for himself and even his family gave him the motivation:

If you go to a law school like UT, you can start out making $190,000 a year, and you can go on to be a judge and change your family's trajectory. That motivates me to help people become lawyers, change the trajectory of their lives forever. The other thing is what motivates me is, I have a family now, I have a wife and two kids, and I want them to prosper. Moving up in higher ed motivates me, doing a better job, that motivates me as well.

Dr. Samuel also clarified that his motivation to be successful in completing his degree was the potential to Pay it Forward to others, which embodies the second characterization for Employment Viability. Dr. Samuel explained the benefits and what he has seen as being

A couple of different things. I'm still passionate about helping people and helping them get to their goals and bettering themselves and their families, because a law degree can change them and their families' histories. You can go from growing up poor, low SES, you get a JD, no matter where you get a JD from, you can make, on average, probably, $70,000 a year as a lawyer.

Dr. Samuel felt that the benefit of completing his degree was the opportunity that he would have to be able to Pay it Forward to others who came from similar situations as him, and this was an important factor in his success.

The third characterization, which is encompassed in the theme of Employment Viability Trumps All, is the need for diversity and inclusion among the participants and their employers. Not only did several participants seek employment that supports diversity and inclusion at their colleges and universities, but they also sought employers who supported those mission statements. Here, Papi explains how he believes one of the first actions Black males can do is to acknowledge that there are similarities and differences in other races and cultures by stating

You probably wouldn't have interacted with that many black people, let alone one that's coming into a doctoral program, but as you interact with more or different takes, if you will. Like those black and brown people who become, like, you realize that it's like they're just people, just like we are. We might have come from the exact same type of neighborhood or maybe a different one. But it's like they're just people at the end of the day. I just think putting people in contact with one another and having them actually listen to each other and understand that they're not actually that different could be a great way to start.

Papi stated how, if we notice and are put in contact with others who may not look like us, we might find out that there are still very similar experiences, or create connections that can open up into new opportunities that might not have been created or given if we continued to have a closed mindset about diversity and inclusion. Diversity and inclusion also related to the fact that participants kept an open mind to all employment opportunities in order to get the most viable form of employment.

These three characterizations create the theme of Employment Viability Trumps All.

With characterizations of Upward Mobility, Paying It Forward, and Diversity and Inclusion, the participants showed how the need and desire for employment stayed a consistent motivation in them completing their post-baccalaureate degree.

Albert's Experiences

As a young Black man, I started working at 12 years old. I consistently had a source of income for myself. My family encouraged me and found ways for me by working in real estate with my aunt and working in my uncle's Crab Shack restaurant. There was a point when I had two jobs at once when I was 16. I was working for Jack in the Box and Long John Silver at the same time to provide for my family and myself at that age. Even through college, I kept working as a basketball referee, a graduate assistant, and a mover for a Firefighter company at Trinity University. I was able to work on campus at UIW in the master program with graduate assistantships. I also held other positions such as an apartment Manager for Lynd Company in San Antonio, selling pillows and knives at Sam's Clubs, and then a guest teacher for Las Vegas, NV and now Houston, TX. The importance here is that, as a Black man, I was taught and trained even from a young age, that I had to seek employment to sustain. This transitioned into the natural responsibility that I gave myself to find funding and employment to reach the completion of my degrees. When it comes to financial preparations and financial education as in investments, all are important.

Figure 4

Major Themes of Imposter Syndrome

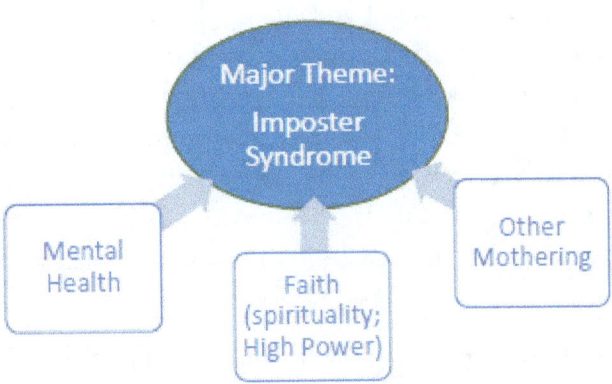

An important theme that developed was participants' perception that they had Imposter Syndrome. Eighty-eight percent of the study participants experienced some form of Imposter Syndrome. Bothello and Roulet, (2019) explain that the term Imposter Syndrome was termed by Clance and Imes (1978) as:

A condition where high-achieving individuals either ascribe their accomplishments to luck and contingency rather than individual skill and merit or find their profession to be a 'bullshit job' that provides little social value. This condition leads to a sense of anomie; in more severe cases, individuals live with the constant fear that they will someday lose all credibility, either when they are exposed as charlatans or when their occupation is revealed to be a sham. (p. 854)

The fact that 14 out of 16 of the participants mentioned Imposter Syndrome draws a connection to the characterizations of Other-Mothering, Mental Health, and Faith (Higher-power).

Interviewees who regarded the Imposter Syndrome as having an upside viewed it as an opportunity to delve deep into their perceptions of themselves as Black, gifted young men who were challenged to find their footing in new and sometimes unwelcoming environments. The first characterization of Imposter Syndrome can be described as Other-Mothering. Dr. Kobe and other participants saw Imposter Syndrome within terminology, grammar, and writing style; they felt like they were not fully equipped or were up to the caliber of the other students. One participant, Dr. Igbo, had a friend who told him "They just use big fancy words." However, Dr. Kobe explained what he went through with his experiences in having a Black female professor who gave him grace on some aspects of education that made him feel like an imposter by saying

One of the things about being a black man in America is like being able to kind of live it day to day. Having like those extra pressures that their peers may not have to think about or worry about. I'll talk a little bit about having imposter syndrome, stereotype threat, being able to kind of have that along with thinking about like if you truly belong there. Knowing what the statistics say and knowing what some of the research says and being able to be like, you're not supposed to be here. Someone that looks like you is not supposed to [clears throat] excuse me. Someone that looks like you are not supposed to achieve at this level.

Dr. Kobe had a deep understanding and perception of the "imposter syndrome." Not only did he understand the term, but he also implicitly explained the term with his personal experience descriptions. According to the U.S. Department of Health and Human Services Office of Minority Health and Mental Health America,

"African Americans are 20% more likely to experience serious mental health problems than the general population. In the United States, the historical manifestation of racism has

had a significant impact on psychological and mental health services." (Smith, 2021, P.47) The mental health of Black males is more likely to be negatively affected than their racial counterparts. Mental health can be directly impacted by the feelings of the Imposter Syndrome because when someone feels alienated from a group that can lead to depression, anxiety, racial fatigue, or even identity issues. Here the characterization of Mental Health becomes directly correlated to the feeling of Imposter Syndrome. Participants echoed the notion of these studies by explaining feelings such as anxiety, homesickness, and depression. Bruce described how he felt about Imposter Syndrome or a sense of not belonging when he began his program. Bruce explains the situation as:

The biggest challenge was imposter syndrome because coming in from where I came from, I didn't think I was supposed to be there. I didn't know if I belonged, I didn't know if-- and a little bit of self-doubt, as well, like, "Oh, you're not supposed to be here, you shouldn't be getting in this. Nobody's ever done this before for you all and you're not going to be the first, you shouldn't be the first." A lot of negative self-talk. Next thing was depression and anxiety, in addition to homesickness, which a lot of it was fueled by homesickness.

These feelings become a concern for Mental Health. If students don't have the freedom to feel like they can be themselves it can become a restraint to progress, whether it's a real restraint or a perceived restraint. The one who feels like an imposter begins to try to act like others to fit in, as they have concerns that being themselves is not enough or not correct for the educational settings, they are in. Bruce continued to say

I work at a predominantly white institution, and I can see how there's a lot of imposter syndrome in a lot of black students that they may have to code switch, they may have to do all these different things to clip their own wings to fit inside of the traditional college mold. It was an outlier in the sense that I went to a Hispanic serving institution, but it still had a lot of Eurocentric or predominately white institution ideals that it was still operating in the same vein, in my opinion, where you're not necessarily discussing black artists all the time or seeing how your culture could fit into a lot of the things that you're doing.

He explained how sometimes Black males must "code switch" meaning, they have to wear different hats depending on their audience. He felt like they had to dial themselves down for the others around. He also mentioned that they would have to "clip their own wings," suggestive of an angelic figure. This is interesting in pertaining to faith, because almost all the participants had a link to faith or spirituality of some kind that helped to bring them through the process to graduation. However, in an educational setting, it is not always viewed as acceptable to discuss faith, religion, or spirituality so they have to mute those perspectives of themselves because they could be an imposter in the educational setting if they did not. This is how the last characterization of Imposter Syndrome relates to faith and spirituality.

Conclusion on Major Theme Relationship with SBMPD Model

The model's understanding or interpretation was that connections exist between relationship terms and vice versa. Consider the relationship between the three themes: Imposter Syndrome vs. Employment Viability Trumps All and Black Immersion (See Us). When the Imposter Syndrome is brought under control, the chances of taking more risks with different jobs, confidence, and willingness to take more risks increase. Resilient risk-taking is essential for people to achieve positive outcomes with others and in business. It demonstrates a willingness to learn and apply new approaches, and the student will be more confident in presenting new ideas and challenges to the traditional way of doing things.

In addition to making sense of the model, consider the relationship or connection between the two: Imposter Syndrome Vs. Black Immersion when black mentorship is seen in academic settings, it reduces the feeling of imposter syndrome in the classroom. It fosters the development of individuals and talents through a pipeline, which is critical in the development of leadership and legacy. The following section will review the inter-weaving relationships of characterizations of the participant's study's three major themes to understand and produce knowledge.

Summary

As we, malleable people, move into higher levels of consciousness and education, we transform as we are becoming and coming to our next level. Knowing that there is no shortcut to transformation illustrates how these participants shift through from student to educator and scholar. This Rite of Passage not only unifies all scholars who have endured this same experience, but even more specifically this indomitable group of participants is uniquely bonded as Black men with post-baccalaureate degrees with unique experiences.

The harmonized group of men understand their existence, as well as have the wherewithal of their history relating to their current state of life. We understand that narratives are often used to as discuss differences in culture as Hofstede, (2011) "explain to outsiders what practices, places, or symbols mean to the people who hold them, then in turn, the findings produced may lead to the development of new theories that resonate more with people's lives" (p. 386).

To elaborate on what the participants were not only thinking, but also how they were feeling with examples of the way they behaved in certain situations. Through understanding, analyzing, and culminating their experiences with the narrative data, we get closer to understanding why and how this group of Black males was successful in accomplishing their goals of a post-baccalaureate degree. Although each participant spoke of their invisibility, being misunderstood, the lack of knowledge from others, the cries, emotions, and stress found at their graduate institutions, the triumph of their individual narratives was highlighted by the pinnacle of their success, which was seen on their shoulders and in their lavish smiles.

The participants were transparent, authentic, real, and honest. Most of the participants shared a characterization of spirituality as a higher power. They displayed vulnerability about their graduate process, with its challenges and successes. The combination of the environment inside of the classroom and outside on the campus was parallel. They relentlessly focused on pursuing research and studies, while at the same time overcoming the challenges of financial struggles day to day. The importance of working while in school and finding a variety of funding opportunities was apparent, as nine out of the 16 participants found a way to economically finance their post-baccalaureate degree with either graduate assistantships, Res Life, or help from their parents/relatives. Employment Viability Trumps All, the power of need and want highlights the fact that winners do not quit. The ever-present story of finding power in celebrating small victories was iconic.

Recognizing the link between physical and mental health, the participants were able to find balance and not only build themselves up, but to build those around them within the community. 16 participants understood the idea of Empowerment and Paying It Forward.

They have received support, information, and guidance from others who look like them, as well as from those who do not look like them. In entirely all the participants felt it was extremely important to have a black mentor/advisor. A few participants did not have the experience of having a Black advisor/mentor during their post-baccalaureate studies, but they did express how that could have better shaped their experience in a positive way. Detailed answers were achieved for the study's research questions and the study's purpose statement rationale: the need for Black men to achieve their post-baccalaureate degrees. The need for Black males in academia to come out of the shadows of their program and become visible to faculty and administrators, with genuine effort and interaction from both the student and the institution's representatives, was highlighted. The narratives shared major themes, such as overcoming the feeling of not belonging or Imposter syndrome and providing examples on how to alleviate stress to create good mental health, the importance of Black Mentors, and the importance of family or peer encouragement/support as motivation.

A captivating discovery, that could not be understated, is the fact that, of the 16 individual participants, more than half stated that their fathers had the highest degree attained within the household. Not only are Black males making a difference, but there was also a common theme among the women faculty of color was extending their expertise and advice in helping to mold these participants' decision-making and pursuit of a degree. Assisting not only with classroom but also outside of classroom involvement. The importance of Other Mothering in academics goes beyond the normal requirements and puts a student under their wings and allows them to grow and flourish beyond their imagination. Regardless of a parent's highest level of educational attainment, participants were motivated and/or encouraged to continue their graduate education.

The 10 characterizations and the three major themes of descriptive data, narratives, and philosophical statements are all interwoven into one, and not only benefited in the triangulation of research, but were also beneficial in allowing me to thoroughly describe these highly motivated individuals who enjoy learning and learned to keep their eyes on the prize of attaining their degree. The 16 individuals are a story of overcomers and optimizers with a growth mindset and high self-esteem. The importance of being proactive and either finding a way to have joy and laughter throughout their shared experience was advantageous. The 16 participants were asked questions that allowed analysis of their characteristics and attributes, which contributed to their success in garnering a graduate degree. All 16 participants felt strongly tied to their need to be seen and to see other Black Mentors within their field of choice, a sense of belonging in the academic setting of the graduate degree programs that can be contradicted by their feeling of the Imposter Syndrome, and the passion about their employment viability that trumps all during and after graduation.

The Model for Successful Black Males with a Post-baccalaureate Degree (SBMPD) was developed based on the experiences and narratives of the study's 16 Black men. SBMPD laid out a road map for individuals and institutions to follow to ensure that Black men's post-baccalaureate success. In the next chapter, you will witness the evolution of the SBMPD Model for implementation and grounded theory. As of now, it is only raw data that is on its way to becoming theoretical and empirical findings.

Chapter 5

Discussion, Implications, and Recommendations

In prior chapters, participants' narratives were used to create a set of findings that can help open the eyes of those who wish to support black males to thrive in graduate school. James Baldwin stated that "People who shut their eyes to reality simply invite their own destruction, and anyone who insists on remaining in a state of innocence long after that innocence is dead turns himself into a *monster*" (Griffin & Fish, 1999, p. 178). With the knowledge and recommendations within the research, it will not be a viable or sustainable choice to turn a blind eye without the people, administrators, faculty, and institutions becoming an enabling part of that monster. The research will benefit educational policymakers, researchers, practitioners, and faculty who can contribute basic and applied knowledge to help key stakeholders in education better serve Black males in post-baccalaureate schools and beyond.

This chapter will discuss the transformation of the SBMPD (Successful Black Males with a Postbaccalaureate Degree) model into the emergent Furlow Engagement and Endurance Theory, what it means, how it works, and the interpretations of the new phases that the model and theory went through. There are important ways in which the theory can be implemented at the College education and University level. This final chapter discusses the literature, its implications, and future recommendations in a way that generates new knowledge. To understand the study's findings, the discussion will provide solutions and recommendations based on higher-level ideas that emerged from the discussion of Chapter 4 and the literature.

A considerable amount of research and literature on Black males in education is devoted to the achievement gap. This study shines a light on Black men who not only are succeeding in post-baccalaureate programs but a framework for that success. Changing the way the SBMPD model is anchored in literature and research results in a theory that is particularly named after me, the researcher, Albert Furlow. The "Furlow Engagement and Endurance Theory" uses a conceptual map to describe the dynamics of this phenomenon. By continuously developing the research findings, it became apparent that speculations which I assumed might only be relevant to a few Black men, were consistently sustainable with this new theory. Even though it is named as "Furlow", this theory is interchangeable with the best practice and open to changing the first letter for adaptability for an institution or curriculum implementation.

Background of Research

In post-baccalaureate education, Black males have historically and continuously been underrepresented. Focusing on research on African Americans working in higher education in the United States, the *Journal of Blacks in Higher Education* (2020) published a new report demonstrating a rise in graduate school enrollment which finds

Enrollment in U.S. graduate schools increased from 2018 to 2019, before the onset of the global pandemic. African Americans made up 12.1 percent of all first-time graduate enrollees in 2019. Yet African Americans were just 6.1 percent of all incoming graduate students at doctoral universities with very high research activity... In 2019, there were 188,478 blacks enrolled at all levels of U.S. graduate schools. Of these, nearly 70 percent were women. (p. 1)

This illustrates how black men fall behind when it comes to post-baccalaureate degrees, even when compared to black women. Few studies specifically focus on black males who have completed post-baccalaureate degrees, and even fewer highlight their success stories.

Nonetheless, this study highlights the evolving SBMPD model and introduces the creation of the Furlow Engagement and Endurance Theory (FEET) to better understand the lived experiences that led to the participants' degree completion success.

Additionally, the purpose of this study is to inform educators and faculty about the aspects and characteristics of Black male students that contribute to success in post-baccalaureate school. The goal is to gain a better understanding of Black males who have completed a post-baccalaureate degree or higher within the last 5 years' perceptions of their lived experiences and attributes. The themes in this study emerged from the 16 participants' lived experiences and information on the monumental turning points that aided in their educational access and mobility. With this study, it will be possible to share this information and grow the retention rates of Black Males and increase their success in obtaining post-baccalaureate degrees.

The research questions were in place to follow as a guide to gain insightful and rich data from the participants. The three research questions that were developed for the study were as follows:

1. What are the characteristics/attributes/practices of Black males who completed a master's degree or higher within the past 5 years?
2. How does honest reflection on their academic degree program enable Black male graduate students to advance academically despite their obstacles?
3. How did/does your identity as a Black male affect(ed) your experiences in graduate school?

The methodology of narrative inquiry and autoethnography was used to gather stories, perceptions, and reflections of the 16 Black male participants as well as myself. Through their descriptions of their experiences, I gained an understanding of the characteristics that led to their success in completing a post-baccalaureate degree. With the participants' ability to reflect on their feelings, interactions, and experiences, narrative inquiry and autoethnography were the appropriate methodologies for describing their post-baccalaureate journey.

Based on the three key themes presented by the interviewees, it became paramount to have Black representation in the academic setting, especially as mentors, to create an inclusive and accommodating experience for Black males. Secondly, it is greatly important to generate tools and resources to overcome imposter syndrome, which most respondents expressed as being in a place or in a program where they did not belong even though they had all the criteria to be there. The notion that Employment Viability Trumps All was also correlated as a necessary criterion for the success of Black males in completing their programs. Since post-graduate study comes at a financial cost, the respondents discussed the need to develop ways to create employment options during the process of acquiring a degree, especially for those without family support. The research also supports the need for continuing resources for networking for employment after graduation.

The arrows in Figure 5 (below) connecting one theme to another represent the value each theme has for the other. In a reciprocal matter, they are all dependent on each other. The arrow's direction, like a triangle, meets at all three points, always revolving between the three major themes. The arrows of Knowledge, Connections, and Confidence were added to the SBMPD Model as important factors that connected the major themes in making sense of the participants' experience in completing their degrees.

Purpose of Knowledge

The SBMPD model now includes important relationships and connection with the word Knowledge. The word knowledge encompasses the concepts of self-knowledge and belief, as well as knowing your own worth, which all contribute to graduation success. A student's environment can increase or decrease their base of knowledge, which will directly affect their knowledge of imposter syndrome and their need to be seen as a Black male within their program. If a student has an ineffective environment for learning and gaining knowledge, then their negative feeling of imposter syndrome will increase, and they will feel less seen or not believe that their presence as a Black man is worthy of the program.

Figure 5

The SBMPD Model with Added Words

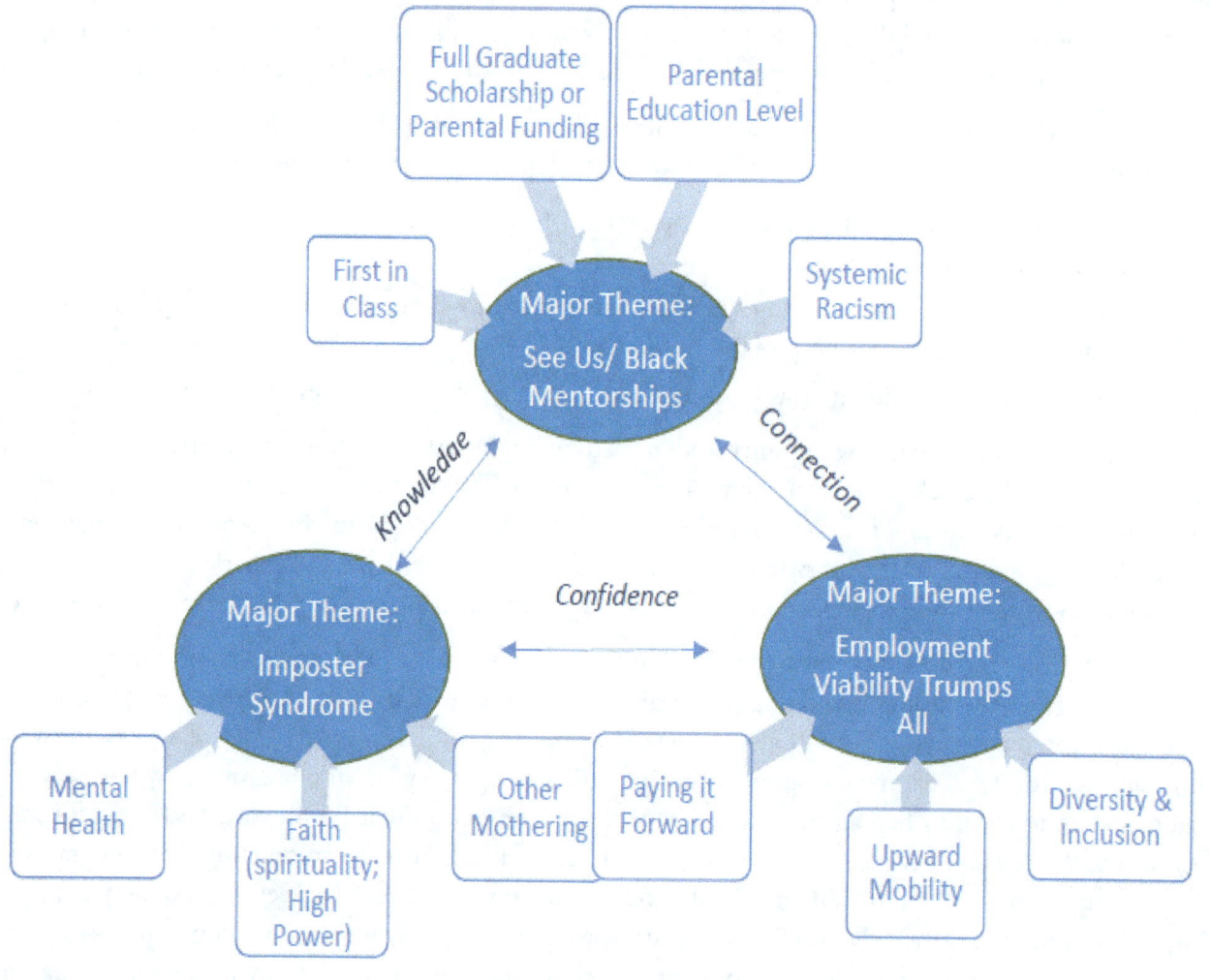

Note. The evolution of the SBMPD Model has additions for clarity and understanding of the functionality of the model.

When participants understand the knowledge and encouragement from their mentors and peers, their confidence levels rise, which helps to alleviate feelings of imposter syndrome and allows them to begin dealing with ongoing issues such as systemic racism and being the first or only Black Male in their class. Gaining knowledge from mentors or peers regarding these issues who may have already dealt with such issues can give them the information that was needed to emotionally process the subjects. Ray described his experience of feeling like he belonged when having a black mentor/advisor.

It gives you a sense of belonging, if I can connect with the faculty, it gives you a sense of belonging. It made me want to be a part of things. It made me want to volunteer. It made me want to continue. At times there's, at one point, I was ready to quit my PhD program because I was like, "You know what, I'm tired, my job at Reslife, I'm already doing diversity work and I'm working in the morning and then at night, I got night classes staying up. Doing a program, like this is for the birds." I got my current major thesis, it was like a 180. It was like, "Yes, you're tired but he's up there with you too." He calls you at 10 o'clock at night because he knows you up and asks you how you're doing or sending you stuff or doing stuff…Navigating these spaces, especially at a predominately white institution. Again, a land-grant, predominately white institution in Louisiana that wasn't created for me. Also, within my research, having someone that understands or is able to at least have their own experiences to be like, no, critical race theory is important as well as the research that he's doing. I have to advocate at one point to one of my advisors why I wanted to do my dissertation on Black Lives Matter. He was like, "What do you mean?" Well, we think that's doing a disservice to the academics and it's almost, she was to give me the whitewash for my research…Then also to me, it gives me a sense of security and safety where I've been able to be vulnerable in certain spaces with my major professor and my committee members too about certain things that are going on and they understand it. This summer, when everything was happening with George Floyd and Ahmaud Arbery, I worked -- I was the assistant director of multicultural affairs, so I'm organizing protests, I'm leading protests, foreign students. My research is on it. I am black, so there's like at 1- point, Dr. Kennedy was like, "Hey, you need to take 2 weeks and not do anything research- or school-wise," but he understood why. Like, He was saying, "I can see it in your face; you're trying to be strong. Now we're not worried about your dissertation." So, they pushed back my general exams. Then he told me, "Your proposal will come, and your general exam will come. Just right now, focus on you." If there had been another professor that wasn't black, they wouldn't understand that or seen that.

Ray explained the concept of the compelling Black Lives Matter movement, relating it to his professors rather than looking down, and the importance of focusing on rightfully gaining a seat at the table. The juxtaposition of being disregarded and devalued causes a disconnection from the established process of learning. The interviewees who experienced imposter syndrome created a barrier between themselves and their instructors and classmates and responded with silence as opposed to engaging in classrooms. They felt strongly that their presence was unwelcome and therefore, they should be seen and not heard. Consequently, learning in a safe/welcoming environment that acknowledges the student and values their attributes as a person diminishes the anxiety students experience. When Black mentorship is seen in academic settings, it lowers the feeling that they are experiencing imposter syndrome in the classroom which in turn develops individuals and their talents through a pipeline that is vital in creating leadership and legacy.

While advising is a short-term process where the focus is on giving information and guidance to the learner, mentoring is a more intricate, long-term, 1-on-1 relationship that goes well beyond simply providing information. True mentoring is a complex process between a professor and a college adult learner that supports a mutual enhancement of critically reflective and independent thinking. (Johnston, 2010)

Mentorship is an intricate and friendly relationship at any level. However, the more a Black man excels in educational programs, these relationships can begin to be even more complex due to social inequalities. The affiliation between black mentees and imposter syndrome becomes even more apparent the further along a student becomes in his educational journey because the further he goes the less likely he is to see someone that looks, acts, or understands like him. As a participant, Dr. Samuel explained,

I believe we call it impostor syndrome. I'm sure that came up every now and again, but I probably, I taught myself, and I had others who told me, who encouraged me that you do belong, you are worthy, you should be here, especially when I did my dissertation, because I did my dissertation on, basically, how our law school handled-- We had to admit students without affirmative action for about 6 years.

As many people experience these feelings throughout their educational process, I am aware that I can now understand and relate more fully to those who may experience imposter syndrome. I can empathize with and articulate the nervousness I feel when preparing for a presentation or waiting for feedback from my committee members that makes me feel like I will never be finished or the doubt that perhaps I cannot complete this venture. That quality of meticulousness, in conjunction with systemic racism or microaggressions, leaves the feeling that I will never be able to finish this process because I am "not meant" to be here in the post-graduate program in the first place, which is an example of my feelings of Impostor Syndrome. Identifying impostor syndrome as an internal factor or cognitive mentality that affects a person's psychological aspect way of feeling/thinking which is a complex concept that anyone can face.

Even if it is stronger in others, it is still an issue; some see it as motivation, while others see it as one of the worst feelings they have ever experienced. They believe they are deceiving or conning others and one day their character or value will be called into question. The approval of others can cause natural anxiety but having the confidence to keep going and being self-assured is essential.

Stakeholders such as university administrators and professors can see the value or significance of "Knowledge." As shareholders who are in the business of education, it is obvious why the knowledge of the post-baccalaureate process is important in order for success. Not only do these individuals want to see success from the colleges or universities, but it also behooves them financially to invest in the Black population to ensure success for minorities and retrieve additional funds through scholarships and grants. Understanding the implications of the necessary knowledge to link the feelings of imposter syndrome and the need for Black mentors is much more functional knowledge than just comprehending verbal or written language. This understanding the significance of the relationship between the two themes of Imposter and See Us: Black Mentorship relies on the need to have knowledge regarding the emotional and social experiences of a black man.

If we continue to build on our progress and strive for truthful narratives rather than dismissing the Black male experience in terms of knowledge and how it relates to the two themes previously discussed, there in fact would be an increase in postbaccalaureate success for Black males.

Real World Connections

Continuing with the SBMPD model additions, the second added word was "Connections". Similarly, when the participants received valuable knowledge from a mentor or advisor, their network expanded, creating real-world connections, allowing them to boost their chances of landing a job, and increasing their opportunities for Employment Viability.

(As mentioned in chapter 4, Dr. Igbo (age 35-44) holds a Ph.D. from Arizona State University in Educational Policy Evaluation, Educational Evaluation, and Research. (He was the first in his family to earn a Ph.D.) Dr. Igbo described his experience of gaining knowledge of reality and feeling as if he had finally figured it out, stating,

They don't check for me, which is a good thing, they are, like, you know, "We don't care about you," right? Because they're usually trying to get all the Latinx people, or, like, they're doing policies against Latinx people, all that sort of stuff. But you'll see that other marginalized groups do a lot of stuff to black people, and you'll be looking, like, "Oh, I kind of – I see it, now. I see – if everybody's fighting for crumbs, then you're going to start trying to take somebody else's crumbs so you can feed your family," you know. I don't think, I mean, I'm not justifying it, but I understand it. But I also understand that we're not trying to look at – we're kind of constantly looking down at the crumbs, instead of looking up and trying to get to the table.

Dr. Igbo explained the concept of competing for the opportunity to just be seen. In his words, if he could be seen and get opportunities that were not outrightly afforded to him, then he could sustain his family. Situational issues such as the lack of engagement or interest that an educator demonstrated towards their student often resulted in a feeling of alienation, which contributed to the imposter syndrome experienced by many students. Ultimately, the goal for students is to secure viable careers which, if not seen or appreciated, becomes a dismal pursuit. It is important to focus on gaining a legitimate seat at the table that will lead to long-term employment viability. Successful Black males have the environmental factor of an effective Black mentorship, their connections, and due to their new knowledge increase, which provides the students with better chances for employment and satisfies the need to be seen and heard by successful faculty. This creates the arrows between See Us-Black Mentorships and Employment Viability Trumps All.

More specifically, "Real Connections" would help one achieve their goals. Even so, university administrators and professors, as well as anyone who cares about black male graduate school success, must recognize the pivotal role that they can play. Operationally, this is accomplished by cultivating relationships and networking with people from diverse backgrounds and different fields of expertise. The connections between the two themes and the implications of their relationship for people to recognize that there are benefits to strengthening relationships with students, the faculty and the community.

It will be difficult to continue to strive for success if you are not aligned with the right people or team on your side, or if you are not connected with anyone. Wherever there are people with whom you can connect, the student is more likely to stay and continue to strive for success. The famous saying goes, "it's not what you know, but it's who you know" holds true for this set of individuals as well. Having a black mentor not only gives them connections into the educational setting, but also connections outside of their educational needs into personal and financial needs as well. People who have experience with the process will be familiar with scholarships, grants, financial aid, or job opportunities that will increase their employment viability in the short-term and long-term with long-standing careers. If the students aren't the only ones advocating for themselves but also have someone on their side advocating for their success, then their likeliness for completing their degree will increase.

Gain Confidence. The word "Confidence" has been added as the final addition to the SBMPD model. When feelings of imposter syndrome are reduced, confidence rises, allowing participants to maintain employment or create new opportunities because of increased confidence. When a student is in a mentally healthy environment, his or her confidence grows, which not only appeals to employers but also ensures the student's persistence in finding viable work. Participant Chris (*MBA current student from LSU*), for example, had to overcome depression issues although he needed to go to work.

I had depression the first 2 or 3 months I got here, but it was coming definitely to the point where, OK, maybe need I'll talk to mental health counselor or something like that or colleges….Let them know what was going on. Because, you know, I was lonely here, you know, I wasn't talking to anybody. I would just go to work or go to class. I will participate in class. But it got to a point to where, you know, some days I may not just want to, you know, get up and go to class or I will always get up and go to WORK though, which was what was really surprising. I see. But some days, you know, when it was class time. I'll find myself in bed AH, I'm not going in. OR, I will be sad some days. I wouldn't say it was really depression that I was dealing with. It was more so like having that anxiety and just dealing with like a lot of stress. You know, I was lonely, too. So trying to figure out, OK. Like, who can I talk to what organization can get involved with here?

Participant Chris described how, when his mental health was poor or he felt like an imposter, he would sometimes refuse to go to class or work but would do so because he knew he needed money to survive. This illustrates how important employment is to a student and their possibilities for success. At times, the participants mentioned having to be more concerned with the viability of their employment than their motivation to continue their education process.

In all prospects, the operational aspect of confidence concerning the themes of imposter syndrome and "employability viability trumps all" is a critical link with great value. When confidence increases for a student, then the feelings of the "imposter syndrome" subside as they grasp the notion of the importance of their presence in their educational programs. Confidence also allows a student to take more chances and risks for new opportunities that could open up for employment during their educational program but also solicit employers to hire the student after graduation. When pursuing success, however, administrators and professors must consider the impact that confidence has on students. If administrators, professors, and others concerned about the success of Black men do not recognize that confidence grows and improves over time by removing self-doubting situations and inspiring their students, they will fail. Functionality through confidence and its connection to the two themes functions through trust, openness, and a shared interest or commonality was by actively participating, providing genuine feedback, discussing existing barriers, and working on relationships so that barriers no longer exist. Encouraging confidence within the students will enrich their lives and career paths.

Therefore, with the addition of the word's knowledge, connections, confidence, and clarity to ensure how the SBMPD model functions, the additional important associations for this model to cohesively work together should not be overlooked. The three major themes, "See Us- Black Mentorship," "Employment Viability," and "Imposter Syndrome," were derived to stand alone, but they also work together as one ever-evolving model with networks and relationships that provides a deeper understanding of black male experiences.

Theoretical Frameworks: Astin's IEO Model and Critical Race Theory

Using Astin's IEO Model and Critical Race Theory as interpretations and dialogue as a framework, the study's three research questions were revealed. Both theories were equally important as the united frameworks to interpret and make sense of the findings.

Astin's IEO Model

To enlighten the Astin Student Involvement Theory and its application to this study, Astin claims:

What desirable outcomes for institutions of higher education are viewed in relation to how students change and develop as a result of being involved co-curricularly. The theory's core concepts are made up of three components. The first are a student's "inputs," which include demographics, background, and previous experiences. The second factor is the student's "environment," which includes all the experiences a student will have while in college. Finally, there are "outcomes," which cover a student's characteristics, knowledge, attitudes, beliefs, and values after graduation from college. (Astin, 1985)

First, the data, according to Astin's Input–Environment–Output (IEO) model, finds the participant's common characteristics and evaluates them with their environments to create a formula that ends in the desired result for Black men who have completed a post-baccalaureate degree. "This model offers a classification scheme to evaluate how inputs (e.g., student characteristics) and environment (e.g., program attributes) may influence desired outputs (e.g., results of programs)" (Callahan et. al., 2017).

The first major theme of See Us-Black Mentorship coincides with Astin's Student Involvement Theory. Knowing and understanding who the student participants and that are identifying with Black faculty and students helped Black men successfully navigate through their programs and institutions to earn their post-baccalaureate degrees. For instance, the I-E-O model states that:

The model contends that outcomes in terms of student development are determined by both inputs and learning environments; at the same time inputs also influence outcomes. The model also suggests that the environment could function as a mediator. Moreover, Astin (1993) explains that the relationship between the environment and student outcomes cannot be understood without taking into account student inputs. (Yanto et al., 2011, p. 4)

In other words, the central point is that Black mentorship, within the major theme of See Us- Black Mentorship, is critical to the student's success. The interdependence between input or the identity of the student (a Black male student) and the environment (an engaging Black mentorship with faculty) directly influences the success of Black males in completing a postbaccalaureate degree. Through the findings, it was discovered that Black mentorship was an important part of the participants' environment which contributed to their success. Specifically, Black mentorship with Black students not only helps to further their academic process, but it inherently also affects their overall well-being with acclimations into the real world.

Finally, the major theme of imposter syndrome was synergized with the Astin framework. It can be connected in several different ways. If a student comes in as a first-generation or first-time post-baccalaureate student, that would be their identity, which can be defined by the lack of other familial experiences. In other words, those students must transform and figure out the next steps and educational material in anticipation of the completion of their degree. This in turn influences and aligns with Astin's outcome. Again, this is where their environment can be so crucial to their success. Also, in another explanation, the Black male in his Black identity, could encounter imposter syndrome by not believing he fits into the academic post-baccalaureate program he is involved in due to the lack of environmental involvement of other Black students or faculty members. Therefore, the students who suffers from imposter syndrome can tend to overwork themselves because they believe their assignments or materials are inadequate, never good enough for completion, which can exhaust them to the point of incompletion of their degree. Again, the missing component of a successful outcome for that Black male is his environment, which can be influenced by healthy Black mentorship. Within this study, the students' input and environment have a significant component of correlation to the output or outcome of success.

Astin's IEO Model was presented regarding the participants' consensus that seeing Black faculty and mentors was crucial to their drive for success due to the health and mental stability provided by the acceptance of their imposter syndrome and cultural/societal issues that are common among other black males. Due to the study's connections to the major themes and theories, I found it beneficial to have this study use a 2-fold theoretical approach. Adding Critical Race Theory along with Astin's IEO Model allowed for this study to further expand on the success narratives and findings from this study.

Critical Race Theory

In 1995, Gloria Ladson-Billings and William Tate introduced Critical Race Theory in education as defined as an "Interdisciplinary approach that seeks to understand and combat racial inequity in society." As mentioned in Chapter 2, Critical Race Theory "does not attribute racism to white people as individuals or even to entire groups of people. Simply put, critical race theory states that U.S. social institutions (e.g., the criminal justice system, education system, labor market, housing market, and healthcare system) are laced with racism embedded in laws, regulations, rules, and procedures that lead to differential outcomes by race" (Ray & Gibbons, 2021).

To help fill in the gaps in the complexity of surrounding environments outlined by the participants of the study, it was crucial to align Critical Race Theory for the additional purpose of expanding on further analysis. Critical Race Theory was utilized to analyze the different forms of social inequities reinforced through the institution of higher education. Combined with Astin's IEO Model, the Critical Race Theory helped to guide the framework of the study by adding to the body of literature and research to explore and use to understand how Black men successfully navigate through higher education to rewarding post-baccalaureate options of success.

Critical Race Theory makes the notion of the inequalities in higher education as the study is intertwined with the three major themes. For instance, the first major theme, See Us- Black Mentorship, "Acknowledges [that] racism is normal and endemic in U.S. society…to expect racism and oppression throughout institutions" (Bell, 1992). To further highlight the importance of Critical Race Theory, most of the participants understood that this was bigger than us (and not only a United States issue). As Michael stated:

Let's see here, considering our current situation, like I said, with COVID and employing distance learning, I think this is a great opportunity to show how critical race theory could be applied to different males in different countries. I'm not saying it's limited to African American males, but you can also use that as an opportunity or gateway into other different types of males. Say, in Australia. In Australia, they have African American males who also have dual citizenship. Because they're there, their skin color and their ability to be recognized as indigenous populations has been marginalized in a way.

Being marginalized in their own country is something black males can understand in our own country. Having that understanding that this can be a very global situation can expand and begin a way of seeing diversity not just by skin tone, but also as an issue for other people to remove that allegory.

Even though Michael compares Critical Race Theory to Australia, he shows the presentation of the Critical Race Theory in other countries and other races other than Black Americans. CRT is not only an American issue, but it is a societal paradigm that judges people based on their skin tone and affords either less or more opportunities depending on the constructed spectrum. If Critical Race Theory is accepted, then open and honest conversations with reflection can be had regarding situations or institutions which are affected by race. Having a conversation about CRT and how to cope with the outcomes of certain situations, for example, helps participants understand how they might have handled a situation differently, as they explained in their interviews. In addition, the participants mentioned that seeing someone or being able to talk to someone about what they were going through was the best option for them. Most of the participants suggested that it works in their favor that they acknowledge racism and their understanding that the ideal option is to eliminate racism to make way for inclusion for all.

Throughout the interviews, there were common threads and emerging factors in participant narratives, highlighting how components of Critical Race Theory point to the lack of inclusivity and diversity in higher education. Therefore, it is important to focus on the enablers of success from the participants. (Ladson-Billings, 2008) It would be the ultimate counter-story to have history repeat itself by repeating the positive successes of Black males who have obtained their post-baccalaureate degrees.

Other Theoretical Frameworks

Scholar Identity Model. The Scholar Identity Model introduced by Whiting and Kennedy (2015) stated that the school counselor is in a singular position to be an integral part of delivering the Scholar Identity Model, describing it as:

(a) Black Male students are more likely to achieve academically when they have a scholar identity; (b) Black male students are more likely to be viewed by educators, their families, and others as not only doing well, but being highly capable, perhaps even gifted, if they achieve at high levels; (c) We cannot close the achievement gap, the opportunity gap, or even begin to pay the "education debt" (Ladson-Billings, 2006) that would place Black male students at promise for achievement unless we focus on their academic identities; and (d) the earlier we focus on the scholar identities of Black male students, the more likely we are to develop a future generation of Black male scholars who are in position to break the vicious cycle of low achievement and underachievement. (p. 196)

In essence, this theory states how important it is to have people believe in the student, not only as good, or able, but as a prodigy or extremely qualified. This prong of the theory specifically speaks to a major theme of imposter syndrome in my research. If a student feels confident in who they are as a Black male, and that they believe in themselves as a scholar, then they will have less anxiety about being an imposter in their education program. They will feel enabled and encouraged to feel like "I got this!" which will inspire their sustainability to reach the finish line.

Urie Bronfenbrenner's Bioecological System Theory. Urie Bronfenbrenner's Bioecological Systems theory is a theory that emphasizes the role of context in development, suggesting that contexts are organized into a series of systems in which individuals are embedded in the environment and that interact with one another and the person to influence development (Kuther, 2018).

We believe that we are active in our development and interact with the world around us. Specifically, Bronfenbrenner's Bioecological Systems Theory poses that development is the result of the ongoing interactions among biological, cognitive, and psychological changes within the person and his or her changing context (p. 21).

Here, who the student is biologically and genetically interacts with their world environment which develops their experiences to create their mental perceptions.

Black Adult Male Learner Success Theory. The Black Male Adult Learner Success Theory is also a theory that was established with the two previous frameworks. The Black Male Adult Learner Success Theory (BMALST) is a "lens to examine the unique experiences of Black male adult learners in higher education and the impact of their various environments on their academic success" (Goings, 2021, abstract). According to Goings (2021),

"Given the preponderance of deficit-oriented discourse about Black men and adult learners in higher education, there have not been any theoretical frameworks put forth to explain the success of Black male adult learners in higher education." (p. 135)

Goings (2021) continues to elaborate on his theory, stating:

Black Male Adult Learner Success Theory, which builds on Gilman Whiting's scholar identity model and Urie Bronfenbrenner's bioecological system theory, was developed as a lens to examine the unique experiences of Black male adult learners in higher education and the impact of their various environments on their academic success. In response to the call for action from adult education scholars, this article introduces an asset-based theoretical approach for researchers to use when studying Black male adult learners. (Abstract)

Even though the Black Adult Male Learner Success Theory was discovered after the construction of this study's literature review, it shows the relevance between Astin's Student Involvement Theory and Critical Race Theory. The combined application of these theories serves as a framework or guide for research. When applied, the answers to the research questions begin to become clearer and more succinct.

The concerns with using the Black Male Adult Learners Success Theory are that it is very sparse, with limited information on the theory, and that it is relatively new, established in 2021. More information is required to determine why Black males are successful. However, this study shows the bigger picture of involvement in interacting with peace and harmony with available resources. By focusing precisely on Black males within the Black Adult Male Learner Success Theory, I believe this can begin a discussion in higher education for the future.

Theoretical Connections Table

To take it a step further, the SBMPD Model was synthesized through literature and theoretical frameworks in collaboration with Astin and Critical Race theory. After finishing Chapter 2 and analyzing Chapter 4, I decided to investigate other theories that could better help to understand or explain my experiences. Table 3 shows additional or alternative theories for future research to fully understand the Black male experience.

The data for the table provided a valuable opportunity to synthesize the experiences, as well as to contextualize them with detailed descriptions. As shown in Table 3, the generated discussion was guided by theoretical connections from the study and theories for future research. Rather than connecting theories, this table describes how they relate to one another and how the theories transform or become more effective when combined or mixed with other theories when analyzed as a whole.

Table 3

Theoretical Connections From the Study and Theories for Further Research

Theories Used & Theories for Further Research	Theoretical Knowledge	Study's Findings & Connections to Theories for Further Research
Astin Student Involvement	Student input compared to the environment and outcome.	The effort you put in is very important. More so Faculty/staff must meet students where they are at.
Critical Race Theory	The systemic barriers of Racism/oppression that are embedded in the Academic program's	Microaggressions, and stereotypes always going to be there. It's up to the individual to deal with it professionally.
Black Adult Male Learner Success Theory (Further research)	Lens to examine the unique experiences of Black male adult learners in higher education and the impact of their various environments on their academic success.	Astin IEO Critical Race Theory
Urie Bronfenbrenner's Bioecological System Theory (Further research)	Individuals are embedded and interact with one another and the person to influence development.	Astin IEO
The Scholar Identity Model (Further research)	Black Male students are more likely to achieve academically when they have a scholarly identity; with guidance from a counselor.	Critical Race Theory

Note. Table 3 shows theories already used in Chapter 2, and theories for future research. lead to the outcome. This theory alone allows for no need for people associated with education, such as faculty, staff, administrators, and professors, to grow or adapt under the IEO Model.

Data for the table provided a valuable opportunity to synthesize the experiences, as well as to contextualize them with detailed descriptions. As shown in Table 3, the generated discussion was guided by theoretical connections from the study and theories for future research. Rather than connecting theories, this table describes how they relate to one another and how the theories transform or become more effective when combined or mixed with other theories when analyzed as a whole.

Overlaying the Frameworks

The study's findings and connections to other theories suggest that the common important factor for the student is the amount of effort that is put into the environment is crucial for success. More importantly, faculty and staff must meet the students' needs where they are in their environment. As the theorist Alexander Astin puts it, a student's input and environment lead to the outcome. This theory alone allows for no need for people associated with education, such as faculty, staff, administrators, and professors, to grow or adapt under the IEO Model.

However, when overlaying the lens of Critical Race Theory and the understanding of the systemic barriers of racism and oppression that are embedded in the academic program, the specific need for a Black mentor will move the needle of success for Black males. Although the theories have a common understanding regarding the students' effort to participate in their environment, they do not consider the complexities of an input of the Black male. The objective of the theory that is missing without Critical Race Theory is that Astin Student Involvement theory alone does not make allowance for the systemic barriers that Black males face within their academic program. To eradicate racism in the educational setting, it must be acknowledged by professors, administrators, and policy makers.

Moreover, one factor that Astin overlooked in understanding the gap between Astin and Critical Race Theory was the mixing of Black Culture or people of color. Based on the student's input, Astin may have overstepped or misunderstood the concept that we are all created equal and have equal opportunities. It is quite clear from the evidence and data from the study that a student's effort and Meritocracy imply that "work hard enough and you will get it." Nevertheless, statistics and first-hand accounts from the participants will explain that it is not always that simple. In an ideal simple world, there are equitable and equal opportunities for all, but CRT explains how that is not true which means that there are Black males who work twice as hard as their racial counter-parts but still face obstacles that can hinder their success.

Additionally, to reiterate the need for a mentor, with the consideration of the Black Male Adult Learning Success Theory, it is apparent with composition of the Scholar Identity Model and Urie Bronfenbrenner's Bioecological System Theory. This study uses a qualitative approach to examine the unique experiences of Black male adult learners in higher education and the impact of their various environments on their academic success. According to the Scholar Identity Model, Black Male students are more likely to achieve academically when they have a scholar identity and are guided by a counselor or a mentor. According to Urie Bronfenbrenner's Bioecological System Theory, individuals are embedded and interact with one another and with the individual to influence development. The difference between the Black Male Adult Learning Success Theory and the Astin Student Involvement Theory is that the Black Male Adult Learning Success Theory relies on the assistance of a counselor or another person, whereas the Astin Student Involvement Theory relies solely on the student's efforts. Having a Scholar Identity or mindset increases your chances of success. The connections and overlapping meanings of Critical Race Theory, as well as their relationship to the Black experience while Urie Bronfenbrenner's Bioecological System Theory is concerned with the system that Black males must navigate to succeed.

With this study, when the Astin IEO Model, Critical Race Theory, and Black Male Adult Learning Success Theory (BMALST) are analyzed together, it emphasizes the need for students to have support from a mentor, counselor, or professional to help alleviate the pressures of graduate school. It would be of best interest to combine the three theories for a better understanding of the Black male experience. Even though Critical Race Theory brings a perspective for people of color, more specifically the BMALST theory will lead to a more unique explanation of the Black Male experience.

Furthermore, the theories interact to produce the Emergent (FEET) Theory Furlow Engagement & Endurance Theory. The next section below will discuss how the SBMPD Model was transformed with analysis and synthesis through current and existing literature.

The Emergent FEET Theory with Theoretical Frameworks

The redefined model was shaped because of a discussion sparked by an analysis of the study viewed collectively. As the results of the study were taken a step further and expanded deeper, theory building, construction, and the lived experiences became more important. The following section will explain the transformation, the why, the significance, and what happened due to all the data synthesis. This chapter begins by describing the SBMPD in terms of knowledge, connection, and confidence theory data. The following sections will now explain how the SBMPD model goes beyond data and theory.

This study made meaning of the theoretical gaps and defined a deeper understanding of Black males to see the bigger picture for the necessities of success. Upon further review and interpretation, the Successful Black Males with a Post-Baccalaureate Degree (SBMPD) Model was transformed to reflect the theories and the research results. Although Figure 5 (the redefined SBMPD Model with the important added words) articulates the three major themes that emerged from the participants' narratives and interviews, there are needed changes to reflect the importance and significance of the data. Figure 6 shows the connections and the synthesized data working through the model and how it moves and the connections and relationship with other themes and theories combined.

From the top, the model now represents the three major theories that were used when analyzing the data that emerged from the participant's answers. First, Astin's IEO Model was useful in explaining how the students' input, and environment, affected students' output and how they viewed their educational experience. The academic performance of the student is directly proportional to the student's involvement. Therefore, these successful Black males needed to be involved with Black mentors during their educational experience. The *connections* that are created between the student and the mentor create more involvement with the institution, which in turn gives them the best opportunity to be successful in completing their degree.

Secondly, Critical Race Theory was used to explain the importance of Black males having Black mentors. Participants needed to see themselves in the profession they were pursuing and in their academic network to believe and have confidence that they belonged to their institution or university, regardless of whether it was an HBCU, PWI, or an HSI. The importance rests in the fact that the participants either wanted or had Black mentors, which shaped their success in completing their degrees.

Figure 6

The Emergent "FEET" Theory with Theoretical Concepts

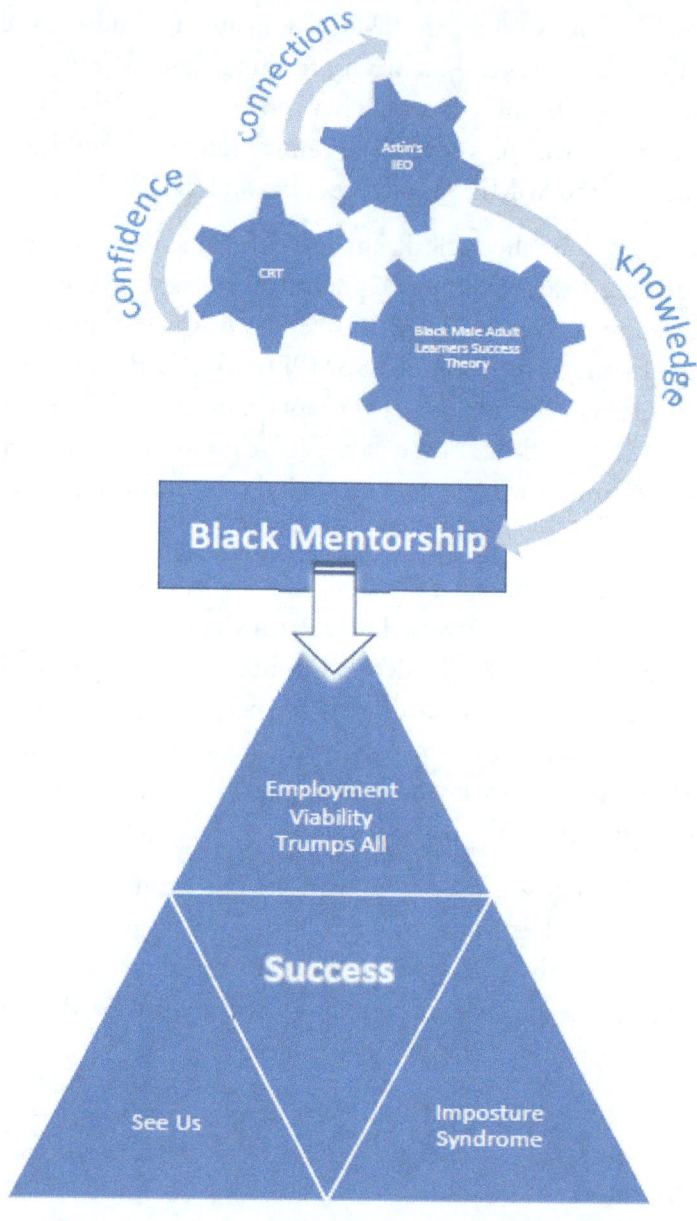

Note. This figure shows how the SBMPD Model and the theoretical frameworks have evolved to show the necessity for Black mentorships is what ultimately leads to the success of Black males. lived experience and serves as an important and useful lens for those who want to support Black people. Furthermore, CRT was beneficial and contributed to the SBMPD model's outcome. CRT is not only useful but also necessary for understanding the depth of the Black males' experiences, and if someone wants to help improve the situation, they cannot do so without thinking about it and applying Critical Race Theory. As a result, there may be a larger issue here than simply assisting black students in succeeding. One of the findings is that fighting for freedom, equality, and equity makes a difference in the educational system.

The third theory, which is suggested for future research on Black Male Adult Learners Success Theory, has a second prong regarding the Scholar Identity Model aligned with the Urie Bronfenbrenner's bioecological system theory, presents how influential and powerful it is to have a Black mentor for Black males because it provides them with someone who believes in them, stabilizes their emotional needs, and gives them *knowledge* regarding topics on and off- campus that are specific to their Black culture.

Specifically, Black graduate students at times had difficulty engaging and accessing White faculty. When interactions did occur, Black graduate students believed that White faculty (a) were naïve and oblivious to the needs of Black graduate students, (b) mistreated Black graduate students, or (c) were outright harmful. In an advising and mentoring context, Black graduate students believed that they received less guidance, more restricted academic options, and inadequate scholarly socialization than their White counterparts. (Stone et. al., 2018, p. 44)

When the connections, confidence, and knowledge increase with the student having a Black mentor, then there is an increase in success and likeliness to attain their post-baccalaureate degree. These three theories with their factors grind out and work together, which creates the necessity for Black males to have a valued Black mentor.

The quintessential need for Black males to have Black mentors requires a model that examines the three themes that made these participants successful in obtaining their degrees. The themes are Employment Viability, the need to See Us and have access to Black mentors, and overcoming the imposter syndrome, which are illustrated within their triangle and positioned within a larger triangle. With a triangle representing the most stable and strongest shape-holding heavy weights—or in this case, ideals—it is the shape that represents the three themes that guard the inner triangle of success. Each of the themes shares a side with the triangle of success, which symbolizes the need to work through these issues to reach the pinnacle of success. The notion that Employment Viability Trumps All of the other success factors is the reason it is situated at the top of the triangle of success. Without the ability to get and retain employment or to find an opportunity to financially fund tuition and living expenses, it is impossible to complete the degree. The participants who succeeded had found a resolution to this factor of Employment Viability. The other triangles in all the See Us, Imposter Syndrome, and We're All in This Together model are those that were common to the participants and found to be important to overall success. There is no necessary order in which these themes were experienced by Black males. However, they were all experienced and overcome at some point in their educational experience.

The findings and data from the Emergent (FEET) theory framework led to the construction of a conceptual map detailing what resonated with my graduate experience. As I am fully a part of this study, not just as an instrument, but also as someone who has lived through these experiences. This is not external, this is from me, authentically me, my intentions capture lived experiences on the part of my participants to help me to validate and compose my own lived experiences. Now, I will explain what that is and then describe or make meaning of what came from that.

Personal Lived Experiences Using Autoethnography

Through the methodology process of Autoethnography, the boxes of "Albert's Experiences" were coded from Chapter four as data. During the analysis, I used my coding process independently of the other codes, as if there were no other codes, and as if the data was generated from the beginning. Ten concepts emerged from the analysis-synthesis for the Conceptual map. Each box's title was displayed in the conceptual model as a box, and those titles were then classified as concepts. Among the 10 concepts, there were four major takeaways based on a review of my personal experience.

Figure 7

Conceptual Map of Personal Lived Experiences

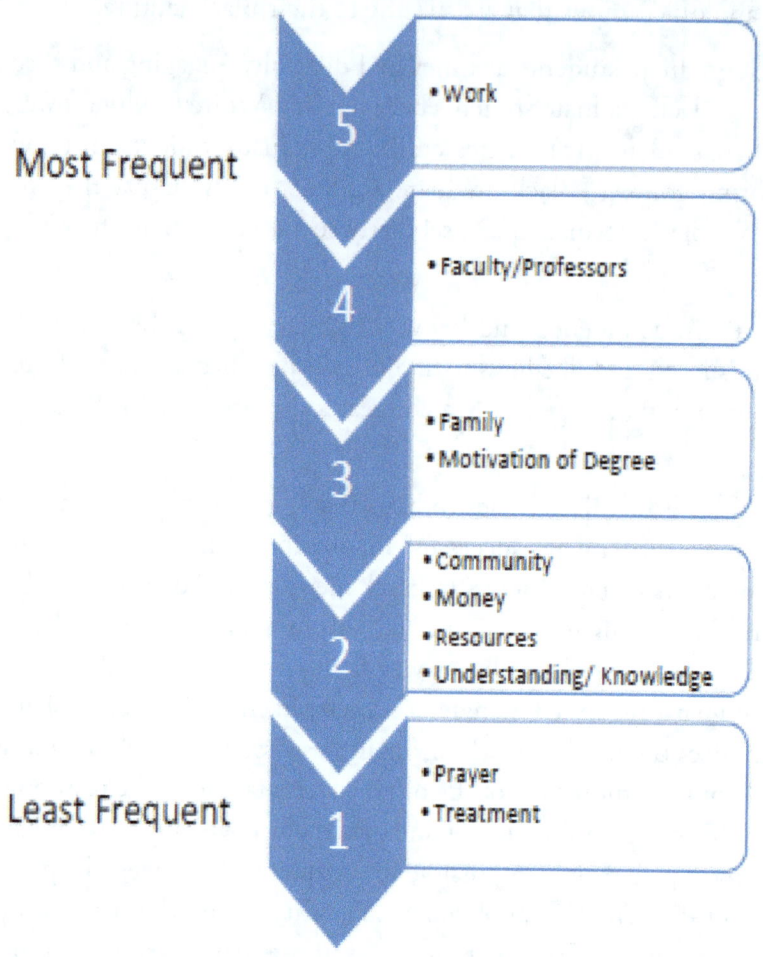

Note. This figure is derived from the text boxes of my experiences that I shared in Chapter 4. I utilized the human processes of coding by utilizing Excel and open-ended processes.

Four of the 10 concepts held most of the weight for those experiences as I reflected on the thoughts and what it meant. Most frequently found was the concept of "Work," then "Faculty/Professors," and at a tie was "Family" and "Motivation for the Degree."

The first and most important concept that emerged, according to the conceptual map consistency, was the concept of "Work". Work, in my experience, brings the entire conceptual map to an opening. When I tried to work on my dissertation without work, I had plenty of time to think. However, not being able to earn money for an extended period is not ideal for my situation. It was imperative and urgent that I put in work because I've always had the mindset of "hard work beats talent when talent is not working hard". With that said, nothing was ever handed to me in my experience. I had to go out there and find creative ways to make ends meet and pay the bills. Even though I don't have any money to give back at the moment, I give back by volunteering in my community. Work was a lifesaver for me because I worked and served others rather than myself. I discovered true joy and happiness at work. Humanitarians, work provided me with a sense of purpose and dignity by allowing me to not only provide for myself but also feed my family. "Work" had a significant and unexpected impact on my life because it provided structure. I learned how to stay focused and set aside time and days to complete tasks. I developed a work ethic in which I wouldn't let my emotions or body get in the way of my work performance. As I work to increase my net worth and the value of my worth, I realize that I am on my own; it is up to me to put in the effort, make the necessary connections, and seek help as needed.

The second concept of mentorship with faculty and professors emerges. Learning from my professors and other faculty members made this a memorable experience. The consistency of the words and the relationship between what the professor and the faculty meant to me were vital.

Fortunately, through my master's and PhD programs, I was able to connect, communicate, and demonstrate commitment to one another's interests with most of my professors.

To succeed as a doctoral student, having a connection with your professor or faculty is critical. They do have the authority to sign off and award you a passing grade or not.

Nonetheless, professors must perform to the best of their abilities. I must do my best, and there are consequences if I do not listen to their advice. A combination of consequences, for example, could be a longer time to complete a degree. Which, because of the domino effect theory, you now have to pay more money and deal with additional issues, such as getting a professor to provide feedback in two weeks

My professors encouraged me to be great and to be aware even when I was finishing my dissertation; they reminded me that I must consider the importance of leaving a legacy. I was informed, and I now understand that. You can't lay a good foundation if you don't know what you're doing and why you're doing it. You're doing it; you must have reasons and rationales to offer for what you do and what you present. My professors provided me with valuable information. I didn't realize it at first, but I wanted to be where my professors were.

As I mentioned in Chapter 4, being without an academic chair and then having two academic chairs switch a month before my final defense was shocking. It felt like I was nearing the finish line, but it kept moving further away. However, I'd like to express my gratitude and honor the fact that my dissertation improved from the first time I thought I was ready for defense. Although it was not at my desired speed or time, I'm grateful for the effective two-way communication my professors and I established during the time I was completing my dissertation. Being open and honest with them about my inability to do something. And, conversely, my professors being open and honest with me, admitting that they didn't know the full scope of the black experience, and suggesting that I elaborate in certain areas, was mutually beneficial. There is enormous value in telling someone that you need to dig deeper to grow as a professional. Gaining their trust and developing a reputation by demonstrating my willingness to listen and improve. As a result, I was able to focus on honing my academic scholarly writing and presentation abilities. Professors taught me how to organize my thoughts and write a written dialogue about what I'm presenting. Assisting in the demonstration of how a person handles nervousness because they may be unsure what to say.

The positive feedback and advice I've received from professors and faculty has been extremely valuable to me. Next, the concept of "family" is as important as assets or a business plan. In my experience, the family has been the backbone, foundation, or structure of success, allowing me to learn and grow through adversity and hardship. By going in the opposite direction of destruction, my family helps me mentally and at times physically. My family is always present, open, and honest with me. What works is family support and the idea of going all in. Combined with uplifting extended family members, my support system, my friends are my family, and my brothers and sisters are all family. I'm confident that I'm on the right track because I see everyone else succeeding around me. To be honest, I wouldn't be me without my family's love and support, even if they hadn't gone through what I was going through. I will continue to strive for it and must keep my eyes on the prize. Every step of the way to completing the degree was a source of excitement and celebration.

I am beyond blessed and fortunate to have a wonderful family that motivated and encouraged me to pursue my doctorate degree.

Also tied for third is the "motivation of the degree" which has equipped and helped me develop a competitive edge in the job market. Being a professional in the field of research has enabled a way of life for all types of decisions. By learning new ways to give back, I'm making good use of my communication abilities. The constant pursuit of the degree taught me that I needed to be more involved in the process than simply trusting it. It was up to me to improve my writing skills, not only to sound intelligent but also to be straightforward and to be loud and clear about what was going on in this phenomenon. Information that I thought was powerful and obvious to me was not so obvious or understandable to others.

Eventually, the conceptual map influenced me in terms of making sense of my post-baccalaureate experience. The four major takeaways created inspiration (Family & Degree), participation (Faculty/Professors), and expectation (Work). Although the Conceptual Map of personal lived experiences is additional data examined through my experiences, it mostly aligns with the data from the other participants and offers additional validity to the SBMPD Model and can be examined through the Furlow Engagement and Endurance Theory, which is the research's most vivid contribution to knowledge.

Contribution to Knowledge

This study offers a concise perspective of the outlook of higher education for Black males in modern times. It serves to mark the progress, achievements, and pitfalls of the educational environment. It also serves to guide us in moving forward with progressive programs and processes to ensure growth. The findings and lessons learned from this study can be used to develop different but critical approaches to understanding and making sense of the experiences of Black males in post-baccalaureate education, which are in serious need of attention. This research better meets the needs of complex social transformation for education, especially post- graduate programs, and it articulates the experiences of Black males with the need to be able to be themselves in their educational setting without feeling that they are out of place or not accepted.

Examining the findings through the important new perspective connecting Astin's IEO Model and the Critical Race Theory is what brings value of knowledge to a new way of thinking. The findings of the qualitative research deepen and broaden the understanding of Critical Race Theory by providing a unique and new application to Astin's Student Involvement Theory. The research also connects the missing ingredient for black males by using Astin's Student Involvement Theory to better understand the importance of black mentors. The difference between using Astin's IEO Model with critical race theory versus the Black male adult learner success theory is the fact that both theories are 26 to 28 years old, showing it is pertinent and grounded even in today's time.

Even with that in mind, Alexander Astin's I-E-O model may have missed or overlooked a perspective from the Black male. For example, the participants mention that their input (Black males) is most likely to be subjected to an embedded form of racism or old traditional ways.

Astin's theory is flawed for Black males because it automatically presumes and assumes inclusion and social equality within an environment that would create an output to inspire career and educational opportunities for all. However, in circumstances that were explained by the participants, there are instances where the increase in engagement with their environment not only would not allow the student to progress, but at times would hinder the student's development to continue with their post-graduate degree. Whether it be due to outside factors of feeling like they are not seen as Black men or cannot be themselves, or the feeling of not belonging in the environment due to going through the imposter syndrome, or the lack of fiscal means as Employment Viability Trumps All, these environmental factors would become barriers if they did not have a Black mentor to help them in some way overcome these external obstacles. Ironically, our country stands on a foundation that speaks similarly to Astin's theory. If you try hard enough and put in enough effort, then you will succeed from any entry point you are placed in. However, Black males and others, know that this prerogative is simply not that true. There are many more factors that have a place in that equation than just 1+2=3. Many Black males that have been trying to add up 1 + 2 together by obtaining their bachelor's degree, obtaining even their master's degree, yet cannot complete a post-graduate degree due to these barriers that can and will be remedied with a Black mentor.

Aside from discussing the theories and ideas, the two, now interwoven, theoretical frameworks aim to show how this body of research (1) contributes new evidence by collecting original data, (2) uses theory as a basis for interpreting and understanding the data, (3) challenges an established theory of Astin's Student Involvement Theory and (4) requires it to be applied with a lens of Critical Race Theory.

The SBMPD model can be understood as a representation of a group of themes from the data. A model provides the individual with a structural representation of the phenomenon, allowing him/her to gain a fuller understanding of it. A model can lay the foundation for a theory. Models can be considered as a representation created to explain a theory. This allows the individual to build his/her theory based on the constructed model.

In turn, with the SBMPD Model, the body of research creates a grounded theory. The theory presented from the findings of the data is to be called the Furlow Engagement and Endurance Theory. The name was inspired by my last name, Furlow, and the acknowledgement of the need for engagement and endurance in order to have black males succeed through the barriers that are created in their journey to obtaining a post-graduate degree. Furthermore, the Furlow Engagement and Endurance Theory a) encourages Black males to find a Black person or group of people with whom they feel comfortable sharing their vulnerabilities regarding their educational experiences; b) embraces that the Black male's struggle has given them the courage to endure through their barriers and allows the student to persist to completion; and, c) reassures the Black male student to find a way to be comfortable with being uncomfortable. The theory in totality promotes a strong community circle by strengthening the student-staff relationships with effective mentorship programs, but also student-to-student relationships by validating similar experiences with their peers that will encourage them to persist. It promotes emotional intelligence by being comfortable with the uncomfortable and improves the overall well-being of the university. The benefits of this theory may support the number and endurance of Black males in post-graduate school by providing institutions and students with a model of tools that will validate Black males to enable success to completion.

Implications for Practice

The Furlow Engagement and Endurance Theory with the use of the Successful Black Males with a Post-baccalaureate Degree model has implications which are imperative for future practices. They are based on chapter four's emergent themes and findings. The use of the Successful Black Males with a Post-baccalaureate Degree (SBMPD) model versus other models can contribute to the vitality of future Black male students, which will encourage the readiness of the student to overcome obstacles and prepare institutions for Black male students. The practice of Black representation in mentorships is the single most important exercise that academic institutions can implement for the Black male population. Finally, the implications for the practice of Foundational Advocacy are broken into three subcategories: financial resources, mental health promotion, and an accepted and accessible climate for Black male students. Three implications for practice are the SBMPD Model versus other models, Black Representation in Mentorship, and Foundational Advocacy.

SBMPD Model Versus Others

The first implication is that the SBMPD model should be implemented by institutions, universities, faculties, and staff. When compared to other models of Black males in higher education, there is a lack of focus on Black Males with post-baccalaureate degrees. Much of the literature and historical research focused solely on undergraduate students. This model allows for concentration on graduate students and professional degrees.

Other Models. Other models that were examined but not comparable were the Socio-Ecological Outcomes Model, the Prove-Them-Wrong Syndrome, and the African American Male Theory (AAMT). For example, African American men in community colleges are the focus of the Socio-Ecological Outcomes Model (Wood & Harris, 2012). This model incorporates domains to tell the story of community college success. The study meets the demographic by focusing on Black men, but it does not make a concerted effort toward post-baccalaureate education (Moore et al., 2003).

Another case in point is the Prove-Them-Wrong Syndrome, which was developed to address the persistence of Black undergraduate males in STEM fields. Prove-Them-Wrong Syndrome participants discussed how they overcame stereotypes and barriers in their major. While Michael, Ray, and Dr. Riley had some specific thoughts about proving others wrong, many of the participants mentioned having been treated unfairly in the past and planning and striving to get through the difficulties they faced. The prove-them-wrong syndrome, on the other hand, did not correspond with the study's purpose or educational level focus. The African American Male Theory (AAMT) by Bush and Bush (2013) looked at the place of African American boys and men in society. AAMT has an ecological approach and is founded on an Afrocentric heritage. While the participants in this study recognized their role and challenges in society, the AAMT did not lend itself to focusing solely on Black males' post- baccalaureate experiences. The AAMT had a restriction when it came to discussing the entire Black men's post-baccalaureate experience (Bush & Bush, 2013; Harper, 2012; Moore et al., 2003). Despite this, none of these models or frameworks addressed post-baccalaureate professional education.

The goal of this study was to concentrate entirely on Black male post-baccalaureate professional education. Reviewing the existing literature on other models, there has been limited focus on PhD students but not in combination of various fields of MBA, in addition to Lawyer and DPT (Doctor of Physical Therapy) professional degrees. In addition to the dynamics of the study, the study also contains current and past students that have completed their degrees or who are on track to finish their degrees.

The difference between the previous models is their focus on undergraduate students, and the SBMPD model is inclusive of post-baccalaureate students. How those differences translate into transformational strategies for professors, administrators, and students to use as a blueprint for the need for survival when it comes to Black males in higher education settings. The participants mentioned a time of isolation when they realized that all they had was themselves and other graduate students to propel them to keep striving and matriculating toward their post-baccalaureate degree. This highlights the importance of the SBMPD model, which is intertwined with the conversion of three components: knowledge, confidence, and connections revolving through the intersections of the study's three major themes.

The Knowledge component evolved, as did the participant's thoughts and feelings. The idea of intrinsic motivation is knowing yourself and understanding others' understanding of yourself. One of the major themes of imposter syndrome was utilized as a tool to attempt to discover what motivates them individually. When they realized their true selves, the value of Other Mothering, with the relentless mentality and spiritual lifting, was evident.

Furthermore, the Confidence component of achievement and independence is the difference between choice and want, but more of a need to survive. Then there is the aspect of faculty and student relationships, such as advising and mentoring, which is connected to the second major theme, Employment Viability Trumps All. Those assisting Black male post-baccalaureate students will be able to identify tangible factors that contribute to their success. Employment is a global need, and the post-baccalaureate achievement segment provided insights into how Black men can be successful with limited resources and by working with what they have. The idea of turning negative situations into positive ones was mentioned by several of the participants. Focus on circumstances or situations that they can control.

Finally, the Connections component of the one of the major themes of Black immersion considers both internal and external influences that must be considered by Black male post-baccalaureate students and those assisting them. Extrinsic motivation, parental education level, full graduate school funding, and the ability to deal with systemic racism are all Connection factors. Continuation of the outer self, factors influencing academic research learning techniques, challenges and barriers, self-awareness, faculty, and support from external factors may impede learning the value of education. Initiatives that are culturally sensitive help to create an inclusive model.

Black Representation in Mentorship

The second implication, the one that will easily make the biggest impact, is to ensure that universities have Black representation in mentoring programs for Black men as they advance through their post-baccalaureate experience. Black males must see other Black leadership figures, especially other Black males, in the roles and positions that they are hoping to become.

Sanders (2016) summarized that Nettles and Millett (2006) found that

African American students choose mentors of the same race more often than they are assigned advisors of the same race. Faculty mentorship needs to be intentional and holistic... articulated mentoring is essential to the professional and academic growth of African American doctoral students. Pairing faculty and students by research interest, personality, research approach, and future aspirations are a few examples that can be utilized to match faculty and students. (p. 6)

In some instances, the lack of Black mentors is not due to a lack of interest from Black professors or leaders in academia, but to the climate that hurts those who are trying to mentor. The need for an institution to see these opportunities as important is just as important as the need for an environment that acknowledges the reasons and ways for which Black mentorship has been deficient. There is not a lack of desire by Black professionals to help mentor other Black professionals, but instead, there are other factors that limit these mentorships from being created. Edwards and Ross (2018) state.

Research-oriented and extensive doctoral-granting institutions have identified concerns that produce stress, dissatisfaction, and a climate of distrust. These concerns established the reasons for a lack of presence (underrepresentation) of the Black faculty and a lack of success of Black faculty at PWIs.

Faculty and institutions can provide support for Black men with an interest in becoming faculty by providing authorship or co-authorship opportunities for publications. Educational institutions would benefit from addressing the lack of Black faculty at their institution and implementing an environment that would create less stress, a climate of trust and satisfaction for Black faculty who wish to become involved mentors of their institutions and thus become critical to the success of Black males completing their post-baccalaureate program.

In connection with the findings from chapter 4, Black Representation was echoed unanimously amongst 16 participants. Bishop expressed his thoughts on the subject in this way,

It's not just going to be like I'm a student because yes, I'm a student but I wanted them to see me as a person as well at the end of the day. Again, this is super important. That was like my top criteria was to have a faculty member or an advisor of color. Couldn't have been any other way. I preferred a man of color, but I also applied to programs for women of color which is I felt like either way I'm going to have a person of color that I can have a good relationship with. I felt like that would support me in the program. I could easily go and talk to them about anything and everything. It was going to be best to set me up to get through the program.

Observing educators and administrators of color is critical to the dynamics of interpersonal relationships for Black male students. It enables them to build upon their strengths. They feel acknowledged, respected, and understood. The relationship offers Black male students a sense of support. Networking with people who are like you can afford students more opportunities. By having the institutions See Us and the opportunity to have Black mentors' support, the challenges and barriers, whether intentional or unintentional, are reduced, and a capacity to deal with and successfully navigate their trials is created.

Foundational Advocacy

This concept was generated from the findings of the data by acknowledging the importance of working and maintaining a healthy life balance was mentioned by all the participants. Dr. Langston stated the importance of employment while in graduate school by stating That's eighty-five percent of it [financial resources], right, there's money. Yes, sir. It's not ours. That's it. I don't think it's that complicated. Watch. You'll get a whole bunch of answers to that question. That'd be like super deep and or rather struggle confidence, toxic masculinity. No. Just give me enough resources to survive and be comfortable.

Having financial resources is the most important factor in pursuing a post-baccalaureate degree. The participants stated that they intend to pay it forward and that they will keep their eyes on the goal. Although the participants did not have equal access to education, they were able to transcend the pitfalls and triumph in the end. Everyone made the best of a bad situation. They are now a part of the 1% of people who made it to the end.

Through these findings and others like them, the final implication for practice is for institutions to have foundational advocacy in place for Black men to succeed at their institutions. Foundational advocacy is established in three ways: through economic resources, mental health promotion, and an accepted and accessible climate. Economic resources, mental health promotion, and an accepted and accessible climate assist Black men in being able to navigate their post-baccalaureate programs and institutions. It also facilitates them having financial support and challenges the norm of accruing debt, while also encouraging a safe and healthy learning environment where they can focus on their educational needs rather than the "isms" of the world outside of the classroom.

Economic resources and opportunities are the crux of where success begins. Being able to provide economic resources in support of Black Males is critical. According to Gasman et al. (2008), "additionally, finances weigh heavily on the minds of African American students and contribute to personal and academic stress in graduate school" (p. 133). Colleges and universities can offer plans at the institutional and program levels that will allow financial assistance but also encourage Black men to focus on their research interests, which will collectively allow them to contribute to the research of their choosing. By making graduate assistantships available for full-time students, or tuition assistance for students working full-time, a world of difference will be made. Additional scholarships are vital as they can contribute to tuition or other financial obligations that Black men may have along the way. Economic resources support will allow Black men to pursue their doctorate without the reliance on loans and obtaining debt. According to Lundy-Wagner et al., institutional financial support appears to be related to the production of underrepresented minority doctoral degree recipients (2013). Having financial freedom and additional options opens doors for Black men that are not always readily available to them. It allows them to pursue their dreams and follow research that is of interest to them.

The second segment of Foundational Advocacy is regarding the promotion of Mental Health Awareness. Mental Health was an important topic that was channeled from the imposter syndrome. Participants suggested that their mental health was affected by the feeling of being an imposter at their level of education. At times, the need to deal with this feeling created a mental framework for the participants to reach out and request help. This need to process their feelings of imposter syndrome led participants to seek help, giving them the confidence to overcome it. Perhaps the negative connotation of the word "imposter" would at times discourage participants from accepting the need to deal with these feelings of feeling less than. If the gentlemen in the study had been prepared for the different programs and obstacles beforehand, they would have understood what they were going through, which was not so much being an imposter as it was preparing oneself for an environment designed for people of a different ethnic background.

When dealing with emotional grievances, levels of confidence, and cultural factors, there are times where Black males need resources to encourage a positive mental perspective. Not only is it important to get Black males into post-baccalaureate programs, but it is important to consider what makes them successful and productive while they are in the programs. Nettles and Millett (2006) were concerned that black doctoral students were having low research productivity in the education, sciences, and mathematics fields. Research opportunities will be critical for Black men as they enhance their curriculum vitae and apply for faculty roles. Having areas of low research productivity is a perspective of the mental health endurance of Black males. With a better relationship with their mental health, Black males can contribute more consistently to the world of academia. Authorship opportunities also give them opportunities to work on their research skills to become better scholars. The promotion of mental health can involve like-minded support groups, faith-based support groups, one-on-one counseling, and even specific Black male groups that can share ideas and create additional partnerships to encourage a positive mindset.

The third prong of foundational advocacy includes ensuring a safe, diverse, and equal environment that creates an accepted and accessible climate. Dr. Samuel reflected on a time when he was abruptly confronted by an alumnus who assumed his admission to law school had absolutely nothing to do with his abilities but instead was due to affirmative action. Dr. Samuel divulged:

I interviewed some alumni from the '60s, and there was this one judge who told me, he said, "Without a doubt, if it wasn't for affirmative action, I wouldn't have been admitted to Texas law, I wouldn't have gotten into law school." He said, "I'll tell you this, affirmative action didn't make A's in the class, affirmative action didn't walk across that stage and get that diploma."

Affirmative action was intended to create opportunities for people who might not otherwise have belonged.

These types of laws allowed black males to overcome the imposter syndrome within the higher educational setting and connect with the Chapter 2 literature review in the section, Access to Black Males in Graduate School. As some participants mentioned, their journeys included dealing with learning how to navigate white spaces within their program, department, and institution. An institution's commitment to a diverse environment can have a positive impact on the experiences of Black male doctoral students. Having institutions intentionally develop an accepted and accessible climate will allow black men to be free and not have the burden of feeling as though they must educate their peers about black men or people of color. To Michael, a participant in this study, the meaning of an accepted and accessible climate has to do with how institutions can focus on not only bringing black males to the completion of their post-baccalaureate degrees but how they can do it even better. Michael explained:

Those are the ways I would think to begin with by making programs, student enrollment for African American males going forward is having it very student-driven…. That's one of those things I said, that's a tough question, because then you're asking faculty members or administrators to look inward and saying, "What am I putting out and what am I repelling? What am I attracting?" I think that level of, say for me, that's after I think, but that's my normal thought process is going into, "What did I do to make the situation better or worse?" I said, "That comes from working with kids," saying, "Did I tell students this way and make them cry, because I hurt their feelings?" Now you translate that into adults of saying, "Did this student leave because I could have done something better?" That's where it's like, "I did my job, but could I have done it better?" Then that's one of those things of saying, "Let's learn from those experiences."

The point is to ask institutions to mediate and request feedback on their programs in which Black males were successful or unsuccessful. Having acceptable and accessible climates for black males means there will be an inclusive environment that will help prevent students from having to self-censor when they are faced with racism, are questioned in the classroom, or are excluded from the support of their academic peers. Institutions must also provide programming (i.e., orientation, seminars, speaker series) geared toward Black men. These programs will assist Black men in having a sense of belonging on campus and in their doctoral programs. Felder and Barker (2013) stated:

When considering the racial and cultural experiences of doctoral students, institutions should embrace policies that support diversity and racial awareness initiatives. These initiatives can be effective only if they are part of the daily institutional operations and are viewed as a priority by stakeholders. (p. 3)

Foundational advocacy is critical for black men matriculating and completing their post-baccalaureate journeys, but it must be an institutional commitment on behalf of the entire university and not the sole responsibility of one person or department.

Recommendations for Future Research

Further qualitative studies with Black men in academia should be done and debated in open forums, not to contextualize their experiences, but to genuinely bring Black men to visibility as true academics. Participants in this study, in a variety of ways, acknowledged that many factors influenced them on their educational journeys, including their positive and negative experiences. Participants explained how they were impacted and able to learn from both experiences within their educational situation. The notion that these students had to endure both experiences is what motivated them to persist with conferring their degrees. This study specifically highlighted the experiences of the participants and narrated a counter-story to the typical message regarding Black males' lack of success. More research may be required to examine how positive and negative experiences influence the failure of Black males to complete their post-baccalaureate degrees.

The study yielded several actions and research recommendations related to Black men's experiences earning their post-baccalaureate degree. Evidence from the findings suggest three recommendations for future research: re-imagine higher education; hire more Black males; and provide Black centers and expand on Black student groups.

Reimagining Higher Education

The first recommendation, to reimagine higher education, and to restructure higher education, is a potential research topic. All 16 participants have the skills, professional experience, and academic expertise to make a difference in higher education. In an insightful contribution to knowledge, what if we reimagined higher education as a set of intuitions that values inclusivity? The idea of being more selective in who is recruited and admitted was exposed during the research. Institutions must develop a more conscious and thoughtful communication style with Black male students. Separate from a conventional orientation, support services must provide in-depth access to what university life is like before registering at their graduate institutions. Tim suggested that,

They have to get to where they are. So, I was told about grad school and pushed and supported again. But I don't remember like a recruiter anything coming to me. So I need to get to where these students are, but also create a great support system. So for me as a black male, it was tough and I had to find and feel my network, if I wasn't as resilient and as resourceful as I was, who would have said that I would have graduated or if I wanted to graduate with, I finished with a positive mindset that I do have. So we had to do better with our recruitment, but also we got to create systems in place to be able to support and retain our black men.

Black men who are serious about pursuing a post-baccalaureate degree could thrive with additional academic support programs. Helpful resources for Black males who identify as being Black and faith-based, first-generation graduate students should be included in these initiatives. This would help with the imposter syndrome and dive deeper into research regarding additional contributions and how to combat the feeling of the imposter syndrome for black male students.

Reimagine higher education with an embedded experience that will provide a positive environment for students, as well as a network of faculty and peer connections. It would also mean creating a purposeful curriculum to introduce black students to their potential networks and groups.

Consider this scenario with 16 participants: Higher education is adaptable and prepared for changes, such as how classes are becoming more asynchronous. Having classes online and face-to-face, a hybrid style of curriculum, being able to reach out to everyone through technology and communication while working through the pandemic safely. The overall picture of education for undergraduate and graduate attainment is changing at a rapid speed. According to data from the 2020 National Student Clearinghouse, undergraduate and graduate students' post-pandemic prospects are bright. "In terms of undergraduates, there was a 3.3 percent drop in college enrollment from 2019 last fall, and there appears to be a 2.9 percent drop from 2020 this spring (NSC, 2021, p. 1). Graduate enrollment appears to have increased by 4.3% this spring in comparison to 2020. The National Student Clearinghouse reports that, surprisingly, graduate enrollment has increased since the pandemic. According to the Pew Research Center,

Graduate enrollment is up in 38 states since the pandemic, with double-digit increases this fall in Mississippi (+17.9%), Virginia (+10.6), and New Hampshire (+10.1%)." On the other hand, 11 states are experiencing declines ranging from 0.2 percent to 4.7 percent. Idaho, New Hampshire, Utah, and West

Virginia all saw increases in undergraduate and graduate enrollment. (Mitchell, et. al, 2020)

As a direct consequence, it makes sense to rethink higher education so that more focus is placed on research involving Black males. If the goal is to gain a better understanding of black educational needs, the possibilities for future research are endless. Although this one study cannot address all issues that emerge during this investigation, it is hoped that it will evolve into and will be a continuing evolution of ongoing research and progressive initiatives.

Hiring More Faculty and Professors of Color

Another future recommendation is to hire more faculty and professors of color at the graduate level and beyond. Hiring more black professors as role models for black male students is imperative. According to Underwood (2019):

Increasing the number of black male teachers in schools across the nation requires strategic planning, including collaborative efforts at the national, state, district, and local levels. A long-term commitment to resources and continuous championing for diversity in our nation's classrooms remains the most promising way to effectively staff schools with Black male educators. (p. 7)

The presence of people of color, especially Black males, in administrative positions and as professors on campuses can increase the morale and involvement of the entire campus. The disparity between the number of white educators and educators of color is astronomical. The make-up of employees in an organization gives insight into the culture of that organization. The National Center for Education Statistics (2020) details:

The racial/ethnic and gender distribution of faculty varied by academic rank at degree-granting postsecondary institutions in fall 2018. For example, among full-time professors, 53 percent were White males, 27 percent were White females, 8 percent were Asian/Pacific Islander males, and 3 percent were Asian/Pacific Islander females. Black males, black females, and Hispanic males each accounted for 2 percent of full-time professors. (NCES, 2020)

Black educators, as seen in the numbers, are sparse. This implies that either they are not sought out to be educators in universities and colleges or the culture or climate of the institution has not proved welcoming or feasible to eligible candidates. Bishop expressed his interest in seeing more people of color in this manner:

I think the biggest piece is hiring more men of color and women of color first so we just see ourselves in these positions and not just be like, "I went to college and I only had like two Black professors out of the hundred classes I took. If you're not at an HBCU, obviously when you go to an HBCU, it's very different. By the same token, I think hiring more will also open that door for people to think, "Oh man, I could do that. "Again, it comes back to that relationship. If you're hiring more and there are people that build a relationship with students, students are going to want to stay around or be more involved and be like, "Hey, how did you get to be a faculty member or how did you get to do this?" That opens the door to be like, "Oh, I did this." Then individuals can get interested that way and get into these programs. I think it first comes with institutions hiring more of us because they're out there, but again the struggle was real with getting these jobs, getting these tenure jobs, or getting dean of students or vice president jobs or those different types of things.

The importance of having a black mentor or advisor had a significant effect on the participants' experiences as well. Participants voiced the importance of seeing themselves represented in the educational population they attend. According to Anjali Adukia of the *National Bureau of Economic Research*, a similar sentiment was shared by stating:

I think of representation as a fundamental need: if you don't see yourself represented in the world around you, it can limit what you see as your potential; and similarly, if you don't see others represented, it can limit what you see as their potential; and if you only see certain people represented, then this shapes your subconscious defaults. (Adukia, et. al., 2021, pg. 4)

In recognition of the value of mentors in this research, Dr. Igbo made the following statement on the importance of seeing someone who looked like him by saying

If I want to be a professor, but I've never seen a black professor, I don't – I say, personally, me, I have to see what I'm going to be. So, I want to see a black professor, so my advisor, most likely, or my mentor is most likely going to be a black advisor. The same situation with, you know, anything I ever did, if I want to become a president of a university, most likely, I'll have a mentor who was a president, so they could help me understand what it means to be a black male president, and what ramifications come with that.

It would help to raise the success rate of Black males in graduate school if we recruited in Black areas and employed more Black professors. To address the challenges of attracting, keeping, and advancing Black male educators, policymakers, and school administrators we must explore and adopt long-term solutions aimed at creating inclusive, fair, and welcoming school environments in which all students can excel. Universities that acknowledge how the presence and positive example of more Black professors on all campuses can make students believe that they, too, can become professors or even earn a post-baccalaureate degree can help students believe in themselves.

Black Engagement Centers and Curriculums

The final recommendation is to establish or construct Black centers where Black students can go to receive useful information about resources and funding opportunities. For example, it could be in a student center, welcoming center, and/ or a website page; a part of the institution that could provide this information for Black students. It may prove impactful as well to implement a program or curriculum in which programs within institutions prepare a curriculum for Black males that is designed to encompass their demographic. Building a Black center or more Black colleges or institutions should be a priority in revolutionizing higher education. Dr. Langston stated:

We should build more Black colleges. We should build more graduate programs with funding at Black colleges.... I believe wholeheartedly what I just said. But in all honesty, I was having a moment. No, I just think they should do what they should, which is build more black colleges. They should build programming at Black colleges. But I also think that if you don't have parallel institutions, then there needs to be very strategic "intro- institutions" There need to be institutions within the institutions that service black communities that have some level of security and independence but still work within the mainstream. If we're talking about a white school, you know that we're working within a mainstream program there at that PWI.

The concept of a place where Black male graduate students can learn and prepare for graduate school while correspondingly easing the pressures of graduate school may help raise mental health awareness. 16 participants suggested constructing or integrating a Black center where they could go to interact with people of similar backgrounds. Dr. Langston's key thoughts are similar to those of other participants; they won't feel so alienated, and they'll be able to distinguish between undergraduate and graduate school. Even the encouragement of Black organizations off-campus but still related to the university, such as Black fraternities, would be beneficial. While there are almost always white fraternities sponsored or encouraged by the campuses, rarely are those same groups established or encouraged for Black students. The significance of networking and establishing contact with a suitable colleague or professor in the fraternities is of key importance. They provide that support system, brotherhood, reliability, and mentorship among peers. Also, a group could be created to be an open, safe space to discuss mental health issues that specifically arise in the Black population. It is simple inclusions like this that can change the inclusivity and culture of the institutions by offering and encouraging such groups to form.

Furthermore, while the value of having a black center varied, the main challenge for most participants was speaking up and wanting the same resources and connections as their peers. It is important to create a balanced curriculum that includes everyone and brings everyone together. Having a place to prepare graduate students for what lies ahead was frequently mentioned by participants in this study. As Ray said:

When I compare it to other institutions, I have friends who are in doc programs at other institutions, the support that they get is totally different. Right now, I'm figuring it all out by myself really about publishing and research and navigating grants and all this stuff and it's like, looking at other people's like, I have friends who are at Georgia, Florida State, Colorado State. They're like, "Oh no, this is built into our program. Well, this is what we're doing. Doing this and that". My program is more they say we are faculty base but the higher-ed part of LSU does not have that assistance. Other programs at LSU, where I have friends who have political science and sociology like," Dang, you all doing all this? I don't know what this is." It's been a lot of figuring stuff out on my own. Navigating stuff. I've had some battles with some of the faculty.

These are unfortunate circumstances that have affected not only Ray but also the majority of the participants. Even though a university lacks the same resources and services as others, there is always the possibility of adopting a more inclusive and diverse graduate curriculum. The participants indicated that, while it is the student's responsibility to network and seek advice from upperclassmen and people who have completed the program, there is a need for a space where Black graduate students can collaborate and collectively steer the program in the right direction.

Conclusion

This study is a thorough body of research based on the experiences of 16 Black males who have completed a post-baccalaureate program and received their degrees. Exploring this phenomenon with rigor and boldness, this study highlights the instances that were empowering and seeks to set a precedence for addressing and correcting situations that impaired not only the participants of the study but also myself. As a Black male, I unknowingly became an observer/researcher and an active participant who could contribute to the data of the research.

Even though my experiences were similar to the 16 participants in the study, some situations differed. However, similar experiences took place for all participants within these graduate institutions. This research showed the importance of the Black community, which is usually not discussed, in how it is important to see others that look and have similar experiences or perceptions as the Black male student. It allowed some people to vent and to be heard like they never had been before. Also, understanding the intent of the research is to help future Black male students, encouraging participants to be vulnerable and honest in using accurate observations to make an impact.

This research and the summary of findings present an abundance of information that will transform Black males' educational experience. Upon analyzing the participants' philosophical statements and their interviews, the most prevalent and important factors of success for Black males were the notions that employment viability trumps all, the occurrence and overcoming of the imposter syndrome, the need to See Us within the higher educational institutions, and the need for Black mentorships for students at colleges and universities within post-baccalaureate programs. With educational institutions, colleges, and universities having access to this information, post-baccalaureate programs need to be transformed to reflect the positive findings of this research. Not only will it make the black male a better and more viable candidate for graduation, but it will provide the student with tools that can be carried outside of the classroom and into their successful, productive careers.

The research's implications that can be used for practice should be present in every post-baccalaureate program, whether an HBCU, HSI, or PWI. The three implications for practice compare the SBMPD model to other models to show its imperial superiority, and ensuring black representation in mentorship programs creates a foundation of advocacy that is established in three ways: through economic resources, mental health promotion, and an accepted and accessible climate within the post-graduate programs. These future practices are tangible changes that can transform the environment and entice black males into post-baccalaureate programs. The implications for practice in conjunction with the summary of recommendations for future research will reveal the secret formulas for the success of black males in post- baccalaureate programs. If educational institutions learn more about reimagining higher education, hiring more black males, creating black engagement centers or curricula, and if more research is done on the Black Male Adult Learner Success Theory, more black males will complete their desired programs, which will in turn attract even more black males to stay devoted to their programs.

What distinguishes this data from others is that it goes beyond the opinions and experiences of just a few. Instead, it is filled with innovative ideas, solutions, and accurate, in-depth, valuable data from 16 participants (in addition to myself) interacting with theories and real-world situations to understand the complexities of the Black male graduate experience phenomenon. Moreover, additional contributions of knowledge that substantially enhance research on the success factors for Black males who have completed a post-baccalaureate program are outlined in Figure 6, The Emergent (FEET) Furlow Engagement and Endurance Theory. The contributing knowledge from the Furlow Engagement and Endurance Theory a) encourages Black males to find a Black person or group of people with whom they feel comfortable sharing their vulnerabilities regarding their educational experiences; b) embraces that the Black male's struggle has given them the courage to endure through their barriers and allows the student to persist to completion; and, c) reassures the Black male student to find a way to be comfortable with being uncomfortable. This model is the new pinnacle for all institutions to use to include and increase the success of Black males in post-baccalaureate programs. By increasing the connections, confidence, and knowledge of Black students with Black mentorships, scholars can overcome imposter syndrome, embody the need to See Us through Black partnerships on campuses, and find financial solutions to the fact that Employment Viability is necessary as it trumps all.

This collection of research offers ground-breaking information that is required as well as insight, given in the narratives and personal experiences, into why it is crucial to concentrate on the positive representation of black men in graduate education. The benefits of increasing Black males' success in post-graduate schools are abundant; such as increased retention rates of Black males, increased minority grants for the post-graduate programs, raising income and net wealth of Black families, and creating a more thriving and balanced educational system.

Each of these men shared their knowledge and experiences with this study in the hopes of positively influencing the lives of future Black men pursuing post-baccalaureate degrees. Within ourselves as Black students and as educators, there is a wealth of meaning, knowledge, and understanding about what contributes to Black male success in graduate school. The actions of institutions, faculty, key stakeholders, and students will be directly affected by the power of this truth and knowledge within these research findings.

As the famous Denzel Washington (2007) said when he played Melvin Tolson, a professor at Wiley College:

I believe we are the most privileged people in America because we have the most important job in America: the education of young people. We must impress upon our young people that there will be difficulties that they will face. They must defeat them! They must do what they have to do in order to do what they want to do. Education is the only way out. The way out of ignorance. (Washington, 2007, 0:50:21)

In similar fashion to Professor Tolson, with the continuance of educational studies, I aspire to continue to bring that passion to other generations through teaching. The ultimate objective here is to facilitate the reconstruction of the mind to construct reform of justice in areas of social, collegiate, and economic equality. Continue learning, continue evolving, and continue educating to create opportunities for Black men in America! Words are lovely, but now it's time to act. Changes must be implemented that, above all, allow one to be true to oneself and to one's truth.

References

Adams, J. (2018). *A narrative study of black males' sense of belonging in graduate counseling programs.* (Publication No. 4816) [Doctoral dissertation, University of South Carolina]. Scholar Commons. https://scholarcommons.sc.edu/etd/4816

Adams, T. E., Ellis, C., & Jones, S. H. (2017). Autoethnography. In J. Matthes, C. S. Davis and R. F. Potter (Eds.), *The international encyclopedia of communication research methods*, (pp. 1-11). John Wiley & Sons, Inc. https://doi.org/10.1002/9781118901731.iecrm0011

Adukia, A., Eble, A., Harrison, E., Runesha, H. B., & Szasz, T. (2021). What we teach about race and gender: Representation in images and text of children's books (No. w29123). *National Bureau of Economic Research.* https://doi.org/10.3386/w29123

Arroyo, A. T., & Gasman, M. (2014). An HBCU-based educational approach for black college student success: Toward a framework with implications for all institutions. *American Journal of Education, 121*(1), 57-85. https://doi.org/10.1086/678112

Astin, A. W. (1984). Excellence and equity in American education. *National Forum, 64*(2), 1-30.

Astin, A. W. (1993). *What matters in college? Four critical years revisited* (1st ed.). Jossey-Bass.

Astin, A. W. (1999). Student involvement: A developmental theory for higher education. *Journal of College Student Development, 40*(5), 518–529.

Baker, F. L. (2019). *Exploring African American student retention at predominantly white institutions: Qualitative exploratory case study.* (Publication No. 27735809) [Doctoral dissertation, University of Phoenix]. ProQuest. https://www.proquest.com/openview/6e52da5e092f1f02c5e8c03a2b48b1ef/1?pq-origsite=gscholar&cbl=18750&diss=y

Bauknight, T. (2020). *The experiences of successful black males in higher education who have completed their bachelor's degrees* (Publication No. 28260238) [Doctoral dissertation, Grand Canyon University]. ProQuest. https://search.proquest.com/openview/8bfff42276bd308474d922404a7460e3/1?pq-origsite=gscholar&cbl=18750&diss=y

Bell, D. (2008). *And we are not saved: The elusive quest for racial justice.* Basic Books.

Bell, D. (2018). *Faces at the bottom of the well: The permanence of racism.* Basic Books.

Berger, J. B. Ramirez, G. B., & Lyons, S. (2005). Past to present. In Alan Seidman (Ed.), *College student retention: Formula for student success* (2nd ed., pp. 7-34). Rowman & Littlefield Publishers.

Bialik, K., & Fry, R. (2019, February 14). Millennial life: How young adulthood today compares with prior generations. *Pew Research Center.* https://www.pewresearch.org/social-trends/2019/02/14/millennial-life-how-young-adulthood-today-compares-with-prior-generations-2/

Birt, L., Scott, S., Cavers, D., Campbell, C., & Walter, F. (2016). Member checking: A tool to enhance trustworthiness or merely a nod to validation? *Qualitative Health Research, 26*(13), 1802-1811. https://doi.org/10.1177/1049732316654870

Blake-Beard, S., Bayne, M. L., Crosby, F. J., & Muller, C. B. (2011). Matching by race and gender in mentoring relationships: Keeping our eyes on the prize. *Journal of Social Issues, 67*(3), 622-643. https://doi.org/10.1111/j.1540-4560.2011.01717.x

Blanton, R. (1960). Marching, singing, and road imagery in Martin Luther King's involvement in the civil rights movement. https://salempress.com/Media/SalemPress/samples/mlk_pgs.pdf

Blockett, R. A., Felder, P. P., Parrish III, W., & Collier, J. (2016). Pathways to the professoriate: Exploring Black doctoral student socialization and the pipeline to the academic profession. *Western Journal of Black Studies, 40*(2), 95–110. https://www.proquest.com/scholarly-journals/pathways-professoriate-exploring-black- doctoral/docview/2049976526/se-2

Boylorn, R. M. (2014). From here to there: How to use auto/ethnography to bridge difference. *International Review of Qualitative Research, 7*(3), 312-326. https://doi.org/10.1525/irqr.2014.7.3.312

Bochner, A. P., & Ellis, C. (2006). Communication as Autoethnography. In Gregory J. Shepherd, Jeffrey St. John & Ted Striphas (Eds.), *Communication as...:Perspectives on Theory* (pp. 110-122). SAGE Publications, Inc. https://doi.org/10.4135/9781483329055.n13

Bothello, J., & Roulet, T. J. (2019). The imposter syndrome, or the misrepresentation of self in academic life. *Journal of Management Studies, 56*(4), 854-861. https://doi.org/10.1111/joms.12344

Braun, Virgina & Clarke, Victoria. (2006). Using thematic analysis in psychology. *Qualitative Research in Psychology, 3*(2), 77-101. https://www.tandfonline.com/doi/abs/10.1191/1478088706QP063OA

Brooms, D. R. (2016). *Being Black, Being Male on Campus: Understanding and Confronting Black Male Collegiate Experiences*. Suny Press.

Brooms, D. R., & Davis, A. R. (2017). Staying focused on the goal: Peer bonding and faculty mentors supporting black males' persistence in college. *Journal of Black Studies, 48*(3), 305-326. https://doi.org/10.1177/0021934717692520

Brown v. Board of Education, 349 U.S. 294 (1955).

Brown, M. C., & Ricard, R. B. (2007). The honorable past and uncertain future of the nation's HBCUs. *Thought & Action, 23*, 117-130.

Brown, T. (2017). *"My brother's keeper" A presidential initiative designed to improve life outcomes for boys and young men of color (BYMOC): A case study to critically assess its implementation fidelity*. [Doctoral dissertation, University of Morgan State].

Brown II, M. C. (2013). The declining significance of historically black colleges and universities: Relevance, reputation, and reality in Obamamerica. *Journal of Negro Education, 82*(1), 3-19. https://doi.org/10.7709/jnegroeducation.82.1.0003

Bush, L. V., & Bush, E. C. (2013). God bless the child who got his own: Toward a Comprehensive Theory for African American Boys and Men. *Western Journal of Black Studies, 37*(1), 1-13. https://www.academia.edu/download/36548062/God_Bless_the_child_WJB_AAMT_Lbush_Ebush.pdf

Callahan, C. N., LaDue, N. D., Baber, L. D., Sexton, J., van der Hoeven Kraft, K. J., & Zamani-Gallaher, E. M. (2017). Theoretical perspectives on increasing recruitment and retention of underrepresented students in the geosciences. *Journal of Geoscience Education, 65*(4), 563-576. https://doi.org/10.5408/16-238.1

Clandinin, D. J. (2016). *Engaging in narrative inquiry* (1st Ed.). Routledge. https://doi.org/10.4324/9781315429618

Clandinin, D. J., & Connelly, F. M. (2004). *Narrative inquiry: Experience and story in qualitative research*. Jossey-Bass.

Clandinin, D. J., & Rosiek, J. (2007). Mapping a Landscape of Narrative Inquiry: Borderland Spaces and Tensions. In D. J. Clandinin (Ed.), *Handbook of narrative inquiry: Mapping a methodology* (pp. 35–75). Sage Publications, Inc. https://doi.org/10.4135/9781452226552.n2

Connelly, F. M., & Clandinin, D. J. (1990). Stories of experience and narrative inquiry. *Educational Researcher, 19*(5), 2-14. https://doi.org/10.3102/0013189X019005002

Creswell, J. W., & Creswell, J. (2003). *Research design*. Sage Publications.

Crimmins, G. (2016). A reflection on a humanistic approach to narrative inquiry into the lived experience of women casual academics. *Reflective Practice, 17*(4), 483-494. https://doi.org/10.1080/14623943.2016.1175342

Cuyjet, M. J. (2006). *African American men in college*. Jossey-Bass.

De Laine, M. (2000). *Fieldwork, Participation, and Practice: Ethics and Dilemmas in Qualitative Research*. Sage Publications.

Denzin, N. K., & Lincoln, Y. S. (2008). Introduction: The discipline and practice of qualitative research. In N. K. Denzin & Y. S. Lincoln (Eds.), *Strategies of qualitative inquiry* (pp. 1–43). Sage Publications.

Delgado, R., & Stefancic, J. (2012). *Critical race theory: An introduction* (2nd ed.). New York University Press.

Druery, J. E., & Brooms, D. R. (2019). "It lit up the campus." Engaging Black males in culturally enriching environments. *Journal of Diversity in Higher Education, 12*(4), 330-340.

https://doi.org/10.1037/dhe0000087

Du Bois, W. E. B. (1898). The study of the Negro problems. *The Annals of the American Academy of Political and Social Science, 11*(1), 1-23. http://www.jstor.org/stable/1009474

Du Bois, W. E. B. (1903). *The Souls of Black Folk.* Cambridge University Press, John Wilson.

Dwyer, R., & Emerald, E. (2017). Narrative research in practice: Navigating the terrain. In R. Dwyer, I. Davis, & E. Emerald (Eds.), *Narrative Research in Practice* (pp. 1-25). Springer.

Edwards, W. J., & Ross, H. H. (2018). What are they saying? Black faculty at predominantly white institutions of higher education. *Journal of Human Behavior in the Social Environment, 28*(2), 142-161. https://doi.org/10.1080/10911359.2017.1391731

Felder, P. P., & Barker, M. J. (2013). Extending Bell's concept of interest convergence: A framework for understanding the African American doctoral student experience. *International Journal of Doctoral Studies, 8,* 1-20. http://ijds.org/Volume8/IJDSv8p001-020Felder0384.pdf

Fleming, J. S., & Courtney, B. E. (1984). The dimensionality of self-esteem: II. Hierarchical facet model for revised measurement scales. *Journal of Personality and Social Psychology, 46*(2), 404–421. https://doi.org/10.1037/0022-3514.46.2.404

Francis, J. J., Johnston, M., Robertson, C., Glidewell, L., Entwistle, V., Eccles, M. P., & Grimshaw, J. M. (2010). What is an adequate sample size? Operationalising data saturation for theory-based interview studies. *Psychology and Health, 25*(10), 1229-1245. https://doi.org/10.1080/08870440903194015

Gasman, M., Hirschfeld, A., & Vultaggio, J. (2008). "Difficult yet rewarding": The experiences of African American graduate students in education at an Ivy League institution. *Journal of Diversity in Higher Education, 1*(2), 126–138. https://doi.org/10.1037/1938- 8926.1.2.126

Gibbs Jr, K. D., & Griffin, K. A. (2013). What do I want to be with my PhD? The roles of personal values and structural dynamics in shaping the career interests of recent biomedical science PhD graduates. *CBE—Life Sciences Education, 12*(4), 711-723. https://doi.org/10.1187/cbe.13-02-0021

Given, L. M. (Ed.). (2008). *The Sage encyclopedia of qualitative research methods.* Sage Publications. http://dx.doi.org/10.4135/9781412963909.n332

Goings, R. B. (2021). Introducing the Black Male Adult Learner Success Theory. *Adult Education Quarterly, 71*(2), 128-147. https://doi.org/10.1177/0741713620959603

Grant-Thompson, S. K., & Atkinson, D. R. (1997). Cross-cultural mentoring effectiveness with African American male students. *Journal of Black Psychology, 23*(2), 120-134. https://doi.org/10.1177/00957984970232003

Griffin, F. J., & Fish, C. J. (Eds.). (1999). *A Stranger in the Village.* Beacon Press.

Hague-Palmer, T. (2013). *Academic and campus experiences of African American males: Implications for collegiate satisfaction and student engagement.* (Publication No. 3671364) [Doctoral dissertation, Bowling Green State University]. ProQuest. https://search.proquest.com/openview/11abf0c090645a0447f5eb475c465d64/1?pq-origsite=gscholar&cbl=18750

Harper, S. R. (2012). Black male student success in higher education: A report from the National Black Male College Achievement Study. *Center for the Study of Race and Equity in Education*, University of Pennsylvania Graduate School of Education. https://rossierapps.usc.edu/facultydirectory/publications/231/Harper%20(2012)%20Black%20Male%20Success.pdf

Harper, S. R., & Porter, A. C. (2012). Attracting Black Male Students to Research Careers in Education: A Report from the Grad Prep Academy Project. *Center for the Study of Race and Equity in Education*, University of Pennsylvania Graduate School of Education. https://race.usc.edu/wp-content/uploads/2020/08/Pub-17-Harper-and-Porter.pdf

Harper, S. R., Smith, E. J., & Davis III, C. H. (2018). A critical race case analysis of black undergraduate student success at an urban university. *Urban Education*, *53*(1), 3-25. https://doi.org/10.1177/0042085916668956

Harris III, F., & Harper, S. R. (2014). Beyond bad-behaving brothers: Productive performances of masculinities among college fraternity men. *International Journal of Qualitative Studies in Education*, *27*(6), 703-723. http://dx.doi.org/10.1080/09518398.2014.901577

Harvey-Smith, A. B. (2002). An examination of the retention literature and application in student success. *Promoting Inclusion*, *5*, 14-26. https://www.ccsse.org/center/resources/docs/research/harvey-smith.pdf

Hedgepeth Jr, C., Edmonds, R., & Craig, A. (1978). Overview: Teaching and learning. In C. Willie & R. Edmonds (Eds.), *Black colleges in America: challenges, developments, and survival* (pp. 29-50). Columbia University Teachers College Press.

Heilig, J. V., & Reddick, R. J. (2008, August 12). Perspectives: Black males in the educational pipeline. *Diverse Issues in Higher Education*.

https://www.diverseeducation.com/home/article/15087532/perspectives-black-males-in-the-educational-pipeline

Hofstede, G. (2011). national cultures, organizational cultures, and the role of management. *Values and Ethics for the 21st Century*, (pp. 459-481). Madrid: BBVA. https://www.bbvaopenmind.com/wp-content/uploads/2013/02/BBVA-OpenMind-National-Cultures-Organizational-Cultures-and-the-Role-of-Management-Geert-Hofstede.pdf.pdf

Holmes, A. G. D. (2020). Researcher positionality: A consideration of its influence and place in qualitative research: A new researcher's guide. *Shanlax International Journal of Education*, *8*(4), 1-10. https://doi.org/10.34293/education.v8i4.3232

Howard, T. C. (2014). *Black Males (D): Peril and Promise in the Education of African American*

Males. New York: Teachers College Press.

Howard, T. C., Flennaugh, T. K., & Terry Sr., C. L. (2012). Black males, social imagery, and the disruption of pathological identities: Implications for research and teaching. *Educational Foundations, 26*, 85-102. https://files.eric.ed.gov/fulltext/EJ968819.pdf

Inouye, C. J. (1989). *Understanding the law school experience: Enhancing student achievement and satisfaction*. University of California, Los Angeles. https://www.proquest.com/openview/a98a3e89596ec18d67262fd8317cfbca/1?pq-origsite=gscholar&cbl=18750&diss=y

Jackson, J. F., & Moore III, J. L. (2006). African American Males in Education: Endangered or Ignored? *Teachers College Record, 108*(2), 201-205. https://doi.org/10.1111/j.1467-9620.2006.00647.x

Jefferson, T. A. (2020). *Advancing Black men in higher education: A narrative inquiry on perceived success in doctoral education* (Publication No. 28163869) [Doctoral dissertation, Kent State University]. ProQuest. https://etd.ohiolink.edu/apexprod/rws_etd/send_file/send?accession=kent159483159111194 27 &disposition=inline

Johnston, B. (2010). *The first year at university: Teaching students in transition*. McGraw-Hill Education (UK).

Kim, E., Newton, F. B., Downey, R. G., & Benton, S. L. (2010). Personal factors impacting college student success: Constructing college learning effectiveness inventory (CLEI). *College Student Journal, 44*(1), 112-126.

Kimbrough, W. M., & Harper, S. R. (2006). African American men at historically Black colleges and universities: Different environments, similar challenges. *African American men in college, 1*, 189-209. Jossey-Bass.

Krishna, R., Maithreyi, R., & Surapaneni, K. M. (2010). Research bias: A review for medical students. *J Clin Diagn Res, 4*(2), 2320-2324.

Kuh, G. D., Kinzie, J., Buckley, J. A., Bridges, B. K., & Hayek, J. C. (2011). *Piecing together the student success puzzle: Research, propositions, and recommendations: ASHE higher education report* (Vol. 116). John Wiley & Sons. http://dx.doi.org/10.1002/aehe.3205

Kuther, T. L. (2018). *Lifespan development: Lives in context*. SAGE Publications.

Ladson-Billings, G. (1998). Just what is critical race theory and what's it doing in a nice field like education? *International Journal of Qualitative Studies in Education, 11*(1), 7-24. https://doi.org/10.1080/095183998236863

Ladson-Billings, G. (2005). The evolving role of critical race theory in educational scholarship. *Race, Ethnicity and Education, 8*(1), 115-119. https://doi.org/10.1080/1361332052000341024

Ladson-Billings, G. (2008). Yes, but how do we do it?": Practicing culturally relevant pedagogy. *City kids, city schools: More reports from the front row*, 162-177. https://fordhamatsdc.files.wordpress.com/2011/08/ladson-billings_g-_yes_but_how_do_we_do_it.pdf

Ladson-Billings, G., & Tate, W. F. (1995). Toward a critical race theory of education. *Teachers College Record, 97*(1), 47-68. https://doi.org/10.1177/016146819509700104

LeCompte, M. D., & Goetz, J. P. (1982). Problems of reliability and validity in ethnographic research. *Review of Educational Research, 52*(1), 31-60. https://doi.org/10.3102/00346543052001031

Levitz, R. S., Noel, L., & Richter, B. J. (1999). Strategic moves for retention success. *New Directions for Higher Education, 1999*(108), 31-49.

Lincoln, Y. G., & Guba, E. (1985). Contextualization: Evidence from distributed teams. *Information Systems Research, 16*(1), 9-27.

Lundy-Wagner, V., Vultaggio, J., & Gasman, M. (2013). Preparing underrepresented students of color for doctoral success: The role of undergraduate institutions. *International Journal of Doctoral Studies, 8*, 151-172. http://ijds.org/Volume8/IJDSv8p151172LundyWagner0381.pdf

Ma, J., Pender, M., & Welch, M. (2016). Education Pays 2016: The benefits of higher education for individuals and society. Trends in Higher Education Series. *College Board.* https://www.getmidegree.org/wp-content/uploads/2018/08/education-pays-2016-full-report.pdf

Mathers, H. J. (2016). Examining Hispanic college students' experiences with perceived discrimination at historically Black colleges and universities. *Cardinal Stritch University.* https://www.proquest.com/docview/1734892014/

Mattise, C., & Willoughby, B. (2004). True blue. *Teaching Tolerance, 25*, 18-21.

Maxwell, J. C. (2021). *Change your world: How anyone, anywhere can make a difference.* HarperCollins Leadership.

Merriam, S. B. (1998). *Qualitative research and case study applications in education.* Revised and expanded from "*Case Study Research in Education."*. Jossey-Bass Publishers. https://doi.org/10.1097/00001416-199101000-00021

Merriam-Webster. (n.d.). Employment. In Merriam-Webster.com dictionary. Retrieved March 3, 2021, from https://www.merriam-webster.com/dictionary/employment

Merriam-Webster. (n.d.). Viability. In Merriam-Webster.com dictionary. Retrieved March 3, 2021, from https://www.merriam-webster.com/dictionary/viability)

Mineo, L. (2017, December 7). The need to talk about race. *The Harvard Gazette.*

Mitchell, A., Oliphant, J. B., & Shearer, E. (2020). About seven-in-ten U.S. adults say they need to take breaks from COVID-19 news. *Washington, DC: Pew Research Center*, 1-5.

https://www.pewresearch.org/journalism/2020/04/29/about-seven-in-ten-u-s-adults-say- they-need-to-take-breaks-from-covid-19-news/

Mitchell, S. K. (2011). *Factors that contribute to persistence and retention of underrepresented minority undergraduate students in science, technology, engineering, and mathematics (STEM).* (Publication No. 3477173) [Doctoral dissertation, The University of Southern Mississippi]. ProQuest. https://aquila.usm.edu/dissertations/657

Moore, J. L., Madison-Colmore, O., & Smith, D. M. (2003). The prove-them-wrong syndrome: Voices from unheard African American males in engineering disciplines. *The Journal of Men's Studies, 12*(1), 61-73. https://doi.org/10.3149/jms.1201.61

Morgan, D. L., Ataie, J., Carder, P., & Hoffman, K. (2013). Introducing Dyadic interviews as a method for collecting qualitative data. *Qualitative Health Research, 23*(9), 1276–1284. https://doi.org/10.1177/1049732313501889

Myers, L. W. (2002). *A broken silence: Voices of African American women in the academy.* Greenwood Publishing Group. https://doi.org/10.2307/3089882

National Center for Education Statistics. (2020). *The Condition of Education 2020* (NCES 2020- 144), Characteristics of Postsecondary Faculty. https://nces.ed.gov/pubs2020/2020144.pdf

National Center for Education Statistics. (2018). U.S. Department of Education, Institute of Education Sciences, *National Center for Education Statistics.* https://nces.ed.gov/pubs2020/2020009.pdf

National Center for Education Research. (2021). *Representation matters: Exploring the role of gender and race on educational outcomes.* Institute of Education Sciences. https://ies.ed.gov/blogs/research/post/representation-matters-exploring-the-role-of-gender- and-race-on-educational-outcomes

Neal, K. D. (2018). *The degree attainment of Black college students graduating from predominantly White institutions of higher education: A qualitative study* (Publication No. 10744772)$[Doctoral dissertation, Northcentral University]. ProQuest. https://search.proquest.com/openview/51ea914958d15f548a8e881b04d28657/1?pq-origsite=gscholar&cbl=18750

Nettles, M. T. T., & Millet, C. M. (2006). *Three magic letters: Getting to Ph.D.* John Hopkins University Press. doi:10.1353/rhe.2006.0050

Nowell, L. S., Norris, J. M., White, D. E., & Moules, N. J. (2017). Thematic analysis: Striving to meet the trustworthiness criteria. *International Journal of Qualitative Methods, 16*(1). https://doi.org/10.1177/1609406917733847

Nwaokoro, A. N. (2010). An investigation of institutional enhancement factors on student college success. *Contemporary Issues in Education Research (CIER), 3*(8), 1-8. https://doi.org/10.19030/cier.v3i8.221

Outcalt, C. L., & Skewes-Cox, T. E. (2002). Involvement, interaction, and satisfaction: The human environment at HBCUs. *Review of Higher Education: Journal of the Association for the Study of Higher Education, 25*(3), 331–347. https://doi.org/10.1353/rhe.2002.0015

Palmer, R. T., Davis, R. J., & Maramba, D. C. (2010). Role of an HBCU in supporting academic success for underprepared black males. *Negro Educational Review*, (1-4). https://www.augusta.edu/aami/documents/role-of-an-hbcu-palmer-davis-maramba.pdf

Pascarella, E. T., & Terenzini, P. T. (1991). *How college affects students: Findings and insights from twenty years of research*. Jossey-Bass, Inc., Publishers.

Pascarella, E. T., & Terenzini, P. T. (2005). *How College Affects Students: A Third Decade of Research. Volume 2*. Jossey-Bass..

Pepper, C., & Wildy, H. (2009). Using narratives as a research strategy. *Qualitative Research Journal,* Vol. 9 No. 2, pp. 18-26. https://doi.org/10.3316/QRJ0902018

Pinnegar, S., & Daynes, J. G. (2007). Locating narrative inquiry historically. In *Handbook of Narrative Inquiry: Mapping a Methodology*, 3-34. Sage Publications. https://www.researchgate.net/profile/Stefinee-Pinnegar-2/publication/232453029_Locating_Narrative_Inquiry_Historically_Thematics_in_the_Turn_to_Narrative/links/0deec53b1698d5c566000000/Locating-Narrative-Inquiry-Historically-Thematics-in-the-Turn-to-Narrative.pdf

Preissle, J. (2002). Ethical Issues in Practitioner Research; Fieldwork, Participation and Practice: Ethics and Dilemmas in Qualitative Research. *Field Methods, 14*(2), 233-240. https://doi.org/10.1177/1525822X0201400208

Quaye, S. J., & Harper, S. R. (2007). Faculty accountability for culturally inclusive pedagogy and curricula. *Liberal Education, 93*(3), 32-39. https://files.eric.ed.gov/fulltext/EJ775570.pdf

Ray, R., & Gibbons, A. (2021, November). *Why are states banning critical race theory?* Brookings Institute. https://www.brookings.edu/blog/fixgov/2021/07/02/why-are-states-banning-critical-race-theory/

Renz, S. M., Carrington, J. M., & Badger, T. A. (2018). Two strategies for qualitative content analysis: An intramethod approach to triangulation. *Qualitative Health Research, 28*(5), 824–831. https://doi.org/10.1177/1049732317753586

Richmond, J. (1986). The importance of student involvement: A dialogue with Alexander Astin. *Journal of Counseling & Development, 65*(2), 92-95. https://doi.org/10.1002/j.1556-6676.1986.tb01240.x

Ryan, F., Coughlan, M., & Cronin, P. (2009). Interviewing in qualitative research: The one-to-one interview. *International Journal of Therapy and Rehabilitation, 16*(6), 309-314. https://doi.org/10.12968/ijtr.2009.16.6.42433

Ryan, G. W., & Bernard, H. R. (2003). Techniques to identify themes. *Field Methods, 15*(1), 85-109. https://doi.org/10.1177/1525822X02239569

Sanders, D. R. (2016). *Mentoring experiences of African American doctoral students at historically Black and historically White colleges and universities* (Publication No. 10158435) [Doctoral dissertation, The George Washington University]. ProQuest. https://www.proquest.com/openview/c246509664b0b30026eea5c9baa008a7/1?pq-origsite=gscholar&cbl=18750

Scherer, M. (2013). Maya and Malala. *Educational Leadership, 71*(1), 7-7.

https://www.ascd.org/el/articles/maya-and-malala

Scheurich, J., & Young, M. (2002). White racism among white faculty. *The racial crisis in American higher education: Continuing challenges for the twenty-first century*, 221-242.

Selden, S. (1999). Inheriting Shame: The Story of Eugenics and Racism in America. *History of Education Quarterly, 40*(1), 104-106. https://doi.org/10.2307/369192

Smith, Rebecca (2019, May 10). Let's talk sales! Inspirational Quote by Michael Margolis – Episode 150. *Criteria for Success.* https://criteriaforsuccess.com/lets-talk-sales-inspirational-quote-by-michael-margolis-episode-150/

Smith, J. R. (2021). Diagnosis issues with African Americans. In M.O. Adekson (Ed), *African Americans and Mental Health* (pp. 47-56). Springer. https://doi.org/10.1007/978-3-030-77131-7_6

Solorzano, D. G. (1997). Images and words that wound: Critical race theory, racial stereotyping, and teacher education. *Teacher Education Quarterly, 24*(3), 5-19. http://www.jstor.org/stable/23478088

Stallion, K. (2013). Brown v. Board of Education and its impact on admissions in higher education. *LOGOS: A Journal of Undergraduate Research, 6*, 65-79. https://www.studocu.com/en-us/document/southern-new-hampshire-university/forensic-psychology/psy205-1-4-journal/25424559

Steele, C. M. (2011). *Whistling Vivaldi: How stereotypes affect us and what we can do.* W. W. Norton & Company.

Strmic-Pawl, H. V., Jackson, B. A., & Garner, S. (2018). Race counts: racial and ethnic data on the US Census and the implications for tracking inequality. *Sociology of Race and Ethnicity, 4*(1), 1-13. https://doi.org/10.1177/2332649217742869

Stone, S., Saucer, C., Bailey, M., Garba, R., Hurst, A., Jackson, S. M., Krueger, N., & Cokley, K. (2018). Learning While Black: A Culturally Informed Model of the Impostor Phenomenon for Black Graduate Students. *Journal of Black Psychology, 44*(6), 491-531. https://doi.org/10.1177/0095798418786648

Strayhorn, T. L. (2008). The invisible man: Factors affecting the retention of low-income African American males. *NASAP Journal, 11*(1), 66-87.

https://www.academia.edu/3997084/The_Invisible_Man_Factors_Affecting_the_Retention_of_Low_Income_African_American_Males

Strayhorn, T. L. (2010). When race and gender collide: Social and cultural capital's influence on the academic achievement of African American and Latino males. *The Review of Higher Education*, *33*(3), 307-332. https://doi.org/10.1353/rhe.0.0147

Strayhorn, T. L. (2017). Factors that influence the persistence and success of Black men in urban public universities. *Urban Education*, *52*(9), 1106-1128. https://doi.org/10.1177/0042085915623347

Strayhorn, T. L., & DeVita, J. M. (2010). African American males' student engagement: A comparison of good practices by institutional type. *Journal of African American Studies*, *14*(1), 87-105. http://www.jstor.org/stable/41819238

Strayhorn, T. L., & Terrell, M. C. (2007). Mentoring and satisfaction with college for Black students. *Negro Educational Review*, *58* (1), 69-83.

Sutton, J., & Austin, Z. (2015). Qualitative Research: Data Collection, Analysis, and Management. *Canadian Journal of Hospital Pharmacy*, *68*(3), 226–231. https://doi.org/10.4212/cjhp.v68i3.1456

Syed, M., Azmitia, M., & Cooper, C. R. (2011). Identity and academic success among underrepresented ethnic minorities: An interdisciplinary review and integration. *Journal of Social Issues*, *67*(3), 442-468. https://doi.org/10.1111/j.1540-4560.2011.01709.x

Trochim, W. M. (2006). Qualitative measures. *Research measures knowledge base*, *361*(1), 2-16. https://doc1.bibliothek.li/aaw/FLMF020216.pdf

Tuitt, F. (2012). Black like me: Graduate students' perceptions of their pedagogical experiences in classes taught by Black faculty in a predominantly White institution. *Journal of Black Studies*, *43*(2), 186-206. https://doi.org/10.1177/0021934711413271

U.S. Department of Commerce, Census Bureau, (2020). Table 4: Estimates of the Population by Race U.S. Department of Education, *National Center for Education Statistics*. The Condition of Education 2020 (NCES 2020-144). https://nces.ed.gov/pubs2020/2020144.pdf

Underwood, K. (2019). *Why America needs more black male teachers.* [Doctoral dissertation, The City University of New York] EdSurge. https://academicworks.cuny.edu/cgi/viewcontent.cgi?article=4875&context=gc_etds

Vaughn, A. S. (2015). *The Obama effect on African American high school males.* (Publication No. 150721249) [Doctoral dissertation, Georgia Southern University]. Teachers College Press. https://digitalcommons.georgiasouthern.edu/cgi/viewcontent.cgi?article=2279&context=etd

Washington, D. (Director). 2007. *Great Debaters [Film].* Harpo Distributions.

Weissman, S. (2021, February 18). This UCLA doctoral student cohort is majority Black. Here's what a group of faculty did to make it happen. *Diverse Issues in Higher Education.* https://www.diverseeducation.com/demographics/african-american/article/15097998/this-ucla-doctoral-student-cohort-is-majority-black-heres-what-a-group-of-faculty-did-to-make-it- happen

Wendling, L. A. (2018). Higher education as a means of communal uplift: The educational philosophy of W. E. B. Du Bois. *The Journal of Negro Education, 87*(3), 285-293. https://doi.org/10.7709/jnegroeducation.87.3.0285

West, C. (1994). *Race matters.* Vintage.

Whiting, G. W. (2006). From at risk to at promise: Developing scholar identities among Black males. *Journal of Secondary Gifted Education, 17*(4), 222-229. https://doi.org/10.4219/jsge-2006-407

Whiting, G., & Kennedy, C. A. (2015). The scholar identity model: Counseling Black male students towards academic achievement. In M.S. Henfield & A. R. Washington (Eds.), *School counseling for Black male student success in 21st Century Urban Schools* (pp. 195-214). Information Age.

Woodson, C. G. (2006). *The miseducation of the Negro.* Book Tree. https://jpanafrican.org/ebooks/3.4eBookThe%20Mis-Education.pdf

Yanto, H., Mula, J. M., & Kavanagh, M. H. (2011). Developing student's accounting competencies using Astin's IEO model: An identification of key educational inputs based on Indonesian student perspectives. *Proceedings of the RMIT Accounting Educators' Conference, 2011: Accounting Education or Educating Accountants.* University of Southern Queensland. https://eprints.usq.edu.au/20077/

Young, L. K. (2010). *The Obama effect and its relationship to the perceptions of Blacks on education and social mobility.* (Publication No. 501) [Doctoral dissertation, Loyola University Chicago]. ProQuest. https://ecommons.luc.edu/luc_theses/501

Appendices

Appendix A Informed Consent Document: IRB PROTOCOL

Subject: Consent to Take Part in a Study of The Black Male Triumph Story: Successfully Achieving Graduate Degrees

Authorized Study Personnel:	Albert Furlow, Education UIW Department 713-703-7010 afurlow@student.uiwtx.edu
Professor:	Dr. Alsandor, Danielle Professor: Teacher Education 210-832-3218 (GB147 UIW) alsandor@uiwtx.edu

Key Information: Your consent is being sought for a research study. The purpose of the research is to explore the experience of approximately 15 Black male graduate students who were successful in completing their graduate program. The researcher composes a basic interpretive study that focuses on how individuals interpret their own lived experiences and what is perceived as they share their narratives (Merriam, 1998).

If you agree to participate in this study, the project will involve:

- Completion of an online survey, providing a written personal philosophy statement, and conducting a semi-structured interview via Zoom, with an accuracy check.

- The interview will take 60-90 minutes

- There are minimal risks associated with this study: Possible risks include mental and emotional stress while discussing their lived experiences.

- There is no compensation for participation.

- Your participation is voluntary, and you may decide not to participate at any time

Invitation: You are invited to volunteer as one of 15 subjects in the research project named above. The information in this form is meant to help you decide whether you choose to participate. If you have any questions, please ask.

Why are you being asked to be in this research study? Congratulations, you meet the Research Criteria for this study. You are being asked to participate in this research study because you self-identify as a Black or African American male and you have also completed a master's degree or higher within the past five years. Using a Narrative Inquiry methodology gives us a front row seat into the minds and experiences of the storyteller. It offers perspectives which are embedded in social, cultural, and institutional practices and behaviors. These narratives surface the ambiguities, complexities, difficulties, and uncertainties to which many have triumphed and sadly many have fallen victim. In this research methodology, participants will construct their own narratives and offer counter-narratives that challenge prevailing assumptions about what it takes to earn a post-baccalaureate degree.

By working closely with an institutional review board and one's colleagues, the researcher can make sure that access to participants is academically and ethically sound. However, at the conclusion of the study, the principal investigator will explain in greater detail what we hope to learn from this research.

What is the reason for doing this research study?

The purpose of this study is to better understand the lived experiences of Black males who have completed a graduate degree. This study will also indirectly acknowledge and address the degree to which historical laws and systemic practices and processes have controlled, and according to some, derailed the execution of quality education for Black male students. Where this study contributes to the literature on Black males in higher education, it is accomplished solely by looking at those who earned a graduate degree to access how to increase the retention rate of Black males in post-baccalaureate programs.

What will be done during this research study? The researcher operates under three different methods in order to collect data from participants. The first method is through responses of the participants from a survey. Next is the method of content analysis which will be utilized during the narration of their personal philosophy statement. This will allow the researcher to collect data through content analysis of written documents. The participant's writing should entail their lived experiences throughout their program that successfully got them through. Lastly, the third method is the semi-structured interview which will take place via Zoom app on personal laptop/cellphone. The interviews are established for a duration of 60-90 minutes in total per participant.

Your remarks may be quoted during presentation or articles resulting from this work. A pseudonym will be used to protect your participant identity, unless you specifically request to be identified by your true name.

What are the possible risks of being in this study? You may feel emotional or upset when answering some of the questions. Tell the interviewer at any time if you wish to take a break or stop the interview.

What are the possible benefits to you?

While compensation is not provided to participants in the study, participants may benefit from reflecting on their lived experiences.

What are the possible benefits to other people? The benefits to society may include acknowledging and discussing the presence of Black males in graduate school and determining how involvement and other skills and traits, along with critical race, influence academic success and degree acquisition.

What will being in this research study cost you? There is no cost to you to be in this research study.

Will you be compensated for being in this research study? You will not be paid for your participation in this research study.

How will information about you be protected? Everything we learn about you in the study will be kept confidential. The only persons who will have access to your research records are the study personnel, the Institutional Review Board (IRB), and any other person, agency, or sponsor as required by law. If we publish the results of the study, you will not be identified in any way. However, if granted, unless you give explicit permission for this below.

What will happen if you decide not to be in this research study or decide to stop participating once you start? You can decide not to be in this research study, or you can stop being in this research study at any time, for any reason. You do not have to answer any question you do not want to answer. Deciding not to be in this research study or deciding to withdraw will not affect your relationship with the researcher or with the University of the Incarnate Word. You will not lose any benefits to which you are entitled.

Deciding not to be in the study or deciding to withdraw will not affect your class standing or grades at the University of the Incarnate Word.

If you decide to withdraw from the study, the researchers will ask you if the information already collected from you can be used or, state that any information collected from the participant will not be used if the participant decides to withdraw before finishing the study.

What should you do if you have a problem or question during this research study? If you have a problem as a direct result of being in this study, you should immediately contact one of the people listed at the beginning of this consent form.

If you have any questions now, feel free to ask us. If you have additional questions about your rights or wish to report a problem that may be related to the study, please contact the University of the Incarnate Word Institutional Review Board office at 210-805-3036 or 210-805-3565.

Consent

If you agree to participate, please complete the online survey and provide a written philosophy statement. If you do not wish to participate, then simply inform the researcher.

Albert Furlow
_____
Name of Principal Investigator/Designee
Albert Furlow

_____   Date_____
Signature of Principal
Investigator/Designee

UIW IRB Approved
UNIVERSITY OF THE   Date Approved:
INCARNATE WORD   8/17/2020

Approval # 20-08-003

Appendix B Informed Consent Document: Invitation

To Participate in Study

Email: FLYER (THE BLACK MALE TRIUMPH STORY: SUCCESSFULLY ACHIEVING GRADUATE DEGREES)

You are invited to participate in a research study about THE BLACK MALE TRIUMPH STORY: SUCCESSFULLY ACHIEVING GRADUATE DEGREES. Completing this online,

nine question survey will only take 5-10 minutes to complete. Your participation is completely voluntary. Please note that there is no direct benefit that will accrue to you from taking this survey; however, your participation will contribute greatly to knowledge on Black males pursing Higher Education.

Things you should know-

Your responses to this survey will be anonymous and the research findings from the data collected will be reported in aggregate form. This survey is for Demographics & Descriptive Purposes for the study. All information will be stored in a passcode personal laptop.

Additionally, all information will be kept confidential and then terminated after a minimum of five years for documentation purposes.

Taking the survey-

Completing and submitting this survey represents informed consent to participate in the research study. You may choose to opt out of the study at any time. To do so, you may refuse to complete the survey. To take the survey, please click on the link below and follow the directions. The survey will be available for your response until September 13th, 2020. https://www.surveymonkey.com/r/YWM8SCV If you have questions at any time about the study or survey, you may contact either myself, the Principal Investigator, at afurlow@student.uiwtx.edu or Dr. Danielle Alsandor at Alsandor@uiwtx.edu.

*Participants will be recruited nationally and will complete a 60 to 90-minute individual semi-structured interview either in person or virtually via telephone (Zoom) and web conferencing tools

*Prior to the interview, participants will be asked to provide a paragraph of philosophical insight on their view of higher education in a minimum of 5 sentences. Please send all survey results and written philosophy statement to afurlow@student.uiwtx.edu.

For questions about your rights as a research participant or to discuss problems, complaints or concerns about a research study, or to obtain information or offer input, contact the UIW Institutional Review Board (IRB) at (210) 805-3036.

UIW IRB Approved

Date approved: 8/17/2020 Approval # 20-08-003

Appendix C: Survey

Data Collection (Survey Monkey) https://www.surveymonkey.com/r/YWM8SCV

1. What is your age?
2. What state do you reside in?
3. If employed, what state or U.S. territory do you currently work?
4. Which of the following categories best describes your employment status?
5. What is the highest level of school your mother completed or the highest degree she received?
6. What is the highest level of school your father completed or the highest degree he received?
7. What is the highest level of education you have completed?
8. What is your Participant pseudonym name if used?
9. At what e-mail address would you like to be contacted?

Appendix D: Interview Questions

This is a semi-structured, dyadic interview with possible follow up questions. The purpose of this survey is to discover your lived experiences and better understand your time in graduate school as a Black man. The questions are divided into three different subheadings: Student Engagement, Critical Race Theory, and Narrative Inquiry. Thank you in advance for taking the time to provide the most accurate and honest answers you can. The results of this survey will help to shape education for current and future students.

Student Engagement:

1. Tell me a little about yourself and how you decided to attend graduate school.
2. Thinking back to when you first began your graduate program, what were your initial thoughts, observations, and impressions?
    - Have your thoughts, observations, and impressions changed over time?
    - If so, why/how?
3. How would you rate your academic program on a scale from 1-100? Why?
4. What would you say is your highest achievement or highlight of your graduate career (thus far)?
5. What motivates you?
6. On the flip side, what would you say were your biggest challenges or struggles during your time in graduate school?
7. There is some research that says students of color have unique experiences compared to their white counterparts. Would you agree or disagree with that and why? – Well, have you ever experienced racism at your academic institution?
8. How would you describe your student engagement while in your graduate program?
9. Who or what resources did you turn to when you had academic questions?
10. What were the barriers or difficulties you experienced inside and outside of the classroom?
11. What about when you were dealing with personal matters, who did you turn to then?
12. What was/is your support network? Were/Are they motivating?
13. Does your support network help you handle the stresses of higher education?

Critical Race:

14. How important is it for you to have a Black advisor or Black mentor?
    - Extremely important
    - Very Important
    - Moderately Important
    - Slightly Important
    - Not at all important Why?

Follow up: Explain if advisor/mentor helped you, influenced you to extend beyond the status quo? From the book "Whistling Vivaldi: And Other Clues to How Stereotypes Affect Us (Issues of Our Time)." The author Steele suggests that we should break down stereotypes. With that being said, did you or do you have an advisor that was not Black, but still able to help you matriculate through the process? (Steele, 2011).

15. How does the ability to relate to a faculty member and/or to communicate about familiar interests affect your engagement as a Black male who completed graduate school, if at all?

16. What do you feel are some of the challenges Black men face regularly?

Follow up: Carter G. Woodson, in his book, "The Miseducation of the Negro," feels as though Blacks are being culturally indoctrinated as opposed to educated. (Woodson, 2006). What are your thoughts on the subject?

17. How would you describe your family culture? Are there any traditions or philosophies you would like to share that you or your family members do?

Follow up: Do you agree with Derrick Bell who used allegory and historical example to argue that racism is built into American society and has no chance of being eradicated as long as white people's well-being is not at stake? (Bell, 2018).

18. Speaking of culture, how would you define what it means to be "Black and Educated" or "Young, Gifted, and Black?" When people say these phrases what does that mean to you?

19. During your graduate academic program, how often did you experience the following feelings?

> 1. **Anxiety:** Very frequent, Frequent, Sometimes, Infrequent, Not at all.
>
> 2. **Depression:** Very frequent, Frequent, Sometimes, Infrequent, Not at all
>
> 3. **Helplessness:** Very frequent, Frequent, Sometimes, Infrequent, Not at all
>
> 4. **Stress:** Very frequent, Frequent, Sometimes, Infrequent, Not at all
>
> 5. **Homesickness:** Very frequent, Frequent, Sometimes, Infrequent, Not at all
>
> 6. **Racial Fatigue:** Very frequent, Frequent, Sometimes, Infrequent, Not at all

20. When you did experience such feelings, how were you able to overcome them and remain committed to pursuing your graduate degree?

<u>Narrative Inquiry</u> –Self-Identity/Educational-Achievement/Financial Support:

21. Do you feel you belong in your graduate program? If yes, why? If not, explain why not?

Follow up: What could have increased your sense of belonging?

22. Do/did you work while in school?

If yes, why? Did employment impact your academic performance?

23. How did you finance your education?

24. How can higher education faculty and administrators work to increase enrollment of and the retention of Black males in graduate programs?

25. What has been your approach to succeeding in graduate education? Meaning, when an event occurred in your life during your graduate program that could be perceived as a setback, how did you rebound from it?

26. How did graduate school prepare you for where you are in your life right now, if at all?

27. How do you sustain that motivation to keep striving?

28. Is there anything you would like to share with me that we have not addressed?

Appendix E: Table 4: Master's Degrees Conferred by Postsecondary Institutions, by Race/Ethnicity and Sex of Student: Selected Years, 1976-77 through 2017-18

Year and sex	Number of degrees conferred to U.S. citizens, permanent residents, and nonresident aliens								Percentage distribution of degrees conferred to U.S. citizens and permanent residents						
	Total	White	Black	His-panic	Asian/ Pacific Islander	American Indian/ Alaska Native	Two or more races[1]	Non-resident alien	Total	White	Black	His-panic	Asian/ Pacific Islander	American Indian/ Alaska Native	Two more race
1	2	3	4	5	6	7	8	9	10	11	12	13	14	15	
Total															
1976-77[2]	322,463	271,402	21,252	6,136	5,127	1,018	---	17,528	100.0	89.0	7.0	2.0	1.7	0.3	
1980-81[3]	301,081	247,475	17,436	6,534	6,348	1,044	---	22,244	100.0	88.8	6.3	2.3	2.3	0.4	
1990-91	342,863	265,927	17,023	8,981	11,869	1,189	---	37,874	100.0	87.2	5.6	2.9	3.9	0.4	
1999-2000	463,185	324,990	36,606	19,379	23,523	2,263	---	56,424	100.0	79.9	9.0	4.8	5.8	0.6	
2000-01	473,502	324,211	38,853	21,661	24,544	2,496	---	61,737	100.0	78.7	9.4	5.3	6.0	0.6	
2003-04	564,272	373,448	51,402	29,806	31,202	3,206	---	75,208	100.0	76.4	10.5	6.1	6.4	0.7	
2004-05	580,151	383,246	55,330	31,639	33,042	3,310	---	73,584	100.0	75.7	10.9	6.2	6.5	0.7	
2005-06	599,862	397,519	59,822	32,578	34,302	3,519	---	72,122	100.0	75.3	11.3	6.2	6.5	0.7	
2006-07	610,703	403,623	63,439	34,962	36,420	3,590	---	68,669	100.0	74.5	11.7	6.5	6.7	0.7	
2007-08	630,844	413,348	65,912	36,899	37,743	3,775	---	73,167	100.0	74.1	11.8	6.6	6.8	0.7	
2008-09	662,082	427,713	70,772	39,567	40,510	3,777	---	79,743	100.0	73.4	12.2	6.8	7.0	0.6	
2009-10	693,313	445,158	76,472	43,603	42,520	3,965	---	81,595	100.0	72.8	12.5	7.1	7.0	0.6	
2010-11	730,922	462,922	80,742	46,823	43,482	3,946	6,597	86,410	100.0	71.8	12.5	7.3	6.7	0.6	1
2011-12	755,967	470,822	86,007	50,994	45,379	3,681	9,823	89,261	100.0	70.6	12.9	7.6	6.8	0.6	1
2012-13	751,718	455,896	87,989	52,991	44,906	3,693	11,794	94,449	100.0	69.4	13.4	8.1	6.8	0.6	1
2013-14	754,582	444,771	88,606	55,962	44,533	3,512	13,417	103,781	100.0	68.3	13.6	8.6	6.8	0.5	2
2014-15	758,804	433,096	87,288	58,752	44,489	3,410	14,628	117,141	100.0	67.5	13.6	9.2	6.9	0.5	2
2015-16	785,757	431,885	88,786	63,060	45,921	3,538	16,589	135,978	100.0	66.5	13.7	9.7	7.1	0.5	2
2016-17	804,542	433,638	89,577	67,026	47,810	3,397	17,674	145,420	100.0	65.8	13.6	10.2	7.3	0.5	2
2017-18	820,102	439,051	91,273	72,470	50,091	3,318	18,850	145,049	100.0	65.0	13.5	10.7	7.4	0.5	2
Males															
1976-77[2]	172,703	144,042	7,970	3,328	3,128	565	---	13,670	100.0	90.6	5.0	2.1	2.0	0.4	
1980-81[3]	151,602	120,927	6,418	3,155	3,830	507	---	16,765	100.0	89.7	4.8	2.3	2.8	0.4	
1990-91	160,842	117,993	6,201	4,017	6,765	495	---	25,371	100.0	87.1	4.6	3.0	5.0	0.4	
1999-2000	196,129	131,221	11,642	7,738	11,299	845	---	33,384	100.0	80.6	7.2	4.8	6.9	0.5	
2000-01	197,770	128,516	11,878	8,371	11,561	925	---	36,519	100.0	79.7	7.4	5.2	7.2	0.6	
2003-04	233,056	146,369	15,027	10,929	14,551	1,137	---	45,043	100.0	77.9	8.0	5.8	7.7	0.6	
2004-05	237,155	150,076	16,136	11,501	15,238	1,167	---	43,037	100.0	77.3	8.3	5.9	7.8	0.6	
2005-06	241,701	153,696	17,388	11,738	16,037	1,253	---	41,589	100.0	76.8	8.7	5.9	8.0	0.6	
2006-07	242,213	154,250	18,340	12,471	16,689	1,275	---	39,188	100.0	76.0	9.0	6.1	8.2	0.6	
2007-08	250,203	157,622	18,759	13,166	17,480	1,294	---	41,882	100.0	75.7	9.0	6.3	8.4	0.6	
2008-09	263,515	162,863	20,146	14,314	18,865	1,349	---	45,978	100.0	74.9	9.3	6.6	8.7	0.6	
2009-10	275,317	170,243	22,121	15,554	19,423	1,419	---	46,557	100.0	74.4	9.7	6.8	8.5	0.6	
2010-11	291,680	177,786	23,746	17,183	19,918	1,409	2,540	49,098	100.0	73.3	9.8	7.1	8.2	0.6	
2011-12	302,484	183,222	25,284	18,633	20,751	1,298	3,518	49,778	100.0	72.5	10.0	7.4	8.2	0.5	1
2012-13	301,552	177,208	26,417	19,441	20,456	1,280	4,472	52,278	100.0	71.1	10.6	7.8	8.2	0.5	1
2013-14	302,846	173,303	26,608	20,565	19,955	1,219	4,890	56,306	100.0	70.3	10.8	8.3	8.1	0.5	2
2014-15	306,615	168,151	26,295	21,384	19,577	1,223	5,438	64,547	100.0	69.5	10.9	8.8	8.1	0.5	2
2015-16	320,574	166,161	27,024	22,749	20,071	1,229	6,129	77,211	100.0	68.3	11.1	9.3	8.2	0.5	2
2016-17	326,857	164,734	26,978	23,749	20,693	1,151	6,453	83,099	100.0	67.6	11.1	9.7	8.5	0.5	2
2017-18	326,870	164,714	27,552	25,255	21,273	1,076	6,658	80,342	100.0	66.8	11.2	10.2	8.6	0.4	2
Females															
1976-77\2\	19,509	16,955	1,237	317	363	58	---	579	100.0	89.6	6.5	1.7	1.9	0.3	---
1980-81\3\	28,428	24,626	1,687	586	678	89	---	762	100.0	89.0	6.1	2.1	2.5	0.3	---
1990-91	41,305	32,979	2,438	1,375	2,082	160	---	2,271	100.0	84.5	6.2	3.5	5.3	0.4	---
1999-2000	53,806	37,676	4,316	2,440	5,215	375	---	3,784	100.0	75.3	8.6	4.9	10.4	0.7	---
2000-01	55,414	38,190	4,380	2,640	5,828	359	---	4,017	100.0	74.3	8.5	5.1	11.3	0.7	---
2002-03	58,849	39,980	4,802	2,832	6,325	401	---	4,509	100.0	73.6	8.8	5.2	11.6	0.7	---
2003-04	62,106	41,681	5,201	3,064	6,751	414	---	4,995	100.0	73.0	9.1	5.4	11.8	0.7	---
2004-05	67,130	45,014	5,623	3,252	7,263	418	---	5,560	100.0	73.1	9.1	5.3	11.8	0.7	---
2005-06	69,144	45,574	5,574	3,352	7,709	500	---	6,435	100.0	72.7	8.9	5.3	12.3	0.8	---
2006-07	73,383	48,010	6,148	3,539	8,278	496	---	6,912	100.0	72.2	9.2	5.3	12.5	0.7	---
2007-08	75,850	49,583	6,160	3,794	8,654	485	---	7,174	100.0	72.2	9.0	5.5	12.6	0.7	---
2008-09	78,890	51,520	6,657	4,109	8,926	518	---	7,160	100.0	71.8	9.3	5.7	12.4	0.7	---
2009-10	81,980	53,712	6,804	4,443	9,376	522	---	7,123	100.0	71.8	9.1	5.9	12.5	0.7	---
2010-11	84,155	54,302	7,096	4,672	9,533	493	694	7,365	100.0	70.7	9.2	6.1	12.4	0.6	0.9
2011-12	87,547	55,877	7,673	5,005	10,104	497	870	7,521	100.0	69.8	9.6	6.3	12.6	0.6	1.1
2012-13	89,946	56,563	7,775	5,635	10,216	500	1,355	7,902	100.0	68.9	9.5	6.9	12.5	0.6	1.7
2013-14	92,002	56,783	8,111	5,877	10,848	496	1,669	8,218	100.0	67.8	9.7	7.0	12.9	0.6	2.0
2014-15	93,626	56,845	8,808	6,252	10,856	474	1,992	8,399	100.0	66.7	10.3	7.3	12.7	0.6	2.3
2015-16	93,894	56,541	8,813	6,659	10,982	440	2,064	8,395	100.0	66.1	10.3	7.8	12.8	0.5	2.4
2016-17	96,706	57,442	9,276	7,072	11,438	439	2,386	8,653	100.0	65.2	10.5	8.0	13.0	0.5	2.7

---Not available.

\1\Includes Ph.D., Ed.D., and comparable degrees at the doctoral level, as well as such degrees as M.D., D.D.S., and law degrees that were classified as first-professional degrees prior to 2010-11.
\2\Excludes 500 males and 12 females whose racial/ethnic group was not available.
\3\Excludes 714 males and 21 females whose racial/ethnic group was not available.
NOTE: Data through 1990-91 are for institutions of higher education, while later data are for postsecondary institutions participating in Title IV federal financial aid programs. Race categories exclude persons of Hispanic ethnicity. For 1989-90 and later years, reported racial/ethnic distributions of students by level of degree, field of degree, and sex were used to estimate race/ethnicity for students whose race/ethnicity was not reported. Detail may not sum to totals because of rounding. Some data have been revised from previously published figures.
SOURCE: U.S. Department of Education, National Center for Education Statistics, Higher Education General Information Survey (HEGIS), "Degrees and Other Formal Awards Conferred" surveys, 1976-77 and 1980-81; Integrated Postsecondary Education Data System (IPEDS), "Completions Survey" (IPEDS-C:90-99); and IPEDS Fall 2000 through Fall 2017, Completions component. (This table was prepared August 2018.)

Appendix F: Participants' Written Philosophy Statements

Participant Bruce: "My statement to live by is to follow a simple idea: to help make a positive change or impact on one's life. If I can change more, that would be great, but one is the goal, and I know that I have done my job here. The main reason for doing this is that I realized my life has been shifted through one idea change at a time, unbeknownst to me."

Participant Dr. Igbo: "My philosophy is pretty simple and can be summarized in these two quotes in no particular order."

"I want my life's resume' to be written by the breaths of those I help." – Gregory Braylock Jr.

"Know this-- there is no shortcut to transformation" – Lasana O. Ho

Participant Tre: "My mantra is to strive for the top because the bottom is crowded."

Participant Bishop: Life: "All I have is the time between the dashes, and I plan on writing an amazing story between my birth and my death."

Career: "It is your responsibility to change society if you think of yourself as an educated person." – James Baldwin

Participant Dr. Kobe: "My philosophy is that education is one path to making a better future for yourself. Education is a way in which someone can write their own narrative for their life and not let it be determined by their family or the zip code they are growing up in. Another motto that I try to live by is do no harm. Every interaction and relationship that I have, I try to go into with the best of intentions. In many aspects, I consider myself a servant leader and having a do no harm mindset allows me to think about what is best for the other person. I try to pray for guidance and then let God use me however he sees fit."

Participant Dr. Samuel: "My philosophy is that of a higher education professional who loves to encourage, inform, and assist responsible individuals seeking a higher learning opportunity to better themselves and their families."

Participant Tim: "My mother taught me a valuable lesson that I still live by: A closed mouth won't get fed. I took that and combined it with the importance of mentoring. Together, the two have allowed me to be successful and have led me to where I am now. No successful person has gotten where they are without the help of someone else, and in my opinion, the best form of help is mentorship."

Participant Chris: "My philosophy with higher education is that I do believe that every student that comes to college has a distinct purpose and a unique aspect of themselves that they will find throughout their college career. Becoming a professional in the higher education world means being aware of the constant change that is happening around us and being able to address and show that change as it still relates to any university's mission or vision statement."

Participant Jeff: "My mantra is from my grandfather's saying, as is my faith. My philosophy of life is to work like everything depends on you and pray like everything depends on God". "My grandfather used to say that to me, and it really shaped my work ethic. I believe good things come to those who work hard and treat others the right way."

Participant Dr. Taylor: "My philosophy is to be a passionate, versatile clinician whose mission is to bridge the gap between the health professional and patient-structured relationship by providing patient-centered, holistic care while maintaining professionalism and adhering to the core values established by the APTA."

Participant Dr. Langston: "Although I am deeply interested in research, my philosophy stems from my passion for preparing the next generation of educators and professionals dedicated to the uplift of their own communities. Currently, I teach courses that prepare physical educators to teach at the secondary level, net games, and individuals with disabilities."

Participant Papi: "My mantra is to strain against the warmth of insignificance."

Participant Ray: "I am that of my ancestors, and their blood that runs through my veins has made me their wildest dreams, which has made me a target for others."

Participant Johari, JD: "My philosophy is that when family members have matriculated within higher education, it is important to understand that they set the foundation for generations to come, and I am proud to have family who helped to pave the way." "The revolution will not be televised," Gil Scott Heron

Participant Tayo: "My philosophy is that building personal brands and encouraging diversity in hiring are two hallmarks of my leadership in global business. A strong background in cross-cultural communications gives me the versatility to work with brands across several cultures and position them for success. There are effective ways to develop global mindsets and strategies to become more inclusive."

Participant Michael: "I am focused on the value of performance philosophy through a qualitative lens. Media and communications as a model for exploration, expansion, depth, and inspiration through logic and imaginative curiosity. Audio-visual user-oriented building information for individual building technology operation and for energy-efficient and comfortable workplace user behavior."

About the Author

As post-baccalaureate education has historically been underrepresented and misrepresented for black men, the objective of this study was to identify common beneficial characteristics of successful black men. By identifying common beneficial characteristics of accomplished black men, this study analyzed the post-baccalaureate performance of 16 Black male participants. Dr. Furlow carefully considered the need to train faculty in the skills Black male students needed to graduate. The target audience for this special research area is those who can help improve services for Black males in higher education and beyond, including educational policy makers, current and future researchers, practitioners, and administrators.

Dr. Furlow was fully involved in the research as it developed, combining his own life experiences, struggles, and triumphs with his professional studies. This book illuminates the importance of emphasizing positive representations of Black men in graduate education, which is best expressed through personal experiences. By providing institutions and students with a model of tools to help Black men successfully complete their degrees, the results of this study will contribute to an increase in the number of Black men enrolled in graduate programs.